Feminism and the Legacy of Revolution

This series of publications on Africa, Latin America, Southeast Asia, and Global and Comparative Studies is designed to present significant research, translation, and opinion to area specialists and to a wide community of persons interested in world affairs. The editor seeks manuscripts of quality on any subject and can usually make a decision regarding publication within three months of receipt of the original work. Production methods generally permit a work to appear within one year of acceptance. The editor works closely with authors to produce a high-quality book. The series appears in a paperback format and is distributed worldwide. For more information, contact the executive editor at Ohio University Press, Scott Quadrangle, University Terrace, Athens, Ohio 45701.

Executive editor: Gillian Berchowitz
AREA CONSULTANTS
Africa: Diane M. Ciekawy
Latin America: Thomas Walker
Southeast Asia: William H. Frederick
Global and Comparative Studies: Ann R. Tickamyer

The Ohio University Research in International Studies series is published for the Center for International Studies by Ohio University Press. The views expressed in individual volumes are those of the authors and should not be considered to represent the policies or beliefs of the Center for International Studies, Ohio University Press, or Ohio University.

Feminism and the Legacy of Revolution

Nicaragua, El Salvador, Chiapas

Karen Kampwirth

Ohio University Research in International Studies
Latin America Series No. 43
Ohio University Press
Athens

The author is grateful for permission to reprint material from the following previous publications:

"The Mother of the Nicaraguans," *Latin American Perspectives* 23, no. 1 (1996): 68–71. Copyright © 1996 by Karen Kampwirth. Reprinted by permission of Sage Publications, Inc.

"Confronting Adversity with Experience," *Social Politics* 3 (1996): 136–58. Reprinted by permission of Oxford University Press.

"Legislating Personal Politics in Sandinista Nicaragua," *Women's Studies International Forum* 21, no. 1 (1998): 53–64. Reprinted by permission of Elsevier.

"Feminism, Antifeminism, and Electoral Politics in Post-War Nicaragua and El Salvador," *Political Science Quarterly* 113, no. 2 (Summer 1998): 267–69.

Women and Guerrilla Movements (University Park: The Pennsylvania State University Press, 2002). Copyright 2002 by The Pennsylvania State University. Portions reproduced by permission of the publisher.

Library of Congress Cataloging-in-Publication Data

Kampwirth, Karen, 1964-
    Feminism and the legacy of revolution : Nicaragua, El Salvador, Chiapas /
Karen Kampwirth.
        p. cm. — (Ohio University research in international studies. Latin Amer-
ica series ; no. 43)   Companion v. to Women & guerrilla movements.
        Includes bibliographical references and index.
        ISBN 0-89680-239-6 (pbk. : alk. paper)
        1. Women political activists—Latin America. 2. Women revolutionaries—
Latin America. 3. Feminists—Latin America. 4. Feminism—Latin America. I.
Kampwirth, Karen, 1964- Women & guerrilla movements. II. Title. III. Series:
Research in international studies. Latin America series ; no. 43.

HQ1236.5.L37K347 2004
305.42'09728—dc22

                                    2004014104

In memory of my dear friend Silvia Carrasco ("Sonia" in this book). Feminist and revolutionary, she left the world a more just place than she found it.

Contents

Preface and Acknowledgments

This book can be seen as a companion volume to *Women and Guerrilla Movements: Nicaragua, El Salvador, Chiapas, Cuba* (Pennsylvania State University Press, 2002). Both books draw on the same collection of over two hundred interviews I conducted between 1990 and 2000. Both tell the stories of many of the women who were mobilized into the revolutionary movements and who went on to become feminist activists. But while the two volumes are informed by the same fieldwork, they are quite different theoretically and historically. In fact, this book begins where the other one left off. This book analyzes the legacy of the revolutionary movements, what happened after the revolutionary wars (in the cases of Nicaragua and El Salvador), and what happened after the guerrillas emerged publicly (in the case of Chiapas, where, as of this writing, the war continues).

In Nicaragua, the Sandinista Front for National Liberation (FSLN), was founded in 1961 to attempt to overthrow the Somoza family dynasty, a family that had ruled Nicaragua since 1936. Nearly two decades later the FSLN succeeded in overthrowing Anastasio Somoza and taking power. The FSLN was to govern until 1990, when the former guerrilla organization lost the second national election under its watch. In 1980 in El Salvador, the Farabundo Martí Front for National Liberation (FMLN), a coalition of five organizations, came together to try to overthrow the military-dominated government, a government that had, like the Somoza dictatorship of Nicaragua, ruled since the 1930s. Both the left and right in El Salvador saw neighboring Nicaragua as a model for what could happen in El Salvador, since the Somoza dictatorship had been overthrown by similar guerrillas just a year before the founding of the FMLN. As it turned out, the FMLN never succeeded in overthrowing the government it opposed but instead demobilized as part of a negotiated settlement in 1992; following more than a decade of brutal war in which at least seventy-five thousand people died. After the war, the FMLN became a political party and now it is one of the two major parties in the country, along with the Nationalist Republican Alliance (ARENA).

Like the FSLN of Nicaragua and the FMLN of El Salvador, the Zapatista Army for National Liberation (EZLN) of the Mexican state of Chiapas could trace its organizational roots to Marxist organizing in the 1960s. But by the time it organized in earnest in the jungles of the Chiapas in the 1980s, it had dropped much of its Marxist orthodoxy, at least in part because the government it sought to challenge, headed by the Party of the Institutional Revolution (Partido de la Revolución Institucional, PRI), a political party that had governed without interruption since its founding in the 1920s, was less overtly dictatorial than the regimes that guerrillas sought to overthrow in Nicaragua and El Salvador. A different challenge required different strategies. The EZLN first emerged publicly in January 1994 with the seizure of seven cities in the early morning of New Year's Day. Less than two weeks later the EZLN withdrew from armed combat and has entered a process of on-again, off-again negotiations with the government. Arguably, given the level of political violence that has plagued the state of Chiapas since 1994, the war continues.

So the three cases differ in important ways: in Nicaragua the guerrillas successfully overthrew the regime and governed for over a decade; in El Salvador the guerrilla war eventually ended in a negotiated settlement; in Chiapas the guerrillas did not overthrow the regime nor was that necessarily their goal. Additionally, the conflict in Chiapas (unlike the conflicts in Nicaragua and El Salvador) has yet to be resolved. But despite these differences, the role of women in the movements is an important factor they have in common. Perhaps a third of the combatants in the FSLN, FMLN, and EZLN were female, a fact that represented a significant change from earlier Latin American guerrilla movements, such as that of Cuba, in which only about 5 percent of the combatants were female.

In *Women and Guerrilla Movements* I asked why significant numbers of women participated in combat positions in late-twentieth-century guerrilla movements in Latin America. I argued that, from the late 1960s onward, a number of factors had changed across Latin America that made it possible for many women to escape the constraints of their traditional lives and to take on the nontraditional role of guerrilla. Economic changes rooted in post-WWII globalization led to greater inequality in land tenure, increased insecurity in the countryside, especially for single mothers, and growing migration to the cities. Once those women and their daughters reached the cities, they found new opportunities for radical organizing, opportunities that had not been open to females in the countryside. That was especially the case after the emergence of the liberation theology movement within the Catholic Church in 1968. Since liberation theologians argued that the Bible should be read as a living text that spoke to the need to work for social justice in this world, the Church actively organized social activists in general and women in particular. Although the Church did not promote guerrilla struggle, many women who later became guerrillas were first mobilized within groups inspired by liberation theology.

Another organizational change that helps explain the jump in women's participation in guerrilla movements in the last thirty years has been a shift of strategies on the part of the mostly male leadership of the guerrilla movements. After the Cuban revolution, Latin American guerrilla movements consistently shifted from the Cuban *foco* (small group) strategy to a strategy of mass mobilization. And as the guerrilla leaders needed more people to carry out the mass mobilization strategy effectively, they were much more interested in mobilizing women than their Cuban counterparts had been.

Finally, I note in *Women and Guerrilla Movements* that while the structural and organizational factors listed above (land concentration, migration to the cities, the rise of liberation theology, and the shift to the mass mobilization strategy) affected all residents of those societies, only a small number of those people were to join the guerrilla movements. I argue that personal factors (something that theorists of revolutionary change rarely pay attention to) can explain how macrosocial changes made activists out of some women. Early childhood experiences of resistance to authority, or what I call family traditions of resistance, are one factor that started many women on the path to radical activism, often many years later. Second, participation in preexisting networks—including families, church groups, student organizations, and labor unions—often was part of a slow transition that led to increasingly more radical activities and eventually to the guerrilla movements. Third, women who participated in guerrilla movements were, on average, significantly better educated than the general population, a fact that may be explained largely by the importance of student groups as a starting point for participation in revolutionary politics. The final personal reason women were likely to be mobilized into revolutionary politics was age at the time of major societal turning points. Young people were far more likely to be willing and able to assume the risks of guerrilla activity than older people.

So in *Women and Guerrilla Movements* I developed a theory of why women were mobilized in large numbers in recent guerrilla movements. My theoretical goals in this book are different. In the pages that follow I ask how and why many of the women who were mobilized within the guerrilla organizations were to break away from those organizations after the wars were ended, going on to create vibrant autonomous feminist organizations.

I HAVE RACKED up many debts over the years it took to research and write these two books. In *Women and Guerrilla Movements* I thanked most of the hundreds of people who helped along the way. Those thanks apply to this book as well. In those acknowledgments I inadvertently left out Guadalupe Sequeira of Nicaragua, who provided important insights, and Tracy Fitzsimmons of the United States, who read an earlier version of this project; I would like to thank them now. Unfortunately I did not meet Michelle Day in time to benefit from her deep knowledge of Chiapas while writing my first book, but she was kind enough to read and comment on the chapter on Chiapas here. And, as always, I am grateful for Duane and Sophie Oldfield's many contributions to this project.

Abbreviations

ADEMUSA	Asociación de Mujeres Salvadoreñas (Association of Salvadoran Women)
AEDPCH (Aedepch)	Asamblea Estatal Democrática del Pueblo Chiapaneco (Democratic State Assembly of the People of Chiapas)
AMNLAE	Asociación de Mujeres Nicaragüenses Luisa Amanda Espinoza (Luisa Amanda Espinoza Association of Nicaraguan Women)
AMPRONAC	Asociación de Mujeres ante la Problematica Nacional (Association of Women Concerned about the National Crisis; predecessor of AMNLAE)
AMS	Asociación de Mujeres Salvadoreñas (Association of Salvadoran Women)
ANIPA	Asamblea Nacional Indígena Plural por la Autonomía (National Pluralistic Indigenous Assembly for Autonomy)
ARENA	Alianza Nacionalista Republicana (Nationalist Republican Alliance)
ATC	Asociación de Trabajadores del Campo (Association of Rural Workers)
CADDIAC	Comité de Apoyo y Defensa de los Derechos Indios, A.C. (Committee for the Support and Defense of Indian Rights)
CD	Convergencia Democrática (Democratic Convergence)
CDS	Comité de Defensa Sandinista (Neighborhood Defense Committee)

CEMUJER	Centro de Estudios de la Mujer "Norma Virginia Guirola de Herrera" ("Norma Virginia Guirola de Herrera" Center for the Study of Women)
CEOIC	Coordinadora Estatal de Organizaciones Indígenas y Campesinas (State Coordinator of Indigenous and Peasant Organizations)
COM	Coordinación de Organismos de Mujeres (Coordinator of Women's Organizations)
CONAMUS	Coordinadora Nacional de Mujeres Salvadoreñas (National Coordinator of Salvadoran Women)
CONPAZ	Coordinación de Organismos No Gubermentales por la Paz (Coordinator of Nongovernmental Organizations for Peace) Dignas Mujeres por la Dignidad y la Vida (Women for Dignity and Life)
EZLN	Ejército Zapatista de Liberación Nacional (Zapatista Army for National Liberation)
FDR	Frente Revolucionario Democrático (Democratic Revolutionary Front)
FIPI	Frente Independiente de Pueblos Indios (Independent Front of Indian Peoples)
FMC	Federación de Mujeres Cubanas (Federation of Cuban Women)
FMLN	Frente Farabundo Martí para la Liberación Nacional (Farabundo Martí Front for National Liberation)
FONIF	Fondo Nicaragüense de la Niñez y la Familia (Nicaraguan Fund for Children and the Family)
FSLN	Frente Sandinista de Liberación Nacional
FZLN	Frente Zapatista de Liberación Nacional (Zapatista Front for National Liberation)
IMU	Instituto de Investigación, Capacitación, y Desarrollo de la Mujer (Institute for Women's Research, Training, and Development)
INI	Instituto Nacional Indigenista (National Indigenous Institute)

INIM	Instituto Nicaragüense de la Mujer (Nicaraguan Women's Institute)
INSSBI	Instituto Nicaragüense de Seguridad Social y Bienestar (Nicaraguan Social Security and Social Welfare Institute)
MAM	Movimiento de Mujeres Mélida Anaya Montes (Mélida Anaya Montes Women's Movement)
MAS	Ministerio de Acción Social (Ministry of Social Action)
MINSA	Ministerio de Salud (Ministry of Health)
MRS	Movimiento de Renovación Sandinista (Sandinista Renovation Movement)
MSM	Movimiento Salvadoreña de Mujeres (Salvadoran Women's Movement)
ORMUSA	Organización de Mujeres Salvadoreñas (Organization of Salvadoran Women)
PDC	Partido Demócrata Cristiano (Christian Democratic Party)
PIE	Partido de la Izquierda Erótica (Party of the Erotic Left)
PRD	Partido de la Revolución Democrática (Party of the Democratic Revolution)
PRI	Partido de la Revolución Institucional (Party of the Institutional Revolution)
RN	Resistencia Nacional (National Resistance)
SEDESOL	Secretaría de Desarrollo Social (Secretariat of Social Development)
UCA	Universidad Centroamericana (Central American University)
UNO	Unión National Opositora (National Opposition Union)
USAID	U.S. Agency for International Development

Introduction

From Feminine Guerrillas to Feminist Revolutionaries

Everything is equal in the EZLN. There are no differences, one day the men make the food, the next day the women make the food, and other days it is all mixed up. . . . Of course, within the houses of the compañeros there is still a little inequality, but there is not much! The compañeros don't abuse women as much anymore.

—Major Ana María, Chiapas, 1994

The problem was that sexism within the FMLN was never seen as it was: as being undisciplined, as being rebellious. Sexual harassment was seen as something acceptable. [They used to say] 'those poor guys, the compas' . . . [Once] a compañero who is now a Congressman from the Democratic Party violently grabbed me . . . Who was I supposed to complain to? He was the leader of the region. But I tell you that I never understood it as a question of gender relations . . . It wasn't until '92 that a case of discrimination clarified things for me.

—Laura, El Salvador, 1996

[After the overthrow of Somoza] I worked in the armed forces. From that point until '84 was a very tense time for me . . . always working twenty-four hours a day to make a dream reality. But I didn't care. . . . The important thing was to carry out the work because you had the hope that everything was going to be better. . . . It was in '84 that I realized that I didn't want to leave the party but [at the same time] I didn't want to stay in the party. I did not reject Sandinismo but I did reject the FSLN. And I did not reject being a leftist. For me feminism was a refuge. Well, not a refuge, better yet it was an alternative. . . . I think feminism is what an authentic left could be.

—Sonia, Nicaragua, 1997

Ana María, Laura, and Sonia have a lot in common. Though they live in three different countries, all three participated in guerrilla movements that sought to overthrow or transform regimes that were characterized by tremendous social inequality. All three became guerrillas at a very young age.[1] None of them joined the guerrilla struggle with the goal of revolutionizing gender relations. Yet years later, the two Central Americans are now both quite critical of the sexual inequality that existed within the guerrilla forces despite the guerrillas' public commitment to reduce social inequality within their societies. These two guerrilla fighters in the seventies and eighties became feminist activists in the nineties and beyond.

Major Ana María of the Mexican state of Chiapas is less critical of sexual inequality within the guerrilla forces. But if the history of similar experiences is any guide, she is already on the path toward a more holistic vision of equality, toward a political agenda that unifies the goals of class equality and social justice typically promoted by guerrillas and other revolutionary groups,[2] with the goals of sexual equality and reproductive rights, typically promoted by feminists. For in a number of Latin American countries, guerrilla struggle and feminism have been linked, though in ways that were often unforeseen by their participants.

New Views of Revolutionary Studies

This book is a step toward addressing what I see as three shortcomings of the literature on revolutions: (1) its relative inattention to the role of women in revolutions and the impact of gender relations on revolutionary movements; (2) its tendency to end analysis at the moment when the old regime is overthrown; and (3) its overemphasis on states and structures, impeding analysis of the impact of revolutionary movements on their participants and on the culture and politics of the societies in which they occur . While the presence of women in revolutionary movements is often mentioned by students of such movements, that presence is less often analyzed. The problem is not that there has been any shortage of recent theoretical works on revolutionary change.[3] Nor is there any shortage of research on the role that gender plays within revolutionary politics.[4] Yet, despite some important exceptions (Foran, Klouzal, and Rivera 1997; Luciak 2001a, 2001b; Moghadam 1997, 2003; Shayne 1999; Tétreault

1994) these findings on gender in revolutionary settings have not been in-tegrated into theories of revolution, except at the level of footnotes.

Valentine Moghadam's work stands out among the theoretical works on gender and revolution in that she takes a broad historical and regional view and begins building a global theory of gender and revolution, clas-sifying revolutionary movements into two categories: "one group of rev-olutions is modernizing and egalitarian, with women's emancipation as an explicit goal; another group is patriarchal, tying women to the family and stressing gender differences rather than equality" (1997, 137; also see 2003). Moghadam categorizes the movements in Nicaragua, El Salvador, and Chiapas as modernizing and egalitarian.

Of course, to say that in the three cases analyzed in this book, women's emancipation was one of the goals of the revolutionary movements is not to say that those movements were perfectly egalitarian or free of contra-dictions. But the important point is that they all contained the seeds of feminist consciousness and organizing, seeds that often germinated after the military stage of the guerrilla movements had ended or subsided. As Moghadam argues, revolutionary movements do not necessarily contain such feminist seeds and, indeed, increased gender inequality is sometimes a legacy of revolutionary movements. So I will also consider two cases—Iran and Poland—in which the legacy of revolution was antifeminism, and one case—Cuba—in which the gendered legacy of the revolution is yet to be determined (see chapter 5). Comparing these cases to cases in which feminism was a legacy of revolution allows me to build on Moghadam's work, suggesting why revolutions leave either feminist or antifeminist legacies.

The second significant shortcoming of much of the literature on revolution (the tendency to end analysis at the moment when the old regime is overthrown) stems from the fact that most of the work on revolution over the past century has been devoted to a single question. From a movement-centered perspective this question is, Under what circumstances have revolutionary movements succeeded in overthrow-ing states? From a state-centered perspective the question becomes, Under what circumstances have states fallen to guerrilla challenges?

That question (which is not addressed in this book) has informed many generations of revolutionary theory and has still not been fully answered to the satisfaction of most participants in the debate. Of course, the hundreds if not thousands of works on revolutionary theory produced over the course of the past century have varied greatly, both in their arguments and in the sort of evidence they utilized, but almost all addressed the same central question.[5] That question, which has intrigued generations of theorists, is clearly a good question, but it is not the only question.

In addition to its intellectual benefits, studying revolutions as movements rather than as points in time is truer to the thinking of revolutionaries themselves. At least in Latin America, the revolution is the period of political, economic, and social transformation that can occur only after the guerrillas succeed in seizing the state. The guerrilla struggle and the revolution are distinct periods, separated by the moment in which the old regime is overthrown. At the same time, they are intellectually linked, for the guerrilla struggle makes little sense without the hope of a later period of revolutionary transformation. While many excellent case studies of particular revolutions have been published, few theoretically focused works have analyzed what happens during revolutions (Colburn 1994; Fagen 1969; Fagen, Deere, and Corragio 1986; and Selbin 1999 are notable exceptions).

A third problem (analyzing states and structures to the detriment of individuals and culture) is directly related to the unfortunate tendency to end analysis at the moment when the old regime is overthrown or when the guerrillas stop trying to overthrow it (either making peace agreements with the state they sought to overthrow or otherwise demobilizing). Ending analysis at that historic moment assumes rather than shows that one can understand revolutionary success in terms of whether or not the old regime is overthrown. But while taking formal power does increase the chance that the revolutionaries will succeed in implementing their agendas, it certainly does not guarantee that they will do so.

Ending analysis at the moment when the revolutionaries march triumphantly into the capital ends up missing much of the messiness of revolution—the real politics that usually occurs only once the revolutionaries have taken power or demobilized. Once the guerrilla struggle has ended, the contradictions that were once papered over come to the surface. Studies that conclude at the close of the guerrilla struggle completely miss the emergence of feminism, along with other legacies of revolutionary movements, intended or not. In contrast, a book like this one, with its focus on the legacy of revolutionary movements, allows for analysis of the impact of such movements on some of the individuals who participated in them and the societies they helped transform.

This argument—that we will better understand revolutions if we study the role of women within revolutions, think of revolutions as movements rather than as points in time, and consider their impact on individuals and cultures—will be documented by considering the experiences of women like Ana María, Laura, and Sonia, whose words were quoted on the first page of this introduction. This book considers the relationship between their memories of participating in revolutionary movements and their involvement in the rise or expansion of women's organizing. Though feminist theorists often think of militaristic movements, like the three guerrilla movements I examine here, as patriarchal and therefore antithetical to gender equality, I will show that they actually played an indirect role in the rise of women's movements. Not only did mobilization in the guerrilla wars lead certain women to become feminists, but the experience of those wars shaped the sort of feminism that developed. This book tells the story of *how* the guerrilla wars led to the rise of feminist movements, *why* certain women became feminists as a result of their experiences with the guerrilla organizations, and *what* sorts of feminist movements they built.

Revolutionary movements have often inadvertently engendered feminist movements for at least three reasons. The first is ideological. For the guerrilla groups and other revolutionary organizations strongly promoted the value of egalitarianism; indeed they valued it so much that many risked dying so as to have a chance at a more just, more equal world. For many women, the time spent as guerrillas or members of other revolutionary groups was a time when they were treated more equally by men than ever before. So it came as a shock to many when it seemed that their male colleagues expected to return to "normal" gender inequality upon the overthrow of the dictator or upon the end of the guerrilla war. It is not that gender inequality was any worse than it had been, but rather that the women who had been mobilized into new ways of thinking and acting were no longer as willing to accept such inequality as natural.

The impact of organizing on individuals was a second reason that feminism was often a legacy of revolution. In the process of being mobilized into the revolutionary movements, many women were personally transformed. Participating in these movements allowed them to gain new organizing skills and new confidence in their abilities to act, even in ways that were not traditional for women. So not only were the women who became feminists unhappy about the return to normal inequality after the wars, many of them felt they had the ability to do something about it.

The power of preexisting networks is a third reason why revolutionary movements often left feminist legacies. During the revolutionary wars, many women's organizations were founded by the guerrillas for the purpose of providing logistical support. Many of those groups that were originally meant to support male-dominated organizations went on to redefine their mission as that of promoting feminist goals. Organizations that were not controlled directly by the guerrillas but that were founded in response to the conflict between the guerrillas and dictatorial states (such as human rights organizations, radical student groups, Catholic groups influenced by liberation theology, neighborhood defense organizations, labor unions) also sometimes took on new goals after the wars started tapering down or when they finally ended. These organizations served as preexisting networks for feminism, networks that were not founded for feminist purposes but that were later used for such purposes, sometimes to the displeasure of those who had originally promoted the organizations.[6]

But though Latin American feminist organizations thrived for reasons that were primarily domestic—including the three just mentioned—those reasons were not entirely domestic. The international context is crucial in understanding why some of those grievances were channeled in feminist ways, since nearly all who were socialized in the revolutionary organizations were aware of the thinking of international leftists. For the Sandinistas of Nicaragua, those international thinkers included Soviets and Cubans but they also included activists of the new left from places like Mexico, the United States, and Western Europe. By the late sixties and early seventies, women of the new left were increasingly feminist, an influence that had an impact in Nicaragua. The same thing occurred in El Salvador in the eighties and nineties, with the explosive addition of revolutionary thought from neighboring Nicaragua, where the Somoza dictatorship was overthrown in 1979. In Chiapas external influences were felt from both the south (Central America) and the north (Mexico City). These influences were carried through books, magazines, international conferences, or through the experiences of living abroad as a student or as an exile.

Given the fact that local feminism is sometimes dismissed as simply a foreign imposition, with suggestions that "our women" never objected to sexual inequality in the past, it is worth emphasizing that foreign ideas were not merely appropriated in a local context. The radical feminism that emerged as an unintended outcome of the guerrilla wars differs in fundamental ways from the more liberal feminism of the north, including its holistic nature, its seeking to transform societal structures as well as ideology, the public as well as the private. Central American feminist thought is notably more concerned with class and less concerned with linguistics than feminism of the north. While there is a family relationship between North American and Central American feminism, the movements are cousins, not mother and daughter.[7] International factors and timing play a critical role in explaining why the Cuban revolution (which came to power before the second wave of international feminism) has not yet engendered an independent feminist movement while the Nicaraguan revolution did engender such a movement.[8] The specific ways in which some members of the international feminist movement helped bring about feminism in Latin America will be taken up in the individual country chapters and in the conclusion.

Why Feminism? Who Are the Feminists?

In Nicaragua and El Salvador, organized feminism[9] can be seen as an unintended consequence of guerrilla struggle. The vast majority of the leaders of the feminist organizations of the nineties were active, in some way, in the revolutionary struggles of the seventies and eighties (or in the revolution of the eighties in Nicaragua). Feminists were not born, they were created. Central American feminists were created by decades of armed and unarmed social struggle for reasons that, originally, had little to do with gender interests. In general, the reasons women gave for joining the guerrilla struggle were similar to those given by men: to end dictatorship, to end exploitation of the poor or indigenous (or both), or to create more just countries for their children. Gender justice was almost never a factor in their initial decision to join. They simply joined so as to live in freer countries and to have more options in life. But for women, the end of the dictatorship or the completion of the civil war did not eliminate many of the forces that limited their options. It was that realization that led many guerrillas and other revolutionary activists to eventually become feminists.

The feminists of the nineties were typically initiated into political radicalism through feminine work in the seventies and eighties. In other words, they made a transition from one kind of women's organizing to another, a distinction that has been nicely defined by Sonia Alvarez, for whom an act is feminist if it "seeks to transform the roles society assigns to women, challenges existing gender power arrangements, and claims women's rights to personal autonomy and equality" (1990, 24). While that definition is broad, it is not meant to encompass all women's organizing. Sometimes women organize in ways that Alvarez calls feminine. Feminine organizing is a way of promoting women's well-being within the context of their traditional roles without directly challenging the gender division of power.[10]

The women who joined the revolutionary movements in Nicaragua and El Salvador were first mobilized through actions that, while stretching the boundaries of their traditional roles as women, did not directly challenge power inequalities between women and men. With time, many went on to confront inequalities based on gender, along with those based on class or politics. Organized feminism might have never emerged, or at least it might have been different, if not for feminists' original politicization through the guerrilla wars. In contrast, in Chiapas the relationship between guerrilla struggle and feminism differs in large part because the timing differs. Organized feminism is not a product of guerrilla struggle in Chiapas, it is a predecessor. Prior organizing of women in Chiapas, especially that of indigenous women, helped set the stage for the rebellion, even when armed struggle was far from the minds of the organizers. So the case of Chiapas demonstrates that guerrilla struggle and feminism are linked in practical and theoretical ways—even when women's mobilization proceeds guerrilla struggle—and not the other way around, as in the two Central American cases.[11]

In Chiapas the relationship between women's organizing and guerrilla politics is reciprocal. Just as women's prior organizing shaped the development of the guerrilla movement, the existence of the Zapatistas is further shaping women's organizing. The Zapatistas' proclamations on gender issues (especially the Revolutionary Women's Law) have been used by women's movement activists as tools for consciousness raising (e.g., Grupo de Mujeres et al. 1994). And not only have the Zapatistas influenced the work of the feminists, but the feminists have on occasion influenced the work of the Zapatistas (see chapter 4).

Finally, the emergence of the EZLN has had an impact on the relationship of women's organizations to each other. A nonindigenous activist with roots in the two previously separate currents in the women's movement—urban groups comprised predominantly of mestiza (mixed-race) women and rural groups comprised predominantly of indigenous women—told me that since the beginning of the uprising, these groups are more likely to flow in a united current (interview, January 1995). Since January 1994 there is more of a movement in Chiapas, where once there were only separate organizations. So the mobilization of women as guerrillas and the later emergence (or development) of organized feminism are intimately related. But while the experience of being a female guerrilla eventually led to feminist activism in many cases, it did not do so in any automatic way. Moreover, not all women became feminist activists as a result of their experience within guerrilla organizations. Why did some former guerrillas became feminists while many others simply demobilized and faded into private life?

Arguably, the founders of the feminist movements were not former guerrillas who had held the positions of most prestige (like commander) nor were they the women who held positions with least prestige (like cook or caretaker of a safe house).[12] Instead, they nearly all were mid-prestige women. My category of mid-prestige women includes what other scholars have called members of the rank and file, or the base, since any woman who served in combat automatically enjoyed some prestige, given the glorification of violence that played a not so insignificant role in guerrilla culture.[13]

In addition to the combatants, the mid-prestige members of the revolutionary coalition were women who either had some authority in carrying out traditional women's work (like the heads of nursing brigades) or who did work that created opportunities for them to make decisions (such as student activism or human rights activism or political education work). Such work was much more likely to be personally empowering than making tortillas. Moreover, their position in the middle meant that, on the one hand, they were not shielded from the brunt of machismo within guerrilla ranks, as were female commanders, but, on the other hand, they had the opportunity to develop political skills and consciousness that might not have been available to very low ranking female participants.

That the rise of feminism is really a continuation or a logical extension of the guerrilla story is implicit in the argument that guerrilla leaders were not those who were previously unorganized but rather those who were organized but who, for various reasons, found themselves marginalized. To use Theda Skocpol's phrase, the leaders of guerrilla movements tended to be "marginal political elites" (Skocpol 1979, 164–68; also Wickham-Crowley 1992, 227; 1997, 50–52). Just as the guerrilla leaders were drawn from the ranks of would-be political elites within their societies, the later feminist leaders were drawn from the ranks of would-be political elites within the context of revolutionary politics.

Empowered through their participation in guerrilla and revolutionary organizations, yet excluded due to sexism, those women helped extend the revolution to one of its logical conclusions. The following table shows why the women who were the "marginal political elites" of the guerrilla period (and the revolutionary period, in the case of Nicaragua), and not those with either more or less prestige within revolutionary politics, were those who went on to become feminist leaders.[14]

	High-Prestige	Mid-Prestige	Low-Prestige
Socialization into revolutionary culture	yes	yes	no
Awareness of international leftist thought	yes	yes	no
Acquisition of organizing skills	yes	yes	no
Affected by guerrilla sexism	no	yes	yes
Few opportunities at end of war	no	yes	yes
Decision to become feminist activists	no	yes	no

The table illustrates the different experiences that women were likely to have when they worked with the guerrilla movements and other revolutionary organizations and the later impact that those experiences had. Certain experiences, in combination, were likely to start women along the path toward feminist activism. One of the most important factors that shaped the sorts of experiences that activists had was the degree of responsibility and status they enjoyed within the organizations. Both high-prestige and mid-prestige revolutionary activists were intensely socialized into the culture of the revolutionary organizations. This socialization involved studying the history of their own countries, reading major works of the international left, and participating in discussion groups in which they interpreted their studies.

Had the organizations been merely military organizations, they probably would have had far less impact on the consciousness of their participants. But the movements in this study were all political-military organizations, so participation in them was often to change the thinking of high- and mid-prestige participants in profound ways. Low-prestige participants were much less intensely socialized, probably because the leaders of the organizations did not believe they needed to be socialized in such ways to effectively carry out their work.

So one factor that led to the rise of feminism was political socialization, and the transformation of consciousness, that occurred within the guerrilla movements. But consciousness alone is not enough to create an activist. A second factor that influenced the future actions of high- and mid-prestige participants was learning organizing skills. Low-prestige participants were far more likely to receive orders than to give them, and so, once the wars ended, they were likely to be far less self-confident and far less politically prepared than their higher-prestige counterparts.

Mid-prestige and low-prestige participants did share one significant experience during the guerrilla wars: sexism within revolutionary ranks. While the political values of equality and social justice that informed revolutionary organizing would seem to preclude such sexism, the reality was that those organizations were the products of highly sexist societies, even if gender relations were often better within those organizations than in the larger society. Sexism in the revolutionary organizations manifested itself in a number of ways, ranging in intensity from overlooking women for promotion, to punishing women for infractions that men got away with, to raping fellow revolutionaries. High-prestige women tended not to be victimized by sexism to the same extent, in large part because the advantage of their prestige overrode the disadvantage of their sex. In fact, some of the high-prestige women I interviewed indicated that they had been unaware that such sexist practices existed within their organizations.

A final factor that both mid- and low-prestige women experienced occurred after the end of the civil wars. While high-prestige guerrillas often moved into high-prestige roles in civilian life (including, in a number of cases, seats in Congress), less famous women were not likely to be presented with such opportunities. In fact, their opportunities were sometimes more dismal than they would have been had those women never joined the revolutionary coalitions, since joining had often meant dropping out of school or turning down opportunities to gain job experience.

Mid-prestige women were the only category who experienced all these factors at once. Like their high-prestige counterparts, they had gained political consciousness and organizing skills. Like their low-prestige counterparts, they had gained grievances, both within the revolutionary organizations and in the larger world that had few post–civil war opportunities to offer them. This combination of skills and grievances was an explosive one.

Methodology of the Study

The women's movement activists I spoke to lived and worked, with a few exceptions, in the capitals of their countries or state: in Managua (Nicaragua), San Salvador (El Salvador), and San Cristóbal de las Casas (Chiapas).[15] Between 1990 and 2000, I spent a total of about two years in the region, divided over many trips (about sixteen months in Nicaragua, four months in El Salvador, five months in Chiapas, and a week in Cuba).[16] During my visits, I conducted a total of 205 open-ended interviews with female political activists (76 in Nicaragua, 69 in El Salvador, 57 in Chiapas, and 3 in Cuba), interviews that ranged in length from fifteen minutes to three hours, with the average interview taking about an hour. In addition I participated in workshops and conferences, did volunteer work in movement offices, and followed the press.

The method I used to find the women I interviewed is sometimes called snowballing. I began by approaching an organization that worked on women's issues, explained my project, and interviewed one or more activists in that organization. Then, at the end of the interviews, I asked for suggestions of other women or organizations that I should include in my study, thus building a sample of major participants in the women's movement, as identified by movement activists themselves. The vast majority of women I interviewed were activists in women's organizations or women's programs within mixed organizations, a few were former women's movement activists, and a number were congresswomen who worked on gender issues or officials in government women's offices.

A significant subset of my sample of activists in Nicaragua and El Salvador were former guerrillas. This was not the case for the women I interviewed in Chiapas, for while I conducted the two Central American studies in the postwar period, I conducted the study of Chiapas while the war was ongoing, at a time when the Mexican military made it difficult for foreigners to spend time in guerrilla territory. The women I interviewed in Chiapas worked with women in various organizations, many of whom had years of experience working in the indigenous communities that were the base of support of the EZLN, some of whom were born in those communities and continued to live there. Though, to my knowledge, none of them participated directly in the EZLN, they could accurately be called participants in what I have called the revolutionary coalition (see endnote 2 for an explanation of the concept of revolutionary activism) or in what Xochitl Leyva (1998) has called "the new Zapatista Movement."

I began all the interviews with a set of questions on the women's childhoods. The questions addressed issues such as when and where they were born; who raised them and what that person (or people) did for a living; their relations with their siblings; how far they had gotten in school; and whether they had worked when they were children. Those initial background questions were followed with a different sort of question: What was your first political experience? Answering that question, which usually required reaching back into childhood memories, typically marked the point when the interviews shifted into long narratives, and my role as interviewer was often reduced to posing occasional clarifying questions and taking notes.

By the end of the interviews, the tone often shifted from the women's intensely personal memories of childhood to a more analytical and abstract analysis of the women's movement in general and their organization in particular. While this book does draw on some personal stories of childhood, most of those stories inform *Women and Guerrilla Movements* (Kampwirth 2002), which analyzes an earlier period in history. Instead, this book, with its more analytical and less personal anaysis, reflects the shift in tone in the interviews.

Three Memories of Gender and Revolution

In Nicaragua, El Salvador, and Chiapas, women were mobilized by the thousands into guerrilla movements and revolutionary organizations in the last quarter of the twentieth century.[17] The organizations they joined in one way or another promoted egalitarian ideas: equality between rich and poor, landed and landless, Indian and mestizo, men and women. Those organizations were revolutionary in that they promised to transform life, to overturn dictatorships, to attack economic inequality, and to challenge social injustice. This is not to say that they were identical in either their goals or their actions, as will be clear in the chapters on each country. And yet, from the perspective of the women who participated in these movements, there were important similarities.

For many women, life within the revolutionary organizations was the closest they had ever come to experiencing gender equality. As many of them explained, it was not necessarily that male guerrilla leaders were deeply committed to gender equality in principle but instead that the needs of revolutionary warfare meant that excluding women just because they were women would have been inefficient: all willing participants had to be welcomed into the revolutionary coalition. This combination—the discourse of egalitarianism with the reality of relative gender equality—was compelling, so compelling as to explain why many remember their days in the guerrilla armies with affection, despite the horror of war.

Yet memory is a slippery thing, a thing that refuses to stay put. Once a crisis like the guerrilla wars has passed, memory may be revisited. It may be reworked in the new light of the postwar era. That is what happened to the women whose stories appear in this book. That process of rethinking their revolutionary past, and reworking their experiences, is nicely illustrated by the three quotes with which this introductory chapter opens.

The first quote was from Major Ana María of the Zapatista Army of National Liberation (Ejército Zapatista de Liberación Nacional, EZLN), a guerrilla army that first publicly emerged in the Mexican state of Chiapas in January 1994. Of the three cases I consider in this book— Nicaragua, El Salvador, and Chiapas—the case of Chiapas is the most recent, for the EZLN is still an active guerrilla movement, albeit one that no longer directly confronts the army. So it might make sense to consider Ana María last since chronologically she spoke last. Yet in the more important sense of intellectual comparability, Ana María's thoughts on equality and gender relations belong first since she spoke in 1994, early in the conflict between the EZLN and the Mexican state, while the two Central Americans, Laura and Sonia, spoke years after the guerrilla conflicts had ended in their countries, years after they had reevaluated their memories of those days.

When Major Ana María commented that everything was equal in the EZLN, exactly what did she mean? The evidence she gave of that equality was that cooking duties were equal, that the men and women of the EZLN either took turns cooking or cooked together. At first glance, that seems to be a domestic observation. Yet Ana María must have been referring to collective or public cooking duties, for she went on to contrast those equitable cooking arrangements with the continuation of "a little inequality" and a small amount of "abuse" in the households of those very compañeros (companions, comrades). How could there be both full equality and continued inequality at once?

Ana María's comments make sense within the framework that has dominated most political thought in the past, the understanding of politics as a public thing that has little or no relationship to the private lives of political actors. Within that framework, it may make sense to proclaim that public equality is the equivalent of full equality. Yet clearly Ana María was uncomfortable with that measure of equality for she did not simply discuss public equality and leave it at that. Instead, almost as an aside, she mentioned the nagging question of private inequality, practiced even by her fellow revolutionaries. When she spoke to a reporter in 1994, the first year of the public rebellion, that information was not enough for her to revise her first claim that there was full equality in the EZLN. It is hard to imagine how she could have focused on that nagging private inequality in 1994; ongoing wars tend to lead people to close ranks, to avoid criticizing their compañeros too vigorously or at all. But the nagging questions might be remembered in new ways once the war comes to an end. That is what happened with many of her Central American counterparts, like Laura.

In 1996, Laura told me of her days in the Farabundo Martí Front, or FMLN. That was several years after the end of the civil war between the FMLN (the guerrilla coalition to which she had belonged) and the government of El Salvador. In the 1980s, Laura was one of the thousands who had joined the FMLN to challenge the military dictatorship that had dominated El Salvador from the early 1930s. Waging war against a deeply rooted dictatorship that was massively funded by the Reagan administration,[18] a dictatorship that was willing to engage in mass murder in order to cling to power,[19] required discipline, commitment, faith in one's fellow revolutionaries. During her years in the FMLN, Laura kept the guerrilla faith, stoically enduring hardships as part of the cost of war. It was only after the war ended that she began to reevaluate some of those hardships, hardships such as the sexual harassment to which she and other female guerrillas were sometimes subject. She began to see such pressures as inconsistent with the FMLN's public commitment to social justice, as even inconsistent with the need for discipline within guerrilla ranks.

The equation of women's mobilization with women's emancipation was common within the guerrilla movements in El Salvador and elsewhere in the late twentieth century (Molyneux 1986). Such mobilization had an impact, sometimes even a significant impact, in transforming the lives of women like Laura, who were mobilized into roles they had never before played. But mobilization invariably stops short in emancipating women for it does not, indeed cannot, eliminate gender inequality. Transforming gender always requires transforming a relationship and that includes men as well as women. Yet the idea that men would also have to change their actions and beliefs was not frequently promoted by the guerrillas.

After the war Laura began to question the equation of women's mobilization with their emancipation. Unlike some of her fellow revolutionaries, whose consciousness of gender relations was awakened in the early nineties, she did not leave the FMLN entirely, instead staying to work within the women's section of the guerrilla organization that transformed itself into a political party in the aftermath of the war. But while she did not reject the FMLN, she did reject the FMLN's equation of mobilization with emancipation. As long as FMLN leaders admitted women into guerrilla ranks without requiring that men change their relationships with those women, they were only setting up contradictions between the promise of social equality and the reality of continued inequality. Laura herself did not see that contradiction during the crisis of the war. But she began to see with new eyes in the war's aftermath.

Movements that rejected the mobilization as emancipation model were not the only legacy of the revolutionary wars. Sonia referred to yet another unintended legacy in discussing how she rethought what it meant to be a revolutionary after the organization to which she belonged, the Sandinista Front for National Liberation (FSLN) came to power in 1979. Sonia and many other political activists were to rethink the theory of the vanguard, the all-knowing organization that guides and directs its members in the process of revolutionary transformation.[20] During the war against the Somoza dictatorship, the vanguard party probably played a critical role in the eventual overthrow of that dictatorship. But once the Sandinistas came to power, many committed Sandinistas like Sonia came to see vanguardism as limiting debate and inhibiting revolutionary transformation. Ironically, Sonia eventually decided that living out the legacy of Augusto César Sandino (the nationalist hero for whom the FSLN was named) required rejecting the party of Sandino. Being a leftist, as she had come to understand the term, led her to reject the party of the left in favor of the new feminist movement, which she saw as an example of "what an authentic left could be."

Like Laura, Sonia chose to live out her political values through the feminist movement that in Nicaragua, like El Salvador, grew dramatically in the aftermath of the war. While Laura chose to promote feminist ideals within the former guerrilla party of El Salvador, Sonia was to promote feminist ideals apart from the former guerrilla party of Nicaragua. While Laura came to feminism through her rethinking of seemingly private relations in the guerrilla movement—through the issue of sexual harassment—Sonia came to feminism through her rethinking of the public politics of the guerrilla movement and the revolutionary government—through the issue of vanguardism. Despite those differences, in fundamental ways, their stories are similar. Both were mobilized as teenagers in ways that stretched or even broke the constraints of traditional female roles. Through that mobilization, both gained new organizing skills, skills they were to draw upon as they became feminist activists. While mobilization in itself was not equivalent to emancipation, it was an important prerequisite.

THIS BOOK TELLS the stories of many feminine guerrillas who became feminist revolutionaries. Those stories might be surprising to some who are not familiar with the history of revolutionary and feminist movements in Latin America. But really, it should not surprise us that sooner or later feminism would make inroads into guerrilla politics. For the two phenomenon have much in common.

Guerrilla struggles aim to transform social relations, to reduce economic and political inequality, in short, to turn the world upside down. Feminist struggles might be described in the same way, qualified only by the addition of the phrase, "between men and women." Perhaps no social movement, in theory at least, is as revolutionary as feminism, for the world it seeks to turn upside down is that most intimate world, the world of daily life and the home.

Chapter 1

"Building the New Fatherland, We Create the New Woman"

Gender Politics in Sandinista Nicaragua

THE GUERRILLA WAR that ushered in the Sandinista revolution (1979–90) was to mark that revolution in profound—and contradictory—ways. One image from the guerrilla period that would be repeated over and over during the decade of revolution nicely captured the gendered legacy of the guerrilla struggle. The idealized Sandinista woman was a mother. A young woman, she grinned while holding a nursing infant; over her shoulder a rifle was slung. Originally a photograph, the image of the nursing guerrilla was reproduced in many forms, including public murals, postcards, and the official poster that commemorated the tenth anniversary of the revolution. That this image was so widely reproduced throughout the revolution is a testimony to its symbolic importance. It captured both the extent and the limits of the Sandinistas' feminism, as seen through their own eyes.

In this revolutionary image, the nursing mother was armed and powerful. But she was also, apparently, a single mother. No man helped tend to the infant and, in fact, images of men and infants were few and far between in revolutionary iconography, both in Nicaragua and elsewhere (Molyneux 1984, 77). Through the revolution that the image promised, women's rights and responsibilities were to be extended in significant ways. Indeed, they often were. But the transformation of gender is necessarily the transformation of a relationship. That relationship, including men's roles, was less often challenged. This near automatic understanding of gender transformation is implied in the name of this chapter, which I took from a phrase that figured prominently in Sandinista discourse during the early eighties.[1] Without directly challenging men's roles, womanhood would be transformed simply by extending the revolution.

While the image of the nursing guerrilla is an image of empowered maternity, it is also, of course, an image of war. Even after the guerrilla struggle, warfare would continue to mark the revolution, often to the detriment of feminist organizing. Guerrilla organizations, like the Sandinista Front that the smiling woman belonged to, are hierarchical by necessity. This may be especially the case for a guerrilla organization like the FSLN that utilizes a mass mobilization strategy and therefore has many thousands of followers who must be organized in some way. The Sandinista guerrillas could have never hoped to overthrow the dictatorship without extremely good coordination. Coordination, in turn, entailed secrecy, verticalism, unquestioning obedience to authority. While the Sandinista project was a democratizing one, it was also a project that was born of a guerrilla organization that was hardly democratic.

So the lessons that were internalized in the guerrilla struggle, and that were reflected in the image of the nursing guerrilla, were laden with tensions. In the guerrilla struggle of the sixties and seventies, thousands of women gained the opportunity to break the constraints of their traditional roles. It was also in the guerrilla struggle that many women who were to go on to be feminist activists first gained the skills and consciousness that made their later activism a real possibility. In some sense the guerrilla war opened opportunities for many women that would have remained closed had the dictatorship entered a third generation, as it almost surely would have done if not for the FSLN. And Sandinismo would forever mark Nicaraguan feminism, even in the case of women who were to reject their formal ties to the party. "Without the revolutionary movement, feminism would undoubtedly still be the province of a privileged few" (Chinchilla 1997, 209).

At the same time, old lessons are hard to forget, especially in times of stress. It is true that Sandinista leaders presented significant evidence, in deeds as well as words, of their commitment to democratization.[2]

That democratizing project often even extended to gender relations.[3] But evidence of their commitment to democratizing gender was most forcefully presented in the best of times, especially in the first two years of the revolution, before the right-wing contras began their attacks on the Sandinistas and anyone who might support them. Once the contra war had begun in full force, the leadership was often tempted to fall back on the lessons it had learned in the guerrilla struggle. Those lessons included the importance of avoiding controversy within revolutionary ranks and of controlling any dissent that might arise. Neither lesson boded well for feminists.

After Somoza, 1979–82

As the Sandinistas—women and men—triumphantly entered Managua on July 19, 1979, waving the rifles with which they had overthrown the hated Somoza dictatorship, it was clear that the balance of power in Nicaragua would never be the same. Even if the Sandinista leadership had wanted to leave gender relations untouched, that would have been nearly impossible. Far too many women had been mobilized in the guerrilla struggle to make a return to the "good old days" easy. But that was never the intention of the Sandinista leadership. From as early as a decade before the overthrow of Somoza, the FSLN had promised that the emancipation of women would be one of the goals of the revolution.[4] And so it was.

Starting in July 1979 the state was transformed in multiple ways, many of which directly affected gender relations. That transformation involved legal reform, the expansion of access to education, the nationalization of health care, and the creation of a wide range of state services, such as day care centers, that opened new opportunities for women. Revising the laws that regulated gender relations was one of the very first things the new revolutionary government did.[5] No doubt this was because changing laws was fairly easy. Also, in the initial excitement of the revolution, many hoped that new laws would rapidly make a new society. Ana María, who would become director of Nicaragua's first state women's institute, the Women's Legal Office, explained: "At the founding of the revolution I thought everything was going to be different, I saw it as a utopia. . . . I thought that by changing the laws they were going to change the people" (interview, May 7, 1991).

On July 20, 1979, the day after they took power, the Sandinista leaders decreed the Law of the Means of Communication, prohibiting the use of women as sex objects in advertising (Junta de Gobierno 1984, 25; Murguialday 1990, 126). On that same day, they passed a law that "established penalties so as to suppress white slavery and prostitution" (Junta de Gobierno 1984, 22), which was followed a few months later by voluntary alternative-job training programs for prostitutes, offered by the Social Service Ministry (Junta de Gobierno 1984, 22). In 1981 the Breast Feeding Promotion Law directed the Ministry of Health to promote breast feeding at the same time as it forbade the advertisement of baby bottles and formula (Lacayo and Lacayo 1981, 286–87; Murguialday 1990, 126). All these legal reforms contained a dual agenda: to improve women's status and to limit what the Sandinistas saw as capitalist excesses.

Another category of laws tried to eliminate insidious distinctions between the children of married and unmarried people. For instance, social security made people in common-law marriages eligible for benefits (Murguialday 1990, 126–27). The 1980 adoption law made it possible for single women or men to adopt without having to be part of a couple (Collinson 1990, 111; Murguialday 1990, 126). Here too, reforms contained a clear class content as well as a gender content since the poor were far less likely to legally marry than rich or middle-class Nicaraguans.

Finally, a third category of laws was directly aimed at transforming gender relations. The Statute of Rights and Guarantees of August 1979 declared the "absolute equality of rights and responsibilities between men and women," banned differential privileges based on legitimacy, and included the right to investigate paternity (Stephens 1988, 153–54). A new labor code forbade the Somoza-era practice of the "family wage," under which the male heads of rural families had received a single wage for the work of their wives and children (Murguialday 1990, 127). And the Law of Relations between Mother, Father, and Children eliminated the Somoza-era concept of absolute paternal authority (*patria potestad*), in favor of shared custody. Mothers and fathers were to have equal rights to, and equal responsibilities toward, their children, except in the case of young children. Mothers would automatically receive custody of children under seven while the preferences of children over seven would be considered (Collinson 1990, 111; Murguialday 1990, 128; Stephens 1988, 156).

The last piece of gender legislation in the early years of the revolution was the 1982 Nurturing Law.[6] Unlike earlier legislation that also proclaimed the shared responsibilities of family members, this law included mechanisms to put those ideals into practice, introducing equal pay for equal work, state pensions, and the right of nursing mothers to take an hour off work every day to breastfeed (Murguialday 1990, 128).

If it had only been for those provisions, the law would no doubt have passed. But the Nurturing Law also required that all household members—including men—participate in housework and childcare. Divorced or separated women who could not work outside the home (for reasons of health or age) would be entitled to a pension to be provided by the former partner. According to the law, adults were responsible for their children while children and grandchildren were to provide for parents and grandparents who were too old or sick to work (Collinson 1990, 111–12; INSSBI n.d., 10; Murguialday 1990, 128–31). This proposal was described as the "most polemical of the many laws that had been proposed at that time" (Murguialday 1990, 130). It never went into effect, although it was approved by the Council of State, because the Governing Junta would not ratify it. The failure of the Nurturing Law marked the end of Sandinista gender lawmaking until the late eighties.

The reason that was most commonly given for the end of the first period of gender lawmaking was the beginning of the contra war. The same women who had been promoting family law reforms agreed with the Sandinista leadership that campaigning to democratize gender and generational relations could be divisive and, ultimately, threatening to the war effort (Stephens 1988, 158). Defending the revolutionary project that had made legal reform possible was given priority over short-term reforms that might undermine the long-term health of the revolution.

No doubt the concern over the war was one of the reasons, probably even the central reason, for ending the early period of legal reform. But another reason may have been the Sandinista leaders' discomfort in the face of increasingly radical, even feminist, demands from their own base. As Governing Junta member (and later president) Daniel Ortega tried to explain, "The social conditions to put these ordinances into effect did not exist" (quoted in Murguialday 1990, 130). Interestingly, Ortega did not raise such objections regarding other potentially divisive issues, like land reform.[7]

So the legal reforms of gender roles had their limits, either due to the war or the leadership's concerns about the development of feminism in the revolution, or both. They were also limited in that law tends to be the preserve of the elite, though that was less true than it usually is, since many of those laws were crafted through mass consultations. Nonetheless, the real revolution in public policy did not occur in the law. Instead, most Nicaraguans pointed to educational and health reforms as the central accomplishments of the Sandinistas. Under Somoza, illiteracy rates were high for everyone, especially for women. While 16 percent of urban men were illiterate, 22 percent of urban women could not read or write. The situation was worse in the countryside: there 64 percent of men and 67 percent of women were illiterate (Stromquist 1992, 27). One of the Sandinistas' earliest goals was to overturn the dictatorship of illiteracy, just as they had overturned the dictatorship of the Somoza family.

Years later, the literacy crusade of 1980 is probably the single most remembered event of the revolutionary decade. And with good reason; such collective social battles are rare occurrences in human history. Through the literacy crusade, tens of thousands volunteered for five months to teach their fellow Nicaraguans to read. The crusade disproportionately helped women since more women than men had been illiterate to begin with. Moreover, the crusade often brought female students together with female teachers: 60 percent of the teachers were female (Collinson 1990, 124). Over four hundred thousand people would learn to read and write during the crusade, reducing Nicaragua's illiteracy rate from over 50 percent to slightly under 13 percent (Brandt 1985, 328; Hirshon 1983, 215; MED 1984, xvii).

But it would be an exaggeration to claim that, because more women than men participated in the crusade, it was therefore a feminist crusade. In fact, one might argue that an opportunity to integrate the transformation of gender relations into one of the Sandinistas' most important public acts was largely missed. The textbook that was used for the crusade, *Dawn of the People,* was highly nationalistic, featuring Sandino in the first lesson and emphasizing the class content of the revolution much more than its gender content.

Nonetheless, women were not completely forgotten. Lesson 19 linked women's liberation to revolution through its key phrase, "Women have always been exploited. The revolution makes possible her liberation" (Barndt 1985, 326–27; Hirshon 1983, 51, 67).[8] This lesson echoed the revolutionary slogan, "Building the new fatherland, we create the new woman." Both identified the transformation of women's roles as part of the Sandinista agenda and at the same time suggested that the transformation of women's roles would be the automatic result of other revolutionary policies.

The literacy crusade did have an impact on gender relations, but that impact was fundamentally an outgrowth of the experience of being a teacher or student rather than a response to the ideas that were promoted through the crusade. Many of those who went on to become feminist activists, especially those who had not been active in the anti-Somoza struggle, pointed to their participation in the crusade as a turning point, the time when they were introduced to a world beyond the constraints of their homes. When I asked América, who at the time of the interview directed the women's secretariat in ANDEN (the Sandinista teacher's union), about her first political experience, she explained that she first became politically involved upon completing high school in 1980: "That was the beginning of my teaching career and also the beginning of my political career. For the first time I came to know the countryside. And from that point on I integrated myself into revolutionary life" (interview, January 22, 1997).

If, in the collective Nicaraguan memory, the literacy crusade is the most important event of the early Sandinista years, then the reform of health care is a very close second. The reasons for that are similar to the reasons for the reverence with which the literacy crusade is remembered. To begin with, health care under the Somozas was miserable,[9] so the improvements of the early eighties were profound. Moreover, the reform of health care is remembered with near equal reverence because those reforms were collective. The revolutionaries placed a high priority on reforming health care, eliminating fees for hospital and clinic visits, and mobilizing the population for preventive health brigades. Through these brigades, children were immunized, latrines and clinics were built, and the population was educated in basic disease prevention (Bossert 1985, 352–53). The campaigns were quite effective. For example, the vaccination campaign nearly eradicated polio and greatly reduced levels of other infectious diseases. While there were only forty-three health clinics in 1978, there were 532 by 1983 (Pérez-Alemán 1992, 241). And women participated in this transformation of the health of the Nicaraguan people to an even greater extent than in the literacy crusade. A full 75 percent of the volunteers in the health brigades of the early eighties were women (Collinson 1990, 96–97).

In the early eighties, thousands of women, often very young women, were mobilized by the Sandinista government for a variety of purposes: to teach others to read, to immunize children, to harvest coffee, to guard their neighborhoods at night. Those campaigns played a critical, if not always planned, role in the challenge to traditional authority that was the revolution. In response to my question about the impact of the revolution on family life, Dinora emphasized the impact of this mass mobilization, especially in the literacy campaign: "Nearly everybody went: in Managua there were no young people left. We went off on our own, we lived independently for five months. All those young people were different when they returned. Their parents felt that up to a certain point their dominance over them was no longer great. After that the coffee-picking brigades came along; the ones who benefited most from them were women. Already women's mentality had changed. That benefited women a lot. It's a very big change, in reality" (interview, April 1991). Dinora's uncle Sergio also linked changes in family life with mobilization into Sandinista activities: "The revolution changed everything. . . . There was a change in parents, in children. Their children went to pick coffee, to the mountains, they went far away. And we felt good about this change. Nobody was forced to go pick cotton, to teach literacy. . . . [There was] freedom for women in the work. That was a tremendous change because they went to work with men. Men and women working. It's a tremendous change in family life" (interview, April 1991).

Opponents of the revolution often agreed about the profound impact that Sandinista mass campaigns had on gender and generational power relations but they disapproved of such changes. The next door neighbors of Dinora and Sergio were two such critics. According to one of their neighbors, Julia, "before the Sandinistas, life was different. Due to the night watch many men lost their women. There was disunion at that time" (interview, April 1991). The night watch, a program run by the neighborhood defense committees (CDS) in the early eighties, was originally meant to guard against counterrevolutionary activities but, as the contras were not active in the capital, Managua's night watch programs mainly served to reduce street crime and burglaries. Julia was quite right that the night watch program caused conflicts in some households: many men objected to their wives carrying guns and being out all night. Julia's sister Luisa had a similar assessment of the mobilization of the eighties: "They [the Sandinistas] prostituted young girls by sending them off to harvest coffee, where they had to practice free love. That was what made those people fall" (interview, April 1991).

Ironically, Julia and Luisa agreed in fundamental ways with the strongest proponents of the revolution that the mass mobilization campaigns—for better or worse—undermined the very foundations of traditional authority in Nicaragua. Looking back on the early years of the revolution, Ana María from the Sandinista Women's Legal Office (Oficina Legal de la Mujer) pointed to the combined importance of these legal, ideological, and structural changes on women's status: "The FSLN made an opening for the establishment of a new base for relations. . . . We women felt we had the right to make demands and to say that we can make our own changes. They made us feel important. At the beginning of the revolution that was extremely important. . . . Later the revolution demystified many myths against women. We awoke with force and with a great awareness of our reality. It wasn't theoretical work, rather [it was] very practical work" (interview, May 7, 1991). Similarly, Janet, who was to arrive at feminism through Sandinista labor unions, traced changes in women's status and consciousness to their mobilization early in the revolution. She particularly noted the importance of women's participation in two of the greatest changes of the early years of the revolution: the extension of free health care to all Nicaraguans and the literacy crusade. These were mass campaigns that helped forge a new identity for both the women and men of Nicaragua: "Since we all participated there was a collective spirit" (interview, May 29, 1991).

Neither Ana María nor Janet claimed that the Sandinista leadership of the early 1980s was centrally concerned with transforming gender relations. Nor did they claim that the hundreds of thousands of women who volunteered to recreate their country thought of public participation as a way of changing their private identities. What was centrally important was that, perhaps for the first time, a majority of Nicaraguans believed that their future was not captive to their past. In fact, that is what is so revolutionary about revolutions. It is not that revolutions, even the most successful ones, manage to truly recreate countries. Post-Sandinista Nicaragua is much like pre-Sandinista Nicaragua: the same mountains, the same volcanoes, and, sadly, the same poverty. But significant revolutions do open up the past to question. They create the collective spirit of which Janet spoke. And for many women, they make it possible to imagine a world, in Ana María's words, in which they have "the right to make demands."

In the early years of the revolution, the Sandinista-affiliated national women's organization Luisa Amanda Espinoza Association of Nicaraguan Women (Asociación de Mujeres Nicaragüenses Luisa Amanda Espinozaor, or AMNLAE) played an important role in teaching Nicaraguans to dream. Founded in 1977 as the Association of Women Concerned about the National Crisis (Asociación de Mujeres ante la Problemática Nacional or AMPRONAC), it was one member of the Sandinista network that helped bring down Somoza. With the revolution it changed its name but its mission did not change significantly. Still a Sandinista support group, the most significant changes in its goals were due to the changes in the FSLN itself, from a guerrilla organization to a governing political party. AMNLAE was to provide support for the male-dominated FSLN without directly challenging sexual inequality. In 1980, AMNLAE hoped that its twenty-five thousand members would "defend the revolution by joining the popular militias; participate in organizations that directed state policy in areas like education, health, supplies, employment and salaries; fight for legal equality and the creation of childcare centers; join the literacy campaign; create health brigades, control contraband and hoarding, and encourage productive collectives of women" (quoted in Murguialday 1990, 104).

While the activities that AMNLAE set out for itself in 1980 all potentially stretched the boundaries of women's traditional roles, most of them did not directly challenge sexual inequality. In short, they were feminine but not feminist. And they certainly did not challenge the FSLN's legitimacy as vanguard of the revolution. Yet with time even women who stayed with AMNLAE, like Ileana, the director of one of

AMNLAE's women's houses,[10] were to question the relationship between the movement and the party: "AMNLAE was practically married to the FSLN; it was the submissive wife. The women's movement was not driven by gender concerns, it was driven by party concerns. But we were born with the revolution and for that reason we were tied, in one way or another, to the FSLN. We can't make a movement away from the FSLN overnight" (interview, March 26, 1991). Significant as Ileana's criticism was, it was far more tempered than that of the majority of the leaders of the women's movement who had left AMNLAE by the early nineties. The analogy of the bad marriage, without Ileana's qualifications, was a common one in the year or two following the Sandinistas' electoral defeat.

Ileana's words to me, in a private interview, differed significantly from her public analysis, when she led one of the neighborhood groups that prepared for AMNLAE's national congress in March 1991. On that occasion, she chose a different sort of family metaphor: "AMNLAE is like a mother who teaches her daughters" (meeting, February 23, 1991). Ileana's use of a double discourse—critical in private while apologetic in public—was illustrative of how deeply ingrained the old guerrilla code of behavior still was.

The hierarchical relationship between the movement and the party (which was largely a remnant of the guerrilla period) and AMNLAE's resulting inattention to gender relations might well have been debated and resolved internally had the revolution been free to continue on the course that was set between 1979 and 1982. The Sandinista revolution, after all, was remarkable for its degree of openness and democracy when compared to other twentieth-century revolutions (Selbin 1999, 46–54).

While there is no guarantee that AMNLAE would have evolved into a more independent organization had the revolution continued on its original course, there is no way to know for sure. For the relatively easy years of the revolution came to an end with Ronald Reagan's inauguration as president of the United States in 1981 and his funding of the right-wing contra guerrillas shortly thereafter, funding that was to have devastating consequences for many Nicaraguans.[11] The contras (short for *contrarrevolucionarios*) waged war against the Sandinista government from 1982 until after the Sandinistas were voted out of office in

1990. The contra guerrillas were led mainly by former members of the Somoza dictatorship's National Guard, people who resented the Sandinistas for having overthrown Anastasio Somoza's government. The rank-and-file contras were largely peasants and indigenous people who for various reasons objected to policies of the Sandinista government, or who in some cases were simply caught up in the war on the contra side.[12]

The War Years, 1982–86

While the contras themselves did not promote an overt gender agenda,[13] the varied responses to the contra war were to transform the women's movement. During the middle years of the Sandinista revolution, women's organizations, like all organizations, had to adapt their strategies and goals in response to the national crisis that was the contra war. And if politics is always an unpredictable sort of thing, it is never more so than during times of war. The role of gender within the revolution was to shift during the war; gone was the early and perhaps naive optimism, the belief that the revolutionary process itself, almost without even trying, without confrontation, would transform gender roles. Hopes that the new woman would be created as a by-product of the new fatherland were fewer and farther between by the mid-eighties, perhaps because the high cost of fatherland building was increasingly clear.

With the onset of the war, gender politics in Nicaragua entered a new phase. Within the evolving women's movement there were at least two different responses to the war, that of what Nicaraguans call the sectors (labor unions or other economically organized groups), and that of the national women's organization, AMNLAE. And their responses to the very same war could not have been more different—just as the women of the sectors were increasingly insistent that the war could never be won without more gender equality, the women of AMNLAE accepted an ever more subservient relationship with the FSLN, on the grounds that the war could never be won without softening demands for gender equality, at least temporarily.

Women's secretariats were formed within all the major unions during the eighties to address the challenges created by the feminization of the workforce that so often occurs during wartime. As fathers and sons were drawn into the war, many mothers and daughters found themselves with new responsibilities. While in 1980, only 22.8 percent of the paid workforce was comprised of women, by 1983, 41.5 percent of the economically active population was comprised of women. The ratio of women to men went down again as the war cooled: by 1987, 31.7 percent of the economically active population were women. Nonetheless, the change in the workforce was more permanent than suggested by the shrinking percentage of working women. Near the end of the war, in 1987, there were twice as many women in the workforce as before the war: 384,466 as compared to 181,900 seven years earlier (INEC 1990, 24). In other words, the lower ratio of women to men, at the end of the war, was the result of the return of men to the workforce rather than the return of women to their homes.

In response to the changes in the workforce, women's secretariats were formed in many labor unions. The Association of Rural Workers (Asociación de Trabajadores del Campo, or ATC) was the first to form a women's secretariat, in 1983, perhaps because the feminization of the workforce was particularly noticeable in the countryside as massive numbers of rural men were drawn into the war, on one side or the other. Prior to the war, women had only comprised about 20 percent of the permanent rural workforce, increasing to 40 percent of permanent rural workers by 1985. Even more dramatically, 60 percent of the workers in the cotton harvest and 70 percent of the tobacco and coffee harvest workers were women (Pérez-Alemán 1992, 245–46).[14] Increasing the productivity of female workers became a national priority, as indeed it had to be, given the importance of agro-export earnings for the national economy and ultimately for the defense effort.

In 1983 the first National Assembly of Rural Women Workers was held, with some hundred women in attendance (Criquillón n.d., 20). That assembly was followed by a year and a half of intensive research to find an explanation for the mystery of why women were less productive than men.[15] What they found was that the double workday—female workers leaving their paid jobs early in the day to begin unpaid work in their homes—was the fundamental root of lower productivity. Amalia, one of the founders of the women's secretariat, explained how gender equality, which had been seen in the early eighties as an outcome of the revolution, was suddenly a goal on which the very survival of the revolution might depend: "We women who worked in the ATC all created a sort of school of thought. It was the first case of feminist work in a mixed sector. The sectorization of the women's movement has been very influenced by the work of the ATC" (interview, June 6, 1991).

The results of their study were presented at the second National Assembly of Rural Women Workers, held in September 1986. The hundreds of delegates were faced with two choices. Either they could demand lower work quotas for women, a solution that would acknowledge their household responsibilities but that would also institutionalize those responsibilities, or they could support equal work quotas for men and women but accompany those quotas with measures to reduce the double workday so as to make it possible for women to meet those quotas. "The second alternative implied that we understood the new role of the working class in the revolution, that we took it on with understanding and, strengthened by the moral authority that we had conquered, that we would demand equal rights, opportunities, and working conditions with men" (Criquillón n.d., 22).

Choosing the second alternative, the delegates called for a series of changes: childcare centers, paid maternity leave, paid days off to care for sick children, installation of running water where it was still unavailable, subsidies for household expenses, public mills for grinding corn, and greater representation for women in leadership positions within the union (Collinson 1990, 46; Criquillón n.d., 25). In response to those demands, rural Nicaragua began to change. While only thirty rural day care centers were in operation in 1985, five hundred were operating by the 1986–87 harvest, though most of those centers did not operate year round. Collective corn mills were installed on state farms, along with seventy-two new public wash basins, and a double page of the ATC's national newsletter, *Machete,* was devoted to the women's secretariat (Collinson 1990, 46–47).

Throughout the rest of the revolutionary decade, the ATC women's secretariat grew in size and radicalism. Some eight hundred women attended the third National Assembly of Rural Women Workers, in September 1987, under the slogan Equality Is Strength (Criquillón n.d., 27). During the fourth assembly, held in 1988, opposition to sexual harassment and in favor of affordable contraception were central issues.

The head of the women's secretariat, Olga María Espinosa, was greeted with applause when she proposed that the "unions incorporate into the contract [with farm managers] sanctions against sexual blackmail at work, rape attempts, and any act that violates our dignity" (Collinson 1990, 48).

While the rural wageworkers union, the ATC, was the leader in making demands for women within the sectors, it would not be long before women's secretariats had emerged in many of the other sectors as well. The peasant farmer's union (UNAG), the health worker's union (FETSALUD), the government workers union (UNE), the urban union confederation (the CST), and the urban professional's association (CONAPRO) would all have active women's secretariats by the close of the revolution.

The varied responses of different sectors of the women's movement to the very same national emergency—the contra war—proved, if nothing else, what an inexact science the study of societies truly is. It illustrated the role of political choices: there was nothing inevitable about the impact of the war on women's organizing. During the war, demands for feminist reforms were made in an increasingly insistent manner within the sectors, while they were heard with decreasing frequency within AMNLAE itself. The decision that AMNLAE's leaders made, in 1982, to cease pressing for controversial reforms in gender legislation, was to set the tone for many of AMNLAE's policies in the mid-eighties.

Why did one group of organized women see the same war through such a different lens than another group? Both were Sandinista, revolutionary, committed to ending the war. They simply made different choices, and why one chooses one road and one another is often difficult to sort out, even for the choosers. One difference that must have mattered is the role that each group played, or did not play, in the national economy. The women of the ATC had a mission, on which the defense effort, and ultimately the success of the revolution, depended. Their mission was to find ways to raise the productivity of the predominantly female workforce and they managed to argue successfully that feminist reforms were the means to fulfilling that mission.

The women of AMNLAE, in contrast, did not produce any material goods with which they could save the revolution. What they could produce were ideological goods: loyalty, devotion, unquestioning commitment to the Sandinista leadership. So, like the women of the sectors, the women of AMNLAE used the tools at their disposal to defend a revolution that was, in their eyes, the prerequisite for continued movement toward gender equality. In the midst of the war, AMNLAE's leaders chose to defend the revolution by subsuming their demands for gender equality and by promoting a traditional model of womanhood.

AMNLAE's already significant ties to the Sandinista Party were only strengthened as the women's organization chose to focus its energies on mobilizing the middle-aged mothers of combatants behind the defense effort. Those women, the Mothers of Heroes and Martyrs (Madres de Heroes y Martires), were to suffer silently and altruistically. Seldom were feminist questions, such as why economically vulnerable mothers of dead or mobilized youth suffered more than the fathers of those youth, posed.[16] Such feminine organizing was distressing to some of the women who had sought to challenge gender inequalities within AMNLAE. Many of those women would eventually break with AMNLAE.

But the disagreement over who and how to organize was not what eventually led to the mass exodus from AMNLAE in the nineties. It was the internal structure of the movement that was to create the greatest resentment. The other conflicts were all subsumed under this one. Had the internal structures of AMNLAE been open to dissent, the other disagreements might have been resolved without splintering the movement. Instead, discontent was lost in AMNLAE's vertical structures. On top of that, visions of vanguardism extended even to AMNLAE's relationship with the women's secretariats. Daisy, an activist in the women's secretariat of the ATC, described a national meeting that was attended by women from both AMNLAE and the sectors: "The division began when they refused to accept suggestions in 1987. There was a very heated meeting with arguments about how we would conduct ourselves. There were suggestions that it was necessary to change the way we worked with AMNLAE, considering the reality of the women workers themselves. AMNLAE just remained like a satellite, going in circles around the structure of the unions. AMNLAE arrived to tell us what to do instead of asking us, What is going on?" (interview, June 10, 1991). During the contra war the links between the state and AMNLAE tightened as both struggled to survive. The war mentality only exaggerated the hierarchy of the movement, shaped in an earlier war. And if the war was not bad enough, the economic crisis that was caused by the war and the U.S. economic embargo was to lead to cuts in services that might have helped extend the revolution's reforms and preserve its legitimacy.

Nicaraguan feminists might have accepted any of those limitations. Almost all believed that the defense of the revolution was a prerequisite for the defense of women's interests. What was harder to accept were the ideological losses identified by Clara, one of the earliest leaders of the independent feminist movement who helped found the Masaya Women's Center in the late eighties. "Because of the war a lot of resources were used up, resources that were not just material but also ideological. And that was part of the fall of the FSLN" (interview, February 3, 1991).

The Close of the Revolution, 1987–90

The end of the eighties was a time when elements of the revolution were institutionalized; it was also when another sort of women's organizing began to emerge. Joining the Sandinista-affiliated women's movement, AMNLAE, whose roots could be traced to the guerrilla period, and the women's secretariats, which grew up in response to the contra war, was a third branch: independent, or autonomous, feminism. This third way—which explicitly rejected links to parties and unions—was an unintended outcome of the debates that led up to the 1987 constitution and a reaction to the 1989–90 electoral campaign, an election the Sandinistas would lose. The contra war would not formally end until the woman who was elected president in 1990, Violeta Barrios de Chamorro, took office, but it had diminished in intensity by the end of the revolution. By the late eighties, the Sandinistas had won the contra war militarily, though they would lose it politically in 1990.

The late eighties was a time of transition, for a number of reasons. It was in 1987 that a process that had begun with the 1984 election culminated in the ratification of a constitution that sought to institutionalize the revolution. The process that led up to the constitution had been highly participatory, including representatives of the political parties along with a range of organizations including women's groups and tens of thousands of other Nicaraguans who participated in a series of twelve televised debates and seventy-three popular consultations in which more than twenty-five hundred suggestions were made, along with the eighteen hundred suggestions that were submitted in writing. Through that long public debate, many of the women who would become autonomous feminists first became known to each other and to the country. The final constitution committed the state to working toward gender equality in a number of ways, though it was not as explicit in certain areas as AMNLAE's leadership and other women's activists had proposed (Barton 1988, 57–58; Collinson 1990, 112–13; *Gente* 1991, 10; Jonas and Stein 1990, 23–25; Kampwirth 1998b, 56–58; Stephens 1988, 158–59).

The first peace accords were signed by the Sandinista government and the contra guerrillas in 1988. While the war was far from over, the end was in sight, opening up more space for women's rights activists than had been available at the height of the war. The third branch of the women's movement, the autonomy movement, began to sprout, and while it would not grow vigorously until after the Sandinistas' electoral defeat, the first hints were already notable in the late eighties, at least in retrospect.

By 1987 the Matagalpa Women's Collective (Colectivo de Mujeres de Matagalpa) already was broadcasting over the radio and performing feminist theater; soon it would offer classes in literacy, midwifery, and legal matters. The Masaya Women's Center (Centro de Mujeres de Masaya) would open in 1988 and the IXCHEN women's center would open offices in two cities in 1989, both providing a range of legal, health, and psychological services at the same time as they advocated for gender equality, on a model that was similar to AMNLAE's women's houses, except that they would forcefully reject ties with the Sandinista Party.

Finally, the late eighties was when the biennial Latin American Feminist Gatherings (*Encuentros*) first met in the northern part of Latin America, in the Mexican city of Taxco. Because the 1987 gathering took place closer than previous gatherings, it was economically feasible for large numbers of Nicaraguans to attend for the first time. That gathering had quite an impact on the women's movement in Nicaragua, as Alicia explained: "For the first time, we autonomous feminists were invited. The Mexicans made a point of seeing that not only the official delegation was there. The organizers set up a quota so that people like me could go. Also, that some lesbians could go, that some women from the departments could go. There were about forty women."[17] The new autonomous feminists returned from Mexico ready to challenge the party. "Upon returning from Mexico the Party of the Erotic Left [Partido de la Izquierda Erótica or PIE] was formed. It served as a sort of internal lobby and it was this group that had promoted the public meetings to debate the Constitution and that waged the fight with the FSLN for the women's proclamation.[18] There were about twenty women. All of us who were members of the PIE went on to found the first women's civil organizations in the country" (interview, January 23, 1997).

It was in this context (with the war waning, the revolution institutionalizing, and autonomous women's activists growing in confidence) that plans were made for the second round of national elections that were held under the Sandinistas' watch.[19] This would be a challenging election for the revolutionaries. While in 1984 the memory of Somoza's overthrow was fresh and many hoped that a fair election was all the Reagan administration needed to call off the contras, things had changed by the end of the decade. In 1989 the memory of the dictatorship had faded for some and, most important, the Nicaraguan electorate was exhausted by the dual burdens of war and economic crisis. The leaders of the FSLN knew it would be a tough election to win and they panicked when it seemed that their women might be slipping out of control.

Amalia told me how the party leaders responded. "In 1989 the women's movement was practically divided in two during the celebration of the eighth of March [International Women's Day]. . . . About two months earlier they had decided they needed a strong woman who would not permit AMNLAE to get out of control during such a critical period as the electoral campaign" (interview, June 6, 1991). So instead of electing their national director, the women of AMNLAE were assigned a new director by the top officials of the party, a director who was sure to be more loyal to the party than to the feminist dissidents within the women's movement. In the words of one observer, "The FSLN overthrew AMNLAE's leadership as in a coup d'état. . . . All the members of the administrative council of AMNLAE were thrown out . . . and AMNLAE was militarized. The feminists had to go underground" (Catia, interview, July 17, 1996).

The new director, Doris Tijerino, a commander in the guerrilla war and later chief of police, was thrust into a very difficult position. While highly respected for her work both within the guerrilla movement and as chief of police, she had not risen through the ranks of AMNLAE or any other women's organization. Moreover, the FSLN had generated considerable resentment by imposing her, resentment that Tijerino would have to face from her first day on the job. Amalia's opinion about the FSLN's attempt to control the women's movement was shared by many: "I think it was a failure. Despite the fact that she was a historical figure her proposals in the first months were not supported by many women. Everyone decided that her sector would continue forward. I think AMNLAE made a very big mistake. . . . AMNLAE wanted to be at the vanguard of the women's movement; it was a strategic mistake" (Amalia, interview, June 6, 1991).

But while the attempt to reunite the women's movement through force clearly failed in the long term (as would become evident after the election), it was not necessarily a failure from the perspective of a party that had a more immediate concern: to guarantee that the women's movement would not publicly fall apart during the campaign, possibly pulling its partisan ally, the FSLN, down with it.

The electoral campaign of 1989–90 ended up being a contest between two major candidates. Daniel Ortega, a guerrilla leader who had helped overthrow Somoza, a member of the Sandinista national directorate, and president of the country since 1984, would once again be the presidential candidate of the FSLN. He faced a challenger who also had personal roots in the struggle against the dictatorship, though her participation had been far less direct. Violeta Barrios de Chamorro, the candidate of the fourteen-party National Opposition Union (Unión Nacional Opositora, or UNO), was the widow of Pedro Joaquín Chamorro, a man who had actively served the struggle against the Somoza dictatorship from the offices of the opposition newspaper *La Prensa*. Chamorro was murdered as he drove to work in January 1978, setting off the last popular uprising that would bring down the same dictatorship that was believed to be responsible for his murder. Symbolically, then, doña Violeta (as she was always called)[20] was a powerful candidate. She had little political experience,[21] but that would turn out to be an advantage, for she could not be blamed for eight years of brutal civil war.

The Sandinistas' concerns as they began campaigning in 1989 were reflected in their choice of campaign strategies. In this campaign, unlike that leading up to the 1984 election, politics was personalized. Daniel Ortega ran as an individual rather than as one of the many representatives of the party's revolutionary platform, in the hopes that a U.S.-style campaign would cheer war-weary voters.

During the campaign, posters of Daniel embracing his baby daughter Camila were plastered across the country. The text that sometimes accompanied the photo promised that "only the electoral triumph of the FSLN . . . will bring stability, reconciliation and unity to Nicaraguan families, without revenge or resentment" (advertisement in *Barricada* January 9, 1990). In their use of the language of familial reunification, the Sandinistas' campaign was surprisingly similar to that of their principal opponent, doña Violeta.

These images did not mesh well with the policy promises of the FSLN. Symbolically, Daniel Ortega took various forms: a loving father, a sex symbol surrounded by young women, a cowboy leading a charging herd of men on horses. Practically, the Sandinistas could not promise an end to the war; that decision was in the hands of UNO's ally (and the contra's funder), the Bush administration. So what they promised was dignity, solidarity, and further anti-imperialist struggle, loosely tied together with the slogan, "Everything will be better," an amazingly bad slogan for a party that had already governed for more than a decade.

A campaign that was silent on issues of gender equality (with the exception of the good-father image), along with the crackdown on AMNLAE, should have been enough to make women's rights activists unhappy. Would they show their displeasure by boycotting the election in February 1990? Or would they vote for the Sandinistas' opponent, a fellow woman? The answer to both questions was no, at least for the vast majority of women's activists.

For all its flaws, most women's activists, including those who would seek autonomy from the FSLN, still believed that the revolution offered their best hope for future progress toward gender equality. So during the campaign the women's movement largely watched from the sidelines. To the extent that the women's movement was an actor in the campaign, it was largely as a cheerleader for the Sandinistas. One mural painted by AMNLAE read "Women and Daniel in one love." It was illustrated with a big red heart pierced by an arrow. Most women's activists felt that they had no choice but to support such a campaign: not only did they think the revolution offered opportunities for future work but doña Violeta made it clear, though her use of antifeminist symbolism, that those opportunities might be closed were she to be elected.

During the campaign, candidate Chamorro presented a series of images of herself, including loyal wife and widow, reconciling mother, and Virgin Mary. Doña Violeta's use of political symbolism made an otherwise implausible argument believable for many: that a member of Nicaragua's landed aristocracy with close links to the United States could effectively represent Nicaragua's poor majority. Gendered images countered class interests. That is not to say that gender was a "mere" disguise for class: both the class and gender agendas of doña Violeta's UNO coalition had their own integrity. Yet this theme—the triumph of traditional femininity over political divisions and the apparent elimination of such divisions through motherhood—has been a thread running throughout right-wing politics in Latin America.[22]

Doña Violeta's widowhood, or the first facet of the symbol, made her an ideal candidate. Of course, it was not widowhood per se that made her an appropriate candidate but the fact that she was the widow of one of the most important political figures in twentieth-century Nicaraguan history, Pedro Joaquín Chamorro. Doña Violeta did not miss an opportunity to remind the public that she was the widow of this heroic figure. For instance, in a rally in Granada, the traditional center of the Conservative Party and her husband's hometown, she told the crowd, "I love this city because it was the city of Pedro Joaquín and of his parents. From Pedro Joaquín I came to know his values and I never thought that I would return to Granada as a candidate, carrying

Pedro Joaquín's bloodied flag" (*La Prensa*, January 22, 1990). The fact that she was the widow of Pedro Joaquín mattered, but the type of wife she had been was important as well. As doña Violeta made clear, she was a good traditional wife. Early in the campaign she told a reporter, "'I am not a feminist nor do I wish to be one. I am a woman dedicated to my home, like Pedro taught me.' Later she would claim 'to be marked with the branding iron of the Chamorros'" (Cuadra 1990).

Not only did doña Violeta present herself as an exemplary wife and widow but as an exemplary mother as well (the second facet of the symbol), who managed to keep her children united against the odds. Those odds were considerable. Violeta had four children, two of whom were as opposed to the revolution as she was. One of her sons, Pedro Joaquín was a director of the contra guerrillas in Costa Rica and also served for a while as editor-in-chief of the anti-Sandinista newspaper, *La Prensa.* Her daughter Cristiana also promoted her anti-Sandinista politics from positions as editor-in-chief and later president of *La Prensa.* In contrast, her other two children were fervent supporters of the revolution. Claudia was the Sandinista ambassador to Costa Rica and held diplomatic responsibilities in the Nicaraguan embassies in Cuba and Spain. Carlos Fernando was editor-in-chief of the daily newspaper *Barricada,* whose masthead read, "the organ of the Sandinista Front" (Christian 1986; Heyck 1990; Larner 1990; Marquis 1990).

Given the difference in political perspectives and the fact that all her children were political activists, it would not be surprising if they did not speak to each other. But it was widely known that members of the family had good relations, despite the odds. And *La Prensa* made an effort to inform any who might be unaware of doña Violeta's reconciliatory skills. For example, the caption of a front-page photograph (January 4, 1990) pointed out that doña Violeta was accompanied on a plane trip by her children Pedro Joaquín and Cristiana and seen off by her son Carlos Fernando. So maternal love triumphed over political divisions. And if it could work for doña Violeta's immediate family, why not for the whole Nicaraguan family? Both messages, the reunification of individual families and the reunification of the national family, were present in the campaign, not just at the level of symbols, but also at the level of explicit policy statements. In a "New Year's Message from doña Violeta," she promised, "[In 1990] the Nicaraguan family will return to reunite with joy. In 1990 the people are going to choose our moral option and there will not be any more war nor misery nor hate, because we will all be brothers" (*La Prensa,* January 5, 1990).

The New Year's message gave little hint as to what reunification would involve, either at the level of the national family or the individual family. Other references to the contra war were equally vague: "There is no Nicaraguan home without a son, brother, or father mobilized to defend a cause that is not of the nation but rather of an adventure-seeking party" (*La Prensa,* January 26, 1990). Neither the contras nor their funders were mentioned as causes of the war, just the whims of an adventurous political party.

While those statements might have been disingenuous as to the causes of the national war, and vague as to the policies that would be implemented to end the unmentioned political conflicts, statements directed at individual families were more forthright. The solutions to individual family problems were hinted at in the above quote in the reference to the "moral option," and they were laid out more explicitly in the Program of Unity, which promised the "[m]oral and social recovery of the traditional nucleus of the Nicaraguan family" (*La Prensa* December 30, 1989).

The third facet of doña Violeta's image, that of the Virgin Mary, was consistent with the first two facets of the image. Throughout her presidential campaign, doña Violeta was photographed in white, a symbol of purity—in this case of her lack of taint by the filth of politics. Doña Violeta, whose supporters even called her "our Mary" on occasion, played on the Virgin Mary symbol in a number of ways, not just in her choice of clothing. Like the Virgin, who suffered the murder of her son, doña Violeta suffered the murder of her husband. While the Virgin was the mother of a martyred savior, doña Violeta was the widow of such a savior.

In running an antifeminist campaign, doña Violeta implicitly equated feminism with the revolution, an equation that would have been surprising to many members of women's movement whose feminism had been nurtured but also obstructed by the revolutionary leadership. Whether she won because of her antifeminist symbolism or because she was the only candidate who could plausibly promise an end to the war is ultimately impossible to answer. The real explanation for her election with 54.7 percent of the vote was probably some combination of factors; political messages cannot be easily separated from the symbolism through which they are expressed.[23] And whether or not the symbolism shaped the electoral outcome, it certainly mattered to women's activists, for it offered a preview of the gender politics of the postrevolutionary period.

Revolution in the Revolution?

The transformation of Nicaragua women's lives in eighties was sometimes called the revolution in the revolution. That is, at the same time the public revolution transformed class and political relations, a private but not less revolutionary movement transformed gender relations. I think we should be cautious before naively accepting this narrative at face value: lots of gender inequality survived the revolution intact, even within Sandinista families. But at the same time it would be wrong to cynically dismiss the narrative out of hand: just because everything did not change does not mean that nothing changed. The surprising twists and turns of the eighties show that nothing is predetermined at the moment when the old regime is overthrown. The story of the Sandinista revolution should be a cautionary tale for those theorists of revolution (the vast majority) who end their stories on the day when the dictator is overthrown. Ending the story at that point misses an awful lot. For once a revolutionary government comes to power, there is no guarantee that it will fulfill its promises, just as there is no guarantee that outside forces will support or even permit their attempts at revolutionary reforms. Additionally, a third scenario is possible; new actors may emerge after the overthrow of the old regime, actors who might carry through aspects of the revolutionary project that the leaders of the revolution could not, or would not, carry out. In the story I have just told, the activists in the women's secretariats within the unions, as well as the autonomous feminists, were just such new actors. The revolution made their existence possible just as it ultimately constrained their actions.

What explains the extent of, and limits to, the revolution in the revolution? First, the FSLN was a revolutionary movement with a commitment to social equality dating back years before the overthrow of the Somoza dictatorship. That commitment led them, at times, to push for radical reforms in gender relations, especially during the easiest years of the revolution, before the contra war had begun. At the same time, the entire national directorate was comprised of men—men who had internalized many of the same sexist norms of the old regime that they rejected.

This tension was complicated by an ideology influenced by classic Marxism.[24] Since they typically understood the transformation of class as something that would automatically lead to the transformation of gender, they were often quicker to defend women's feminine interests instead of their feminist interests. This was also consistent with the class agenda of the revolution. The defense of feminine interests (through national health care or expanded literacy), clearly benefited poor women more than middle-class women. In contrast, feminist concerns were often considered, fairly or not, as being in the exclusive interest of middle-class women.[25]

The preference in Sandinista policy for the addressing of feminine versus feminist interests was not merely a foreign import (as the discussion of classic Marxism might imply) but also a response to Catholicism and to popular demand. Catholicism, in both its traditional and popular forms, was an important factor in the development of Sandinista family policy. The hierarchy of the Church was an important limit on family reforms as it opposed feminist policies, such as enhanced reproductive rights, that would increase women's power within households and decrease the power of the Church's hierarchy over them. But a much more important influence over the Sandinistas was the popular church, that is, the church of the base communities or of liberation theology. The popular church was an important source of support for family reforms, as it encouraged women to take a more active role in public life (Alvarez 1990, 63; Boff 1985, 35–36). Equally important, the popular church lent support to issues of class justice that, for the many female heads of poor families, were in their feminine interests.

On the other hand, the popular church was sometimes an impediment for gender reforms since, while rejecting many aspects of the teachings of the traditional church, it stuck fairly close to Rome's teachings on reproduction and family life (Alvarez 1990, 65). This ideological impediment was quite subtle, compared to the influence of the hierarchical church, since it came from within the ranks of the FSLN itself. Under the FSLN many members of the popular church held leadership positions in the government (such as Minister of Culture Ernesto Cardenal, Director of Sandinista Youth Fernando Cardenal, Minister of Social Welfare Edgard Parrales, and Foreign Minister Miguel d'Escoto, all of whom were Catholic priests). Many more were among the most fervent supporters of the revolution (see, for example, Lancaster 1988).

Another factor that shaped the impact of the revolution on gender relations was the nature of the old regime, in this case the Somoza dictatorship. In other countries, when the old regime used a discourse of women's liberation, as was the case in many Eastern European countries and Iran, the revolutionaries typically rejected gender equality as part and parcel of the old dictatorship. This happened even if the old regime merely talked about women's equality (without doing much to promote it) and even if the revolutionaries supported other policies that were compatible with feminist reforms.[26] Nicaraguan feminists were lucky in that the Somoza regime had not promoted gender equality, to any significant extent,[27] as it attempted to legitimize its rule. As a result, feminism would not be automatically equated with the counterrevolution, though it was not at the center of the revolutionary project either.

So most of the reasons that class reforms were prioritized over gender reforms by Sandinista leaders were internal to Sandinista thinking (the influence of Marxism and radical Catholicism) and to Nicaraguan history (the memory of the Somoza government's gender policies). A final reason for defining social justice as a class project more than a gender project was a practical consideration. As the contra war heated up, FSLN leaders sometimes revised their previous policies so as to consolidate their base of support and to try to win the support of those who had joined the counterrevolutionary coalition. Revising policies typically meant revising economic policies, not gender policies. While many contra supporters were unhappy with FSLN economic policy, they did not oppose the FSLN out of unhappiness with the slow speed of feminist reforms. Quite the opposite; at least some contras were uncomfortable with the mobilization of women under the Sandinistas. "One [contra] commander smugly described this discomfort as a fundamental difference between Contra men, who want to protect their women, and their Sandinista counterparts, who exploit them" (Payne 2000, 211).

For a series of reasons, revolutionary leaders typically prioritized economics over gender. But their policy choices were hardly predetermined: at the beginning of the revolution, it was not clear that the gendered reforms of the revolution would be as limited as they turned out to be. Had there been no contra war, had there been no inflationary crisis, perhaps the Sandinista leadership would have been willing to open up more space to radicals within the women's movement than it did. The record of the Sandinistas at their most radical, in the short period before the contra war began, suggests that the revolution within the revolution might have been more extensive under conditions of peace.

Gabriela, who would be active in the gay and lesbian rights movement that emerged in full force in the nineties, discussed her experiences during the eighties: "The FSLN began a double morality game. There were speeches about women but in practice there was a world of difference. I felt a strong fear of the word *feminist*. I think more than anything it is a fear of losing power, of having to share power with a woman" (interview, June 10, 1991).

Nonetheless, Gabriela discussed a long list of concrete reforms that all served the cause of greater gender equality, including the extension of education to new sectors of the population, the creation of rural and urban day care centers, the transformation of health care from a privilege to a right, and the ratification of the Constitution. On top of those material and legal changes, there was a rhetorical shift during the revolution: "The constant clamor for men to give women their rights was theoretically important. We shall see how much of an effect it had in practice. I don't think they had the ability to change themselves. I think their intentions were good but they couldn't overcome their own machismo. They never proposed that changes had to come from them too. I think it is not enough to have good ideas. It's not sufficient if there is a great discrepancy between practice and theory."

Chapter 2

Reacting to the Revolution

Feminist and Antifeminist Politics in Post-Sandinista Nicaragua

THE GENDERED IMAGES of doña Violeta's presidential campaign were to mark her government, both symbolically and in practice, from the time she took office in April 1990 until she stepped down in January 1997. In honor of her first full year in office, doña Violeta was praised on the front page of *La Prensa,* the daily newspaper owned by the Chamorro family. According to the paper's editors, the president was "neither a guerrilla, nor aggressive, [she's] a woman of the house" (April 25, 1991).[1] This image of maternal reconciliation was to be a powerful one, as the contras did largely demobilize in 1990 and the war came to a formal end. But the peace and prosperity that she had promised were not to come so easily. Sporadic political violence continued, especially in the north of the country—and despite the taming of inflation in 1991, the economic prospects for most Nicaraguans worsened as unemployment rates soared.[2]

The social policies of the Chamorro administration had been foreshadowed by the presidential campaign, though doña Violeta's gender agenda was not always be carried out fully and immediately. Yet despite the variation in gender policies over time and from ministry to ministry, there was a pattern; during the nineties, public policies tended to push family relations toward an older, more hierarchical model than had been the case under the FSLN. In short, public policy was shaped by antifeminism.

Antifeminism is organizing that rhetorically responds to, and attacks, feminism. Antifeminism is not the same as the feminine organizing discussed in the introduction, though both accept power differences between men and women as natural. The difference is that while feminine organizing simply reinforces the status quo, antifeminist strategies are employed in response to a threat to the status quo, in this case the decade of the Sandinista revolution. Responding to the Chamorro administration's antifeminist policies, the autonomous women's movement emerged with a vengeance after 1990. Ironically, a social change that was only ambivalently promoted by the revolutionary leadership—the rise of the feminist movement—turned out to be one of the most long lasting legacies of the revolution. For the women's movement, especially the third branch—autonomous feminism—flourished during the nineties. In part, that is because the leaders of the autonomous feminist movement were highly skilled political organizers as a result of their participation in the guerrilla war and the revolution. It was also because the Sandinistas' electoral loss helped loosen organized women's ties to a political party that was becoming constraining. Finally, it was because the Chamorro administration presented women's movement activists with a clear challenge around which they could mobilize. That challenge was expressed through a range of policies, including social services, education, and health care.[3]

Social Services

For the first two years after the transition from the Sandinista administration to the Chamorro administration, nothing changed within the Nicaraguan Social Security and Social Welfare Institute (Instituto Nicaragüense de Seguridad Social y Bienestar, or INSSBI), at least according to the institute's leaders. The same goals—popular education, participatory research, communal solutions for social problems—that were proclaimed during the Sandinista era were reaffirmed in documents produced in the early years of the Chamorro administration (e.g., INSSBI 1990). But despite continuity at the level of rhetoric, there were policy changes during the first two years of the Chamorro administration that diminished the agency's contributions toward gender equality. Day care centers were closed down outright or economic support for the centers was drastically reduced. Support services for battered women, marriage counseling, and workshops to prevent domestic violence were all eliminated by mid-1991.

But reducing or eliminating services did not mean that the general public ceased to seek help in the offices of INSSBI. One strategy that INSSBI's staff used to address the continued demand that they could no longer meet was to send those who sought services to the women's movement, a classic example of civil society being expected to meet needs that were the responsibility of the state in the days before the dominance of neoliberal policies.[4] Sonia, the director of ISNIM, one of the many autonomous feminist organizations that was founded in the early nineties, explained that women went to the ISNIM center for help with child support claims because they had been sent there by the government agency: "Often they hand them over to us . . . INSSBI calmly hands them over and says to us, 'We're sending you this woman so that you will resolve her problem.' Or they say to the woman, 'Go there. They will resolve your problem.' And the woman arrives to make a claim as if we were a branch of the state that has an obligation to work on her case. We explain that we will work on the case since we are women and this is what we do, but we are not a branch of the state" (interview, July 13, 1991).

INSSBI's policies and the very structure of the agency were transformed even more dramatically in early 1995 when all the social welfare activities of INSSBI were eliminated, reducing the agency to its Somoza-era function as the overseer of pensions, and eliminating the BI (i.e., Bienestar, or Social Welfare) from the name of the agency. Two new agencies replaced some of the social welfare functions of the BI of INSSBI. The Nicaraguan Fund for Children and the Family (Fondo Nicaragüense de la Niñez y la Familia, or FONIF) was devoted to overseeing programs related to children and families, as indicated by its name, while the Ministry of Social Action (Ministerio de Acción Social, MAS) facilitated the creation of short-term employment for stipends or food or both. Neither agency explicitly served women and the goal of gender equality in either their stated goals (as expressed in their documents and interviews) or in their practical policies. If women were to be served at all by the new agencies, it was only by subsuming them in the family. Through the elimination of the social welfare functions of INSSBI along with the creation of FONIF and MAS, the Chamorro administration took a sharp turn toward neoliberalism in the mid-nineties. While the Sandinista administration had cut state services on occasion, it had not, in principle, denied the responsibility of the state to provide for the general welfare. In contrast, representatives of all the new agencies proclaimed, in writing and interviews, that the era when the state was committed to promoting gender equality through its spending decisions was definitively over (for more details, see Kampwirth 1996a, 1996d; 1997, 116–20).

Health Care

Because the Sandinistas had made health care one of their top priorities, providing free services in clinics and mobilizing highly successful grassroots health campaigns, the Ministry of Health (Ministerio de Salud, or MINSA) enjoyed a great deal of popular legitimacy when the FSLN handed it over to the Chamorro administration. The value that the population placed upon health services could be part of the explanation for why MINSA did not change its approach significantly during the Chamorro years, certainly not compared to most other state agencies. Unlike INSSBI, the Ministry of Health remained intact, the basic priorities (services for mothers, children, and the poorest) were untouched, and, while the budget for public health was lower in nineties than it had been during much of the eighties, the number of personnel employed by the ministry remained steady (Bossert 1985, 352–53; Kampwirth 1997, 123–25; MINSA 1991, 1993a; Pérez-Alemán 1992, 241).

But there were some changes in health care during the years of the Chamorro administration. One notable change, beginning in 1991, was the initiation of fees for services, to be paid according to a sliding scale. As even small fees put public health care out of the reach of many Nicaraguans, women's activists often found themselves providing basic health care, another example of civil society filling in the neoliberal gap. Since both AMNLAE and the autonomous feminist movement ran numerous women's houses that offered a variety of services, usually including some health care,[5] many women's activists found that they had become the only source of health care of any sort for some women.

Under doña Violeta's governance, reproductive services became less available, and not simply because of the new fees for services. In the nineties Nicaragua's public hospitals offered no advice on contraception after a woman gave birth. While the health ministry's policy under the FSLN was not that different (only meeting "spontaneous demand" for contraception or contraceptive advice), in the eighties the ministry did give unsolicited contraceptive counseling to "high-risk" patients (such as individuals with multiple sex partners, women who had repeated abortions, and young people). That policy was dropped once doña Violeta took office (interview with the director of MINSA's women's health department, July 23, 1991).

Education in family planning was limited under the Sandinistas but it was a goal of the health ministry, at least in theory; the terms *family planning* and *contraception* appeared numerous times in official health goals published in the eighties (e.g., MINSA 1989). In contrast, when the health ministry analyzed the problem of high maternal mortality rates in the nineties, it did not suggest improving access to contraception, not even for women who were prone to dangerous pregnancies. In its master plan for 1991 through 1996, MINSA suggested twelve different ways to reduce Nicaragua's maternal and infant mortality rates, making no mention of making contraception (much less abortion) available in public hospitals (1991, 114).

Not surprisingly, Nicaragua in the nineties had the highest birth rate in the hemisphere, with the sole exception of Haiti.[6] Large numbers of unplanned pregnancies, combined with the fact that women were seldom granted therapeutic abortions (abortions to save the life of the pregnant woman),[7] meant that illegal abortion was very common in Nicaragua. Health care workers estimated that illegal abortion was the number one cause of death among women of childbearing age (panel on women's health, March 3, 1991).

By cutting or eliminating services such as child support and family counseling (provided by INSSBI during the Sandinista years) or reproductive counseling and abortion when the life of the pregnant woman was endangered (provided by the Ministry of Health during the Sandinista years), the administration of Violeta Chamorro played an unintended role in the expansion of the women's movement in the first half of the nineties. As women sought out the women's houses that had existed for about a decade (mainly run by AMNLAE) and those that were newly formed (mainly run by the autonomous feminists), the prominence and prestige of the women's movement was enhanced. And each time services for women were cut further, women's activists were energized and united around a common opponent: the Chamorro administration. The skills and confidence developed by many during the guerrilla and revolutionary years became consolidated in the early nineties as Sandinista women were simultaneously freed from their ties to the FSLN and confronted with the challenge represented by the Chamorro administration's gender policies.

The final major area of government gender policy, that of the Ministry of Education, was also challenging to the feminists, though in a different sort of way. While the ministry did not provide the sort of services that could be easily replicated by the women's movement, its role in opposing feminist values may have been more important than that of any other government agency, since educators often have a profound impact on the values of the future.

Education

Education was central to Sandinista efforts to transform Nicaraguan society, most notably through the 1980 literacy campaign (see chapter 1). Through the literacy campaign many activists in the women's movement first became politicized; it was in the campaign that they first gained independence. While those women looked back at the campaign with affection, the opponents of the Sandinistas sometimes looked back with horror. They also remembered the literacy campaign as a key moment in Nicaraguan history, but they remembered it as epitomizing the destruction of traditional authority that was the revolution. In a speech given on the fifth anniversary of her taking office, President Chamorro made the surprising claim that the tens of thousands who had volunteered to teach others to read had done so only because the Sandinistas had mixed drugs in the soda pop that the volunteers drank. While she offered no evidence to support her theory, the underlying sentiment, that the campaign was a blow to traditional family values, was commonly held by members of the UNO coalition and their supporters, at least by the social conservatives within that coalition (Kampwirth 1997, 120, 128, n. 26).

In the early nineties the Chamorro administration's appointees to the Ministry of Education wasted no time in trying to reinstill what they saw as traditional family values. Textbooks in a series called Morals and Civics were written, published, and in children's hands less than a year after the UNO took office thanks to a grant of $12.5 million from the U.S. Agency for International Development (AID). The new textbooks were controversial. While they were not partisan (as the Sandinista textbooks often had been), they were nonetheless quite political. In order to inculcate a version of traditional family values, the texts in the Morals and Civics series presented numerous images, as well as direct discussions, of ideal gender and generational relations. Happy mothers were pictured cooking or scrubbing in their middle-class kitchens; happy fathers were pictured sitting in stuffed chairs or engaged in paid employment. The texts emphasized the value of legal marriage, the only form of marriage recognized by the writers of the books (though the 1987 constitution recognized both common-law and legal marriages), as well as the evils of abortion (which had been decriminalized but not legalized under the FSLN).

The sixth-grade text featured an eight-page discussion of the Ten Commandments, in apparent violation of the laws of the secular republic of Nicaragua (Escobar n.d., 4–12). MED officials denied that such discussions could be seen as an attempt to substitute Catholic education for lay education, acknowledging that such a substitution would be a violation of the Constitution. Instead, their goal was simply for the "educational system to be open to values of Christian inspiration" (MED 1990, 13). As an adviser to the minister of education explained, the Morals and Civics series needed to be reinstated since "education [under the Sandinistas] was devoid of a lot of traditional family values that Nicaragua had known under the Somozas. . . . Christian values were lost" (interview, January 31, 1991).

Nowhere was the contrast between the Chamorro administration and the expanding women's movement more sharp than within the field of education. But the conflict was not between Christians and non-Christians. Like the administrators at the Ministry of Education, the vast majority of women's activists were Christian and in fact the liberation theology movement had influenced many of them in profound ways, both during the guerrilla struggle and during the revolution itself. The struggle, ultimately, was over which model of family values would come to dominate in Nicaragua. Doña Violeta's model, forcefully promoted by the Ministry of Education, was inspired by what were sometimes called the Christian values of the Somoza era, an era in which men and women knew their places, in which women traded subordination for security. This ideal might not have ever existed in practice except for an economically privileged few, but that did not keep some from finding the model appealing. In contrast, women's movement activists promoted a different vision of family life, a model for a yet unknown future of gender equality. Yet that model also drew on past experiences, looking back to the egalitarian ideals of the revolution and seeking ways to extend those ideals into places where the revolutionary leadership had hesitated to go.

Feminist Revolution in the 1990s

By the time the revolution came to a close in 1990, the Nicaraguan women's movement was already quite diverse. AMNLAE, the women's organization that traced its roots back to the guerrilla struggle, was still the largest branch of the movement. Through a nationwide network of fifty-two women's houses, AMNLAE provided health care services, psychological counseling, and legal advice, along with workshops in areas such as sexuality, contraception, and job training (Loli, interview, November 1990). AMNLAE was a giant, but a giant that was severely wounded by the FSLN's electoral loss. Because AMNLAE had been so closely linked to the FSLN before the election, it took the electoral loss much harder than the other two branches. That loss meant that AMNLAE lost access not only to a steady source of state funds but also to the prestige that had been inherent in being part of the revolutionary project. The electoral loss was felt both economically and psychologically.

The second major branch of the women's movement was comprised of the women's secretariats that were attached to the sectors—that is, the labor unions and professional associations. The electoral loss hit this branch hard, as it had AMNLAE, though for somewhat different reasons. While never completely independent from the FSLN, the secretariat movement had always enjoyed more autonomy from the party than had AMNLAE. Perhaps that was because, as part of economically productive sectors, the secretariats had the opportunity for economic independence, through union dues, that AMNLAE never had. Or maybe it was because their history differed; during the contra war they had a degree of leverage because of the importance of economic production to the war effort, an advantage that AMNLAE did not enjoy.

But even though the women's secretariats were more independent than AMNLAE, they too were hit hard by the FSLN's electoral fall from power. Under the Chamorro administration, unemployment skyrocketed (see endnote 2). While some of that unemployment may be attributed to the transition to a postwar economy, which might have occurred even if the FSLN had won, at least part of that unemployment was due to a series of policies that eliminated jobs in the state sector (Babb 2001; Kampwirth 1996d, 74–75). Women were particularly hard hit, as they tended to be the first to be fired. For instance, while there were 4,879 women employed in the textile industry in 1990, by the fall of 1991 there were only 2,308 (*Boletina* 1991b, 18).

The transformation of the economy hit women particularly hard for various reasons. One cause was a backlash against Sandinista-era labor reforms. An easy way to avoid having to pay for maternity leave or having to give nursing mothers breaks during the workday was to fire female workers and to favor men over women in hiring. Another reason was that female workers were also mothers, grandmothers, sisters. If they were responsible from the perspective of their families, that meant they were irresponsible from the perspective of their employers. In contrast, male workers could be counted on to be responsible from the perspective of their employers; it was highly unlikely that they would miss work to care for a sick child.

Some of the people who sought to eliminate state jobs hoped that one result of those policies would be to move Nicaragua toward an older model of family life, the model championed by doña Violeta herself.

According to the director of budget planning at the finance ministry, the Plan of Economic Conversion[8] had a series of gendered benefits: "Of course [the plan] is going to have quite an impact on family life. Before, women had to leave their children to work." Women had taken advantage of the plan in disproportionate numbers because it was appealing to "housewives[9] who took advantage of it to return to their homes and take care of their children" (interview, July 18, 1991). Scrambling to protect their jobs from those who wished to send them to their "rightful" places in the home, it was not surprising that union activists were initially hesitant to make radical gender demands.

The one sector of the women's movement that was actually helped (at least in the long run) by the Sandinistas' electoral loss was the third branch: the autonomous feminists. For them, the electoral loss of 1990 was a blessing in disguise, though it took a while to see through that disguise. Initially, the few autonomous feminist groups that had emerged in the late eighties responded as most other women's activists did; they were quite demoralized. Like the other women's activists, the vast majority had been first mobilized in the guerrilla struggle or the revolution, and so they shared a commitment to the revolutionary project, even as they criticized elements of that project. And like the other women's activists, they were concerned about the effects of Chamorro administration's gender policies. It was almost a year after doña Violeta took office when they finally responded to the opportunity created by the new political era. The official coming out party of the new branch of women's organizing was held, appropriately, on International Women's Day.

The Festival of the Fifty-Two Percent, held the weekend of March 8, 1991, was a critical turning point.[10] It represented a definitive and public break between AMNLAE and other currents within the women's movement; a break that was covered on the front pages of the newspapers. At the same time as most women's organizations joined in the festival, held at the "Piñata," a public fairgrounds, AMNLAE held a separate national congress a few miles away. Most of the delegates to AMNLAE's congress, which I attended, rejected suggestions that they transform and open up the structures of the organization. At the close of the meeting, in a nice, if ironic, illustration of the dissidents' complaints, only one candidate was presented for the office of national coordinator, even though, during neighborhood meetings in preparation for the national congress, multiple candidates had been proposed for that office. The official candidate, Gladys Baez, a former guerrilla commander and high-level FSLN leader, was unanimously elected. Those congress participants who had expressed their unhappiness at AMNLAE's political style were to defect to the Fifty-Two Percent shortly afterward. They were joined in that movement by a brand-new lesbian feminist movement.

The Lesbians Come Out

It was at the Festival of the Fifty-Two Percent that the most important innovations in the Nicaraguan women's movement occurred that March weekend. At the festival most of the participants were only confirming their existence and their independence from AMNLAE and the Sandinista Party, though in 1991 that was novel enough. But at least one new current within the women's movement—lesbian feminism—was to make its public debut in the Piñata.[11] At the festival, organizations that defended sexual minorities set up a stand where they sold orange juice and lemon meringue pie. One of the women who sold juice and pie, Lorena, was quite pleased by their organization's reception: "We didn't feel rejected by society even a little bit; additionally, it was good business. We were successful; it was a lot of work. Yes, journalists were present but they didn't have bad intentions" (interview, July 1994). While a few gay and lesbian rights organizations had existed as early as the mid-eighties, they had occupied a precarious space during the revolution, having been ordered by FSLN leaders to lie low and refrain from making waves. It wasn't until after the Sandinista loss in 1990 that the groups became large and vocal. María explained how the end of the revolution led her and others to join the rapidly expanding lesbian feminist movement. She saw that decision as a continuation of her long history of political activism.

In the early seventies María's political career began when she joined her older sister in a student demonstration against the Somoza dictatorship, temporarily taking control of the cathedral of Matagalpa. Her chosen path became clear when in 1973, while a scholarship student at a Chilean university, she found herself caught up in the early days of the Pinochet dictatorship. Taken off to the soccer stadium with thousands of others, she was forced to undress and threatened with sexual assault. As it happened, she was among the lucky few to leave the stadium alive a few days later. María spent some time telling me the story of the stadium, for it marked her: "It was there in Chile that I became convinced there was no alternative other than armed struggle" (interview, January 23, 1997).

Back in Nicaragua that same year, she was taken into police custody for a day because of her involvement in student protests. By 1974 she was a member of the Sandinista Front and an urban guerrilla. "The truth is that at that time I never was concerned about a lesbian organization. For me the most important objective was to overthrow the dictatorship." I asked if she was an open lesbian when she joined the FSLN in 1974 and she responded, "They never asked me, What sort of thing are you? [Laughing.] Never, you simply joined and that was it; it's not like they asked me what I thought, what I believed. I simply joined. . . . So before the triumph I didn't have problems, I simply worked, I took on responsibilities with clear objectives, which were the ones we all pursued: to overthrow the dictatorship. And after the triumph, I still wasn't very interested in lesbian organizations. For me the fundamental goal was defending the revolution" (interview, July 1994). The fact that her guerrilla comrades made little of her sexual orientation does not mean that homophobia was nonexistent within guerrilla ranks, of course. But just as the guerrillas could never succeed with a mass mobilization strategy if they refused to admit women, refusing to admit gays and lesbians could be detrimental to the success of the revolutionary cause. During the sixties and seventies the FSLN was happy to accept help from open gays and lesbians and even to give thanks for that assistance in writing (Randall 1994, 268–69).

During the eighties María made her career within the FSLN and during that period she sometimes faced questions about her sexual identity from within the party. She was even transferred from one particularly conservative region of the country to a less conservative region so the party could avoid controversy. But since she was not demoted, she accepted the transfer. It was not until after the FSLN, the organization with which she had spent her whole adult life, lost the election of 1990, that she thought seriously about lesbian rights: "With the new election, a big emptiness opened up and I think that happened to a large number of Nicaraguan men and women. It was a political emptiness, that they didn't expect a defeat. For us it was very serious, it was a cause for grieving. Your life's work, your political work, your employment, all that fell apart. So for me, this emptiness was filled by the feminist movement. I think that, because of my background, I always looked for somewhere to belong. So I began to work with women, I decided to fill all that emptiness. I participated, I joined in with the movement of the Fifty-Two Percent" (interview, July 1994). For María, a single thread tied together her life as a guerrilla, a party activist, and an autonomous feminist in the Fifty-Two Percent coalition. She never rejected the earlier activism; instead, María moved on from one form to another when circumstances changed: from guerrilla to party activist after Somoza was overthrown and from party activist to feminist after the Sandinistas lost the 1990 election.

Lorena, who also became a lesbian rights activist in the nineties, joined the FSLN about the same time as María:

> From that time on, around '76, I began to work as a nurse in the hospitals in León, because I am a nurse. There I began to work directly with the revolution in a clandestine way: I stole instruments, anesthesia, which I sent to the warfront, which was where my brothers and sisters participated—that is, almost my whole family participated in that. And the only way for me to help was to recuperate medicine, anesthesia, surgical instruments for the clandestine hospitals. Later I began to realize that there were many women who were lesbians and that really we weren't organized, since at that time there was no organization. But really, the presence of lesbians was significant. . . . Politically I haven't seen myself as being affected with respect to the Sandinista Front. Really, I have always dressed like this, I have always looked this way, always as a lesbian. I haven't had many problems in that way. (interview, July 1994)

After the overthrow of Somoza, Lorena continued her activism with the Sandinistas; in the army, in industrial brigades, and in the Sandinista Youth. Like María, she felt free to be both a lesbian and a Sandinista, so she was not interested in organizing for lesbian rights in the eighties. The fact that both women became Sandinistas in the early days, when the guerrilla movement was desperate for activists, probably helped shape their later treatment. Their experiences differed sharply from that of Irene, who was younger and did not become a Sandinista activist until after the overthrow of Somoza.

Around 1985, Irene came to accept the fact that she was a lesbian and to make friends with other gay and lesbian people, all of whom were involved in revolutionary activism in one way or another. "I worked in the armed forces at that time and the truth is that we began to want to organize ourselves because there was a lot of political organizing going on in Nicaragua. At that time women, children [and] shanty town dwellers were all organized. There were various different organizations for Nicaraguans. So we said, why not us as well?" But something made them hold them back from creating a new organization right away, and eventually they figured out what it was.

> We started to think about what was happening, why, if we are within a society where we say there is freedom of expression—there was freedom to organize also—then why couldn't we do it in that way? Then little by little we began to share, we began to realize that there was a big, a big taboo, social oppression, right? But we didn't know what to do about it; the truth is that we were very new at this. Around then we began to make contact with gays and lesbians who came to Nicaragua from different parts of the world. And at that time it turned out that many gays and lesbians from San Francisco were arriving in Nicaragua to pick coffee, to pick cotton, to build schools, to learn Spanish in a project, and that way, little by little, exchanges happened.

In 1987, energized by contacts with foreign gays and lesbians, Irene decided to finally come out as a lesbian in front of everyone she knew: family, friends, coworkers, fellow Sandinistas. And her fellow revolutionaries responded:

> They threw me out of my job and they threw me out of the party as well. I was a member of the Sandinista Front. And from that point on I began to have an . . . attitude of questioning the party. Why did they throw me out of the party if my political, party, and military

records were good? Later on I began to speak, from the local committee even up to the national directorate. But there was no response at that time. Because of that I told the national directorate itself that I was not going to accept my reinstatement in the party nor my job at a personal level because at that moment I was speaking for all the gays and lesbians who had been thrown out of the party, right? And if the party did not make a rule that there would be no discrimination based on sexual preference, then I was not going to belong to the party. So because of that sort of action, from then on I live out my lesbianism as a political struggle.

Now unemployed, Irene had more time than ever to devote to working for the rights of gays and lesbians. She and others formed a collective but shortly thereafter they were called into a meeting at the Ministry of the Interior, where they were told that they could continue meeting only as a social group, not as a political group. "They even threatened us severely, even with the threat of being imprisoned. But since they knew that all of us were involved in the [revolutionary] process, they didn't do anything to us" (interview, July 1994).

That early attempt to organize around gay and lesbian rights was not rejected by all members of the Sandinista leadership, however. In contrast with the negative reaction from the Ministry of the Interior, many in the Ministry of Health saw an opportunity in the emerging group. Under the sponsorship of the health minister, Dora María Téllez, the new collective took on the cause of AIDS education, under the name Colectividad de Educadores Populares contra el SIDA (Collective of Popular Educators against AIDS or CEPSIDA). Yet, as long as the FSLN remained in power, the position of CEPSIDA was somewhat precarious: it could quietly carry out its work, but it was not until after the FSLN was voted out of office that CEPSIDA, along with other gay and lesbian organizations, came out of the organizational closet at the Festival of the Fifty-Two Percent in March 1991.

So gays and lesbians occupied a rather uncomfortable position within the revolutionary coalition, sometimes assigned positions of responsibility and sometimes kept from organizing. On the positive side, gays and lesbians were not condemned as inherently immoral, as has so often been the case with other twentieth-century revolutions. Some even viewed them as especially good revolutionaries since, like Catholic priests, they were likely to have fewer family responsibilities than the average person and could therefore devote more energy to the revolution (Lancaster 1992). And when, in 1992, a particularly nasty antigay bill was pushed through the National Assembly, the FSLN bloc in the assembly voted unanimously against it, though it passed anyway (see Kampwirth 1996d, 1998b).[12]

Yet gays and lesbians, even those who were clearly Sandinistas, were far from free to organize as they saw fit, risking the loss of their jobs and positions within the party if they tried to do so.[13] Two factors influenced the response of the Sandinista leaders to the gays and lesbians in their midst: the length of time they had been part of the Sandinista coalition and whether they organized only for others or for themselves as well. The older lesbians who traced their political roots back to the guerrilla period, joined at a time when all were welcome.[14] Once the Sandinistas came to power, their seniority within the FSLN meant that they were respected members of the coalition and could continue to rise within the party, assuming that they were willing to be discreet about their sexual orientation (though of course heterosexuals were not expected to hide their heterosexuality). Younger women, who lacked the protection that seniority brings, were in a more precarious position within the party.

But the second factor (the need to organize for others not for oneself) may have been even more important than the first (relative seniority). Even young gays and lesbians were welcomed as long as they organized in a self-sacrificing way, devoting their energies to promoting the revolutionary agenda, as defined by the top leaders of the party. In short, they were welcome if they were willing to play an extreme version of the traditional woman's role. Women were also expected to subordinate their personal interests to those of the revolution, though they were not in much danger of being thrown out of the party merely for advocating women's rights. In contrast, gays and lesbians could be thrown out of the party simply for advocating gay and lesbian rights.

The parallels in their experiences during the revolution may explain why the gay and lesbian rights movement ended up being closely allied with the autonomous feminist movement in the nineties. In fact, many lesbians were present when the autonomous feminists declared their full independence from AMNLAE at the March 1991 Festival of the Fifty-Two Percent. That independence was ratified less than a year later, when the groups that came out in the Piñata participated in the first national conference of the autonomous feminist movement, in January 1992.

Autonomy at Last

Expecting about three hundred participants, the organizers of the first National Feminist Conference were pleasantly surprised when eight hundred women arrived instead. Though the title of the conference, Diverse but United, expressed a goal more than a reality, many believed that it was an attainable goal (*Boletina* 1993; Cuadra, Fernández, and Ubeda 1992). By early 1992 the autonomous feminist movement was large, diverse, capable, and increasingly daring.

A workshop on violence provided evidence of just how capable the new independent movement was. The participants in that workshop proposed a series of concrete steps that needed to be taken to confront the problem of violence. One account of the workshop said there were five steps: that rape laws should be changed to make rape a public, rather than private, crime; that the penal code be reformed to defend women; that educational media campaigns be launched; that a women's network against violence be formed; and that the public schools begin teaching sex education (Cuadra, Fernández, and Ubeda 1992, 24). Only months later, at the end of 1992, four of the five concrete steps that were proposed had already been carried out. The only one that was not reached was the one that could not be attained by the autonomous feminists on their own: the demand that the Ministry of Education change its policies regarding sex education.

But the gathering was not free of controversy. Indeed, the public nature of the controversies was a good indicator of how open and free political exchange was at the gathering; gone were the days of the unanimous acclamations that disguised underlying disagreements. At the "Diverse but United" conference, the major conflict that divided the newly autonomous activists was autonomy itself. What exactly did it mean to be autonomous? Some activists—the majority in fact—

were so leery of being controlled once again by an organization like the FSLN or AMNLAE that they rejected all proposals to form any coordinating organization.

The trouble was that, in the minds of the autonomous feminists, the FSLN and AMNLAE had seen themselves as vanguards, organizations that due to their special insights were in unique positions within their movements. The role of the vanguard was to guide, to educate, and, when necessary, to impose the correct line on the well-meaning but uninformed members of the movement. It is probably true that the vanguard model of coordination had its place in the early days of the FSLN and AMPRONAC (the group that became AMNLAE), when those organizations struggled to overthrow the Somoza dictatorship. Guerrilla struggle did require extremely good coordination and even hierarchy in decision making. But the era of the guerrilla war was long over by the early nineties, when many women's movement activists finally demanded autonomy, an end to the days of the vanguard.

Yet even those who were most afraid of reproducing a vanguard within the new feminist movement recognized that efficiency required them to be able to unite their individual groups in some way, at least on occasion. The conference ended with an agreement on an alternative, less centralized, form of organization: a series of networks. Eight networks were formed at the conference, to work on issues such as sexuality, economics, and environmentalism. By the late nineties, two of the networks formed in early 1992—the network against violence and the network for women's health—still were active. At that point, both had formal office space from which they coordinated the work of a significant numbers of member organizations: one hundred twenty to one hundred fifty in the case of the network against violence, and ninety-six alternative clinics, collectives, and women's houses in the case of the network for women's health (*Boletina* 1992, 12–21; 1998, 51; interview with the secretary general of the network against violence, January 17, 1997; interview with the secretary of the network for women's health, February 6, 1997; for an excellent history of the Women's Network against Violence, see Delgado 2003).

So one understanding of autonomy—no central coordination of any sort—was to carry the day at the Diverse but United conference. But there were other ways to interpret autonomy, and proponents of those other interpretations also made considerable strides in early nineties. Those feminists thought that the problem in their relationships with the FSLN and AMNLAE was not as much that those groups had sought to coordinate but instead how they had coordinated: as vanguards. If only a central coordinating body could be created that was strictly controlled by its members, then the advantages of the vanguard—that is, efficiency—might be combined with the advantages of autonomy or intellectual freedom. Moreover, failing to create something more centralized than the networks was risky, from their perspective. Without such a coordinating body, the new autonomous movement might stagnate, continually reinventing the feminist wheel. So, in an effort to combine efficiency and intellectual freedom, they formed the National Feminist Committee (Comité Nacional Feminista) in May 1992.

To join the committee, groups had to agree to support a set of demands, a feminist agenda. Some people criticized this ideological entrance requirement, thinking that the network model, in which all could join regardless of their ideas, was a more fluid model that would allow members to grow in their feminism, rather than treating growth as a prerequisite for membership. In response, the creators of the committee argued that without unity behind a common agenda there was little chance of ever getting those demands met. The members of twenty-five organizations ended up choosing unity over fluidity.

The organizations that belonged to the committee all publicly declared that they were against violence, domestic and otherwise; that they were in favor of gay rights; and that they were in favor of choice (*pro derecho a decidir*), or the right to choose safe abortion and contraception. The first claim—opposition to violence—was not controversial at all; in fact, that was the single demand that consistently united female activists of both the left and the right across the political spectrum in Nicaragua and elsewhere in Latin America. But the second two claims—that gay people should enjoy the same rights as others and that women should have the right to control their own reproduction—were very controversial.

In May 1992, when the committee was founded, Nicaragua's congress, known as the National Assembly, was engaged in a debate over changes to the penal code that ended in one of the most repressive antigay laws in the western hemisphere (see note 11, above). During that same debate in the National Assembly, an effort to permit abortion in the case of women who had been raped was defeated; in its place was a requirement that rapists pay child support. The fact that twenty-five organizations were willing to take such stands, in the midst of quite an unfriendly political atmosphere, says a great deal about the changes in the movement since its origin in the struggle against the Somozas.[15] But the contrary fact, that the committee decided to disband in November 1994 in the midst of infighting over a series of strategic disagreements, also showed how difficult it still was to do organizing work that was feminist, coordinated, and, at the same time, autonomous (COOPIBO-Nicaragua 1995, 11; Kampwirth 1998b, 60–61; Stephen 1997, 61).

As it turned out, the National Feminist Committee rose again, reactivating itself with twenty-five organizations and five individual members in November 1998.[16] Moreover, even during the time when the committee did not exist, the organizations and individuals that had belonged to the committee continued their activism; among other things they were instrumental in organizing the first Central American feminist gathering, held in 1992 in Nicaragua, and the first Latin American feminist gathering to meet in Central America, held in 1993 in El Salvador.[17] Through these meetings, alongside the formation of the five-country Central American Feminist Current (La Corriente Feminista Centroamericana) in 1995, with its office and staff in Managua, Nicaraguan feminism had begun to cross borders in significant and sustained ways by the mid-nineties. So the most significant innovation in Nicaraguan women's organizing in the years following the Sandinistas' electoral defeat was the emergence of an autonomous, feminist movement that was influential well beyond Nicaragua's own borders (see chapter 3).

But the internationalization of Nicaraguan feminism was not the only innovation. The other major innovation in women's organizing in the nineties was the beginning of coalition building across partisan and class lines. It was not that the women who traced their roots to the struggle against the Somoza dictatorship had dropped the commitment to greater class equality that had driven that struggle. But with time they began to reevaluate the relationship between the multiple axes around which inequalities often revolve. Though the classic Marxist understanding of inequality would have a vanguard party lead the class struggle, with the understanding that gender inequality would disappear of its own accord once women had access to well-paying jobs, the experience of the revolutionary period had made a lot of autonomous feminists think that the relationship between class and gender was not so simple. In the eighties gender inequality did not just disappear as class inequality was attacked through measures such as land reform, nationalization of health care, and the literacy crusade. Instead the very vanguard party that was to supposed to lead the struggle for class justice was often hesitant to disturb gender inequality, especially when the interests of the male members of the party were at stake. As a result of their evolving views of the relationship between partisan, class, and gender interests, some members of the emerging autonomous feminist movement made alliances that would have been unimaginable in earlier decades. Two of the most visible examples of the new cross-partisan, cross-class alliances for gender justice were the Women's and Children's Police Stations (Comisaría de la Mujer y la Niñez) and the National Women's Coalition (Coalición Nacional de Mujeres).

In 1993 a series of groups whose relations were normally more hostile than otherwise came together behind a project that helped to make legal protections against domestic violence a reality. Although a series of legal changes in the eighties and early nineties had strengthened the laws against domestic violence, those laws were only paper promises as long as victims of domestic violence were afraid to go to the police stations, which were mainly staffed by men who had not been trained to address such issues. In contrast, the Women's and Children's Police Stations were staffed by women and it offered a holistic range of services including legal, psychological, and medical support, very much like the women's houses that had been originated by AMNLAE in the eighties and like similar women's police stations in Brazil.[18]

What was completely innovative, in Nicaragua at least, was the coalition that made the project possible. On the flyer announcing the inauguration of the pilot project, located on the grounds of the fifth police district in Managua, nineteen different sponsoring organizations were listed. It was a diverse coalition, quite surprising in a country that, as a result of decades of civil war and political strife, was typically characterized by highly partisan social-movement politics.

The first name on the list was AMNLAE, the nationwide women's organization founded by the Sandinistas in the last years of the guerrilla struggle against Somoza. Alongside the most Sandinista of women's groups was Pro-Familia, a nongovernmental organization that dated back to the Somoza period, whose mission was to offer contraception, including sterilization, at the same time as it opposed abortion rights. While Pro-Familia was not linked to any party, as was AMNLAE, it is unlikely that it would have been willing to work with a Sandinista organization only a few years earlier, when Pro-Familia's national director had disparagingly recounted the history of the eighties, when the "communists" were in power (interview, 1991). The rest of the list was similarly diverse. Six autonomous feminist organizations[19] were united in their opposition to domestic violence with seven state agencies,[20] despite the fact that the autonomous feminists were consistently the most vocal opponents of the gender policies that were carried out by those same agencies. The list was rounded off with a health center,[21] and perhaps the greatest surprise of all, FUNIC-MUJER, a women's organization founded by Azucena Ferrey, one of only two women to serve on the National Directorate of the Resistance (or the contras) in the eighties, and a representative to the National Assembly in the nineties.

Despite the apparent instability of the coalition, the Women's and Children's Police Stations continued to grow: four years after the beginning of the pilot project, there were twelve centers in operation nationwide, three of them in the capital. By 2000 thousands of women had been served at one of fourteen centers nationwide (Comisaría n.d.; *Boletina* 2000, 36–39; 1996b, 34–37; interview with a social worker at the Women's and Children's Police Stations, January 16, 1997). At the beginning of the twenty-first century Nicaragua stood out among Central American nations with regard to women and law enforcement: "Nicaragua currently boasts a higher percentage of women police officers, more women officers in the highest ranks, the most institutionalized system of women's police stations, and the most extensive police training on gendered crimes in Central America" (Fitzsimmons 2000, 225).

While in the eighties many of the people who made the Women's and Children's Police Stations possible were busily trying to kill each other—in the most literal sense—a few years after the war and the revolution had come to an end, those same women came to realize that their interests did not always break down along partisan lines. Remarkably, Sandinista women sometimes found that they could make agreements with right-wing women, around their common gender interests, more easily than with Sandinista men. That certainly does not mean that they switched sides in any significant sense; they continued to share the values of most Sandinista men around a host of issues including economic justice and organizing rights. The difference was that their world was no longer starkly divided into black and white, us and them.

The formation of another major coalition in 1995 confirmed that many had come to think that gender interests had an independence from class and partisan interests. The National Women's Coalition sought to extract promises from all the parties in the months leading up to the 1996 national election, which was the first election for any national office since 1990. The coalition included women who belonged to the two biggest parties—Arnoldo Alemán's Liberal Alliance and Daniel Ortega's Sandinista Front—along with women from many of the smaller parties, including the Sandinista Renovation Movement (Movimiento de Renovación Sandinista, or MRS),[22] the National Conservative Party, the Party of the Resistance (the contras), and PRONAL, an alliance of centrist parties. All three currents within the women's movement—AMNLAE, the women's secretariats, and the autonomous feminist organizations—were also well represented.[23]

At a rally of more than two thousand women on March 8, 1996, the National Women's Coalition presented its Minimum Agenda to the parties. Three parties and coalitions—the FSLN, the MRS, and PRONAL—eventually signed the agenda, committing themselves to a series of significant gender reforms. Of course, the most controversial demands—abortion, contraception, gay rights—did not appear on the agenda, as would be expected, given how broad the national coalition was. But even so, had the demands on the agenda been met, politics would have been transformed in some important ways at the levels of the nation and the family.[24] As it happened, the big winner of the October 1996 election, Arnoldo Alemán of the Liberal Alliance (Alianza Liberal), refused to sign the agenda or to even meet with members of the coalition, even though many women from his own party belonged to the coalition (*Barricada internacional* 1996a, 19–20; Blandón 2001; *Boletina* 1996a, 27–28; Richards 1996, 29).

Why did Alemán refuse to even consider signing the Minimum Agenda? While he never really explained, his response to the National Women's Coalition was consistent with the general patterns of his political career. Both as a young man in the Somoza Youth and as the mayor of Managua from 1990 to 1996, his political style was one of right-wing populism: appealing to excluded groups, especially the poorest of the poor, and seeking to mobilize those groups from above. This style of politics suited him well and was probably the most important reason for his election as president. "He does things" was repeated over and over by many Nicaraguans as an explanation for his appeal to them; each time the mayor installed a public faucet in a thirsty shantytown or built a new traffic circle, newspaper and TV advertisements proclaimed, "The mayor's office gets things done!" (e.g., *Barricada* 1992, 2b). And like a certain family of right-wing populists that preceded him, Alemán assumed the presidency under a cloud of electoral fraud,[25] suggesting to many that Nicaraguan politics had come full circle: from rule by the Somozas to rule by a former Somocista.

Arguably, Alemán refused to sign the Minimum Agenda because the women's coalition could not be squeezed into his political framework. It was nonpartisan while he was fiercely partisan; it was an autonomous organization while his organizations were all controlled from above; it demanded rights with no strings attached while he preferred to dole out privileges in exchange for loyalty. Finally, the content of the coalition's demands might have been problematic as well; Alemán was very closely allied with the most conservative sectors of the Catholic Church.

During the first year of the new administration, that church-state alliance was strengthened as Alemán directly confronted the gendered legacy of the revolution. In one of his first acts as president, Alemán named a new cabinet, replacing almost all the ministers from the Chamorro administration with the exception of the minister of education, Humberto Belli. Belli, a member of the right-wing Catholic organization City of God (Ciudad de Dios), had been at the forefront of efforts to combat various revolutionary legacies. Although the constitution of 1987, ratified under the Sandinista watch, had guaranteed free public education, Belli led the drive to privatize public education. While the women's movement promoted sex education, AIDS awareness, and egalitarian gender roles, Belli promoted legal matrimony, abstinence, and traditional gender roles. But if his social policies were not been enough to land him a second term as minister, he had increased his chances by having the Ministry of Education produce and distribute an election study guide for high school students[26] in which the FSLN was explicitly criticized (*Barricada internacional* 1996b, 6–7; Kampwirth 1997, 120–23).

Of course, the retention of Belli did not signal a break with the Chamorro period, quite the opposite. Yet despite her efforts to turn back the clock on gender politics, doña Violeta also was publicly committed to reconciliation. Thus the Instituto Nicaragüense de la Mujer (Nicaraguan Women's Institute or INIM), a state agency formed under the Sandinistas, continued to exist; indeed by the end of the Chamorro administration, INIM was one of the central actors in the coalition that created the Women's and Children's Police Stations. Under Alemán there would be far less ambivalence in state policy.

Before his first year in office had come to an end, President Alemán had announced plans for restructuring state ministries. INIM would no longer be an independent agency; instead it was to be subsumed under the newly created Ministry of the Family. That ministry was to "defend" the institution of the family, defined as the nuclear family, despite the fact that most Nicaraguans did not live in nuclear families (*Boletina* 1997a, 28–30). Among other things, defending the family, meant "to help people in common law marriages to formalize their relationship through matrimony" (Nicaragua, Presidencia 1997, art. 28, point d), despite the fact that de facto polygamy—men with second and even third wives and children—was common. The proposed director of the new ministry of the family, Luis González,[27] was left silent by the question of how the government would decide which wife and which set of children would become the legitimate ones and what would happen to the other women and children (*Boletina* 1997a, 22). According to the law that created the new ministry, the purpose of those nuclear families was "procreation," a purpose that the state was committed to defending (*Boletina* 1997b, 14). For the Alemán administration, defending procreation meant "to defend life from its conception in the maternal womb"

(Nicaragua, Presidencia 1997, art. 28, point e). While it was less direct regarding the contradiction between access to contraception and defense of procreation, logically even contraception threatened this model of family life.

So was the women's movement up to the challenges presented by the Ministry of the Family? Various groups launched educational and lobbying campaigns against the proposal; in April 1997 about three thousand marched on the National Assembly to protest the proposed ministry, which was approved anyway. But later protest campaigns would be more difficult for women's rights activists, given that one of the duties of the new ministry was to "'oversee and coordinate' the actions of all governmental and nongovernmental organizations that work with children, women, youth, the family, elderly people, and disabled people" (*Boletina* 1997b, 15).

Through a single phrase, the balance between the state and civil society was tilted in favor of the state.[28] NGOs that advocated a wide range of family-oriented causes were no longer the legally autonomous entities they had been. Most of those groups were highly dependent on outside financing, usually from foreign countries, to continue their work in one of the poorest countries in the Americas. Yet the Alemán administration had given itself the right to oversee the funds that would reach those groups, creating the opportunity to skim off some of those funds for its own purposes and to deny funds to groups that were too critical of its policies or too radical in their vision of family life. In response, foreign funders sometimes redirected their grants to countries where civil society continued to enjoy the financial independence from the state that it needed to function as an effective critic of the state (for more on the relationship between the nongovernmental sector and the Alemán administration, see Kampwirth 2003). At the beginning of the twenty-first century the threat to oversee and coordinate the funds that foreign agencies granted to women's organizations remained largely a threat, a threat that Alemán dangled over those social activists who challenged the consolidation of his power. But while the Alemán administration had a largely antagonistic relationship to civil society, as had the Somoza administration a generation earlier, the issues over which they waged the struggle had changed. The guerrilla struggle, the revolution, and the contra war had revolved around issues such as dictatorship versus democracy, capitalism versus socialism, national sovereignty versus international intervention. At the close of the twentieth century and the opening of the twenty-first, the contents of the old agendas had been transformed: democracy now included autonomy, socialism was reduced to an anti-neoliberal whisper, international allies were critical supporters of national civil society. As feminism had grown, the old revolutionary alliances had been threatened. And nothing illustrated the realignment of politics in Nicaragua like the scandal that shook the first family of the revolution.

Unrest within the Revolutionary Family

In March 1998, a year into Alemán's administration, all the tensions within the revolutionary project, all its unexpected feminist legacies, were to explode. But the explosion was not set off by either the Alemán administration or by any of the groups within the women's movement. Surprisingly, the spark was ignited from the depths of the first family of the revolution itself when Daniel Ortega's stepdaughter made the astonishing public claim that, from the age of eleven, her stepfather had sexually abused her. Zoilamérica Ortega, a Sandinista party activist who had nothing to gain and everything to lose through her admission,[29] had spoken the unspeakable. This family tragedy then became a national tragedy that illustrated, in its painful detail, how little Nicaraguans agreed about what it had meant to make a revolution, and what it meant to be a revolutionary in its aftermath. It was a far too neat summary of the argument made over the course of this chapter: that some elements in the Sandinista revolution, originally a project of class justice and national independence, had evolved, against the wishes of the original founders of the project, into a revolutionary movement for gender justice.

Most of the original high-level leaders of the revolution, and most of the rank and file that had sacrificed so much for the revolutionary dream, were furious to see their project transformed. Their initial responses were predictable: that the CIA was behind her accusations, that Zoilamérica was a Somocista, that nothing of the sort could have happened since Daniel was a good leader. Months later, those sentiments were still strong: when tens of thousands gathered to celebrate the July

19 anniversary of Somoza's overthrow, many of the young men in the crowd sported Daniel's image on T-shirts that read, "Daniel, I am with you" (*Daniel, estoy con vos*). Based on my count of T-shirts, nobody stood with Zoilamérica that day.

Another position was more complicated, yet equally critical of Zoilamérica. In this version she was not the pathological liar her mother made her out to be; rather she was a woman scorned. Yes, Zoilamérica and Daniel had a sexual relationship when she was a teenager living in his household, but it was "consensual"; the trouble is that she did not "get what she wanted" and so later claimed that he had forced himself on her. This version was more consistent with the well-known secret that had gone around in Sandinista circles since the early eighties, but it was still fundamentally akin to the direct denial.[30] It also was based on a view of the revolution as a purely public project that was not to cross the threshold of the private sphere.

Yet Zoilamérica was not alone. Women's movement activists, especially the autonomous feminists, insisted that a total transformation of Nicaraguan life—a true revolution—had to cross the threshold of the private sphere. By 1998 some of them had been making that argument for a decade; arguably, they had helped to create the atmosphere that allowed Zoilamérica to come forward. Most women's movement activists,[31] and especially the members of the Women's Network against Violence, defended her right to have her say, to have her day in court. For three years she pressed her case in national and international courts while Daniel Ortega enjoyed immunity from prosecution through his position as a member of Congress.

Then, to the surprise of many, Ortega voluntarily gave up his parliamentary immunity in December 2001 so as to appear before Juana Méndez, a judge who according to her own testimony had been a loyal supporter of Ortega's faction within the FSLN since the seventies. To the surprise of few, Méndez threw out the case nearly immediately. So Zoilamérica failed in her quest to be effectively heard in court. But she succeeded in that, as a result of her courageous act, she would no longer have to live a lie. More than a decade of autonomous feminist organizing had made it possible for Zoilamérica and other Nicaraguans to escape a strictly public model of revolutionary change.

Chapter 3

Feminists Break Away in El Salvador

"WHAT DO WE want? We want equality, nothing more, but nothing less." That was how one member of Women for Dignity and Life (Mujeres por la Dignidad y la Vida, or the Dignas) explained her group's mission as she introduced the festivities at the Dignas' sixth anniversary in July 1996. The quest for equality and nothing less should have been an easy, even obvious, demand for a group that, like the vast majority of the groups that made up the women's movement, had been created by one of the guerrilla groups that made up the FMLN in the eighties. After all, social equality had been one of the guerrillas' central goals all along. Yet it was not so easy. It was one thing for women to form organizations in the eighties, under the auspices of the guerrillas, to support the general struggle for social equality. It was quite another when those same women tried to extend general values of social equality to their own personal lives. Many of their former comrades-in-arms responded very badly when they resisted the return to the traditional gender inequality that had characterized life before the war. "They called us traitors, [saying] that we had betrayed the blood of the comrades who fell in battle" (interview, June 28, 1996).

Had the members of the Dignas (and the thousands of women in other groups that also sought autonomy from the guerrilla organizations) really betrayed the blood of the martyrs? The answer, if there is one, requires considering why blood was shed in the first place. Certainly the original motivations for the guerrilla struggle had little or nothing to do with gender equality in an explicit sense. Even the women who later became the most committed feminists had been motivated by the same goals that motivated other men and women when they joined the guerrilla struggle, goals such as democracy, equality, social justice, an end to the dictatorship, and new opportunities in life. Yet once the war ended in a negotiated settlement in 1992, the contradiction between those goals and the reality of continued gender inequality even within the guerrilla organizations, led some to believe that being true to the martyrs required, ironically enough, seeking autonomy from the guerrilla groups and the political parties they became. To be revolutionary meant breaking with the revolutionary leaders.

This chapter will tell the story of some of the revolutionary women who became feminists in the aftermath of the civil war. As in Nicaragua, the explosion of women's organizing in El Salvador in the nineties was an unintended outcome of the guerrilla mobilization of the seventies and eighties.[1] That history bequeathed the movement traits that Salvadoran feminists valued highly, such as rebelliousness and class consciousness. It also left a legacy of more problematic traits like vanguardism or the belief that movement leaders had special knowledge that permitted them to, or even required that they, guide the thinking of the unenlightened rank and file. "[V]anguardist ideas—inherited from the leftist tradition—weighed heavily in [Salvadoran] feminists' considering themselves as the carriers of women's *true* interests and in lack of consideration for the *others,* that is, for those woman who fought for issues like survival, sweatshop labor, or indigenous people's rights" (Garaizábal 1996, 16, emphasis in original).

Sectarianism was another challenging legacy of the guerrilla struggle. The women's movement that emerged from the war was highly sectarian precisely because the guerrilla coalition that had engendered most of the organizations within the movement had been highly sectarian, effectively divided into five guerrilla organizations and a political wing known as the Democratic Revolutionary Front (Frente Revolucionario Democrático, or FDR) which later evolved into the political organization known as Democratic Convergence (Convergencia Democrática, or CD). Large numbers of organizations meant that the movement had an impressive capacity to mobilize across the country, at least in theory, though it also meant that coordination was not always a simple thing.

The following chart documents the roots of most of the major women's organizations that were active in El Salvador in the nineties, illustrating the historical ties between many of them and the insurgents of the eighties and early nineties. Initially, those typically hierarchical links had meant that the leaders of the women's groups could not set their own agendas, instead carrying out tasks assigned by the male-dominated leadership of the group that founded them. Similarly, many elements of that experience were shared by women's groups that were founded by nonguerrilla organizations (churches, unions, other political parties) in the eighties. All references to "links" should be read as "links at time of founding"; by the early to mid-nineties, most of these groups found themselves battling for autonomy from the groups that helped found them.

Groups linked to the Communist Party

ADEMUSA, Asociación de Mujeres Salvadoreñas (Association of Salvadoran Women): founded 1988

IMU, Instituto de Investigación, Capacitación, y Desarrollo (Institute for Research, Training, and Development): founded 1986

Groups linked to the Ejército Revolucionario del Pueblo

ADIM, Asociación para el Desarrollo Integral de la Mujer (Association for Women's Integral Development): founded 1992

AMS, Asociación de Mujeres Salvadoreñas (Association of Salvadoran Women): founded 1987

Comité de Mujeres por una Cultura de Paz (Women's Committee for a Peaceful Culture): founded 1992

Groups linked to the Fuerzas Populares de Liberación

Asociación de Mujeres Rurales "Olga Estela Moreno" (Olga Estela Moreno Association of Rural Women): date founded unknown

CCM, Consejo de Comunidades Marginales (Council of Poor Communities): founded 1984 (active in the women's movement in the nineties but no formal women's section)

CRIPDES, Comité Cristiano Prodesplazados de El Salvador (Christian Committee for the Displaced People of El Salvador): founded 1984?; Programa de Desarrollo de la Mujer de CRIPDES (CRIPDES' Program for Women's Development): founded early 1990s?

MAM, Movimiento de Mujeres Mélida Anaya Montes (Mélida Anaya Montes Women's Movement): founded 1992

Group linked to the Partido Revolucionario de los Trabajadores Centroamericanos

MSM, Movimiento Salvadoreño de Mujeres (Salvadoran Women's Movement): founded 1988

Group linked to the Resistencia Nacional

Dignas, Mujeres por la Vida y la Dignidad (Women for Life and Dignity): founded 1990

Groups linked to the FMLN without party distinction

CONAMUS, Coordinadora Nacional de Mujeres Salvadoreñas (National Coordinator of Salvadoran Women): founded 1986

Secretaría de la Mujer del FMLN (Women's Secretariat of the FMLN): founded 1992 or 1993

Group linked to the Partido Demócrata (the successor to the ERP/RN)

Dirección de la Mujer y la Familia (Directorate of Women's and Family Issues): founded 1995 or 1996

Groups linked to Convergencia Democrática

Instituto Mujer Ciudadana (Women's Citizenship Institute): founded 1990

ORMUSA, Organización de Mujeres Salvadoreñas (Organization of Salvadoran Women): founded 1985

Group linked to the Partido Demócrata Cristiano (PDC)

COMUTRAS, Comité de Mujeres Trabajadoras Salvadoreñas (Committee of Salvadoran Women Workers), a project of the CTD, Centrales de Trabajadores Salvadoreños (Salvadoran Workers' Central): date founded unknown

Groups linked to religious organizations

COMADRES, Comité de Madres y Familiares de El Salvador (Committee of Mothers and Relatives of El Salvador): founded 1977 with support from the Catholic Church

Comité de Familiares de Víctimas de Violacciones Humanas CODEFAM Marianella García Villas (Marianella García Villas Committee of Relatives of Human Rights Victims): founded 1981 with support from the Catholic Church

Flor de Piedra (Rock Flower): founded 1990 with support of the Universidad Luterana Salvadoreña

Groups linked to other women's groups

Asociación de Madres Demandantes por la Cuota Alimenticia (Association of Mothers Demanding Child Support): founded by the Dignas early 1990s

CEMUJER, Centro de Estudios de la Mujer "Norma Virginia Guirola de Herrera" (Norma Virginia Guirola de Herrera Center for Women's Studies): founded 1990 in memory of IMU founder Norma Guirola

Colectivo Lésbico Feminista de la Media Luna (Lesbian Feminist Half-Moon Collective): founded by the Dignas 1992

COM, Coordinación de Organismos de Mujeres (Coordinator of Women's Organizations): founded 1989

Concertación de Mujeres por la Paz, la Dignidad y la Igualdad (Coordinator of Women for Peace, Dignity, and Equality): founded 1991

Groups whose linkages, if any, are unknown

CEF, Centro de Estudios Feministas (Center for Feminist Studies): founded 1990

Comité Femenino de la Asociación de Trabajadores del CEL (Women's

Committee of the Association of CEL Workers): founded 1992; CEL, Asociación de Trabajadores de la Comisión Ejecutiva Eléctrica del Rio Lempa (Association of Workers of the Executive Commission of Electricity of the Lempa River): founded 1984/85?

Mujer Cooperativista (Coop Woman), program of COASES, Confederación de Asociaciones Cooperativas (Confederation of Cooperative Associations): founded 1993

Programa de la mujer de ANTA (Women's Program of ANTA): founded 1990; ANTA, Asociación Nacional de Trabajadores (National Workers' Association): founded 1985

Sources: interviews conducted in 1994 and 1996; CEMUJER 1992, 192; Guerra 1993, 61–62; Hipsher 2001; Moreno 1997, 54–60; Stephen 1997, 67–71; Vázquez et al 1996, 48; personal communications with David Amdur and Vince McElhinny (both October 1999).

Peace at Last

By the early nineties, it was clear to most that the long war, a war that had consumed at least seventy-five thousand lives over more than a decade, was impossible to win militarily. Once both sides decided that it was futile to continue, and once the cold war that had fueled the superpowers' interest in Central America had concluded, the war finally ended in a negotiated peace accord signed in January 1992.[2] What was promised by the accord that marked the passage between war and peace? Some, like Tommie Sue Montgomery, argued that the peace accord was unprecedented in its sweep, that it was "an agreement not simply to stop shooting but to restructure society" (1995, 226). Others, like Clara Murguialday, thought the accord was more limited in its goals, that it "did not claim to resolve all the problems of Salvadoran society; as a result, the unjust distribution of wealth in the country, the problem of structural poverty, environmental degradation, and existing inequalities between men and women, among other things, were not considered in the accord" (1996b, 34).

There is evidence to support both positions. As Montgomery pointed out, the peace accord called for a series of reforms including significant demilitarization of Salvadoran society (through cuts in the size of the armed forces and purges of the most serious human rights violators), legalization of the FMLN as a political party, and redistribution of land to those who had fought on both sides during the war. The last two reforms were directly aimed at the principle roots of the war: the exclusion of the left from electoral politics and the highly unequal distribution of land in the country. As former combatants gained access to political and economic power, they were to be "reinserted" into society.

And yet, as Murguialday observed, a whole host of social problems were not addressed in the agreement signed in January 1992. One of those unaddressed issues was the role of women in El Salvador. "Neither in words nor spirit is there any reference to women, despite the fact that they represent 52.9 percent of the Salvadoran population, 30 percent of the 13,600 FMLN combatants that were verified [by the United Nations], and more than 60 percent of the civilian population that supported the guerrillas during the armed conflict" (Murguialday 1996b, 36). At the start of the transition process, women were not promised equal treatment and, not surprisingly, they did not receive it. Many peasant women found themselves excluded from the postwar land reform as the local FMLN commissions that oversaw the process distributed land in a gender-biased fashion. Initially, titles to land were distributed to heads of families and those heads were assumed to be men, except in the cases of households in which the only adults were widows or single women (Murguialday 1996b, 36). But in the later stages of the postwar land reform some of those inequities were reduced as more female ex-combatants were incorporated into the list of potential land recipients. After carefully studying the results of the land reform, Ilja Luciak concluded that "women received land according to their relative strength in the FMLN at the time of demobilization" (2001a, 45).

After the Peace Accord: Resisting the Return to Normal Life

The first year of peace, 1992, was also the first year when many former guerrillas were reinserted into lives as housewives (Murguialday 1996b, 36). Others found themselves selling fruit on the street or working for wages without the right to equal pay for equal work and without protection from sexual harassment in the workplace. A few, the tiny minority who had risen to top leadership positions by the end of the war, were to take advantage of the FMLN's new political rights by running for office, sometimes ending up in the halls of Congress. I have told some of their stories elsewhere (Kampwirth 2002, 54–81).

This chapter is devoted to another group, a group of people who found themselves in the middle after the war. On the one hand, they were not powerful enough to fully enjoy the benefits of electoral politics, yet they had access to enough resources to avoid resigning themselves to a return to subservience. Those women, mainly the mid-prestige activists of the war years, led women's groups in the fight for autonomy from the former guerrilla groups.

The days and months following the end of the war were pivotal ones for the incipient women's movement. That was the time when many finally found the breathing space to think back on their experiences during the war. Over and over again, women volunteered that 1992 was the year when they reevaluated their unquestioning loyalty to the revolutionary leaders. One of those women was Kristina, who had first become a political activist after enrolling at the Central American University (Universidad Centroamericana, or UCA) in 1977. Although she described her father was an activist in what she called right-wing unions,[3] none of her four older siblings nor her younger brother had participated in politics; "not everybody becomes sensitized." Yet nearly immediately upon entering college, nineteen-year-old Kristina found herself swept up into the Resistencia Nacional (RN), one of the five groups that made up the FMLN.

> At the UCA it was impossible to not know what was happening and, on top of that, I studied sociology. A professor of mine who was already organized got me a job as a secretary in an office. . . . That was how a lot of people entered [the guerrilla movement]. All of a sudden you are involved, learning about materials; by coincidence the office was a meeting point for the RN. . . . the thing is, at that time I didn't question myself much, without thinking about it much you just joined. I participated in producing educational materials. And in some way I prepared conditions for the men; almost all of them

were men. I did not have much gender consciousness at that time. . . . Until 1992, during all that time, I never questioned my participation. (interview, June 18, 1996)

Even though Kristina spent most of the eighties and early nineties doing educational work for the FMLN outside El Salvador (first in Mexico and then in United States), like many others she could not bring herself to question the FMLN, and the role of women within it, until the war had safely reached its end. Eventually her contact with foreigners had an impact on her development as a feminist, but not immediately. It was not until 1992, the first year of peace, that she felt free to rethink her experiences during the war. That was when she decided to join the Dignas in their fight for freedom to organize as feminists, free from the tutelage of the FMLN.

Of all the groups that had been founded by the guerrilla organizations in the eighties, the Dignas was the first to seek autonomy. From the founding of the women's organization in 1990, many of its original members hoped to work for women's rights rather than to serve as helpmates for the guerrillas. Perhaps because the Dignas was the first women's organization to make such daring demands, the RN (the guerrilla party that had founded the women's group) responded aggressively: "In response to our claim that we had the right to choose the path of the organization by ourselves, the party responded by accusing us of being out of line, divisive, and radical. We went from one region to another explaining to local leaders that we had no intention of dividing the revolutionary ranks, but they were not open to our arguments. They made fun of us and of the name we had chosen, they made up stories to undermine our reputations, they closed off our access to the former war zones and to material and financial support, they prohibited the women of the RN from meeting with those of the Dignas" (Dignas 1993, 119–20). While the Dignas were the first women's group to seek and eventually attain autonomy from its guerrilla sponsor, it was soon followed by others. Partly that was because women in many other organizations shared the Dignas' concerns and goals and partly because the Dignas actively sought the support of other groups. "Convinced that on our own we would not be able to win the battle for autonomy . . . we opened the doors to our workshops and seminars [to the other groups], in an attempt to make a practical break with the sectarian barriers that had kept us apart for so long" (122).

The Dignas probably had a bigger impact on the wave of demands for feminist autonomy in the early to mid-nineties than any other single group. Because of the importance of that organization, many have written about its battle for autonomy (Dignas 1993, 115–32; Hipsher 2001; Ready 2001; Stephen 1997, 67–107). But although it was the Dignas' autonomy struggle that drew the most attention, it was not the only group that struggled over the issue of autonomy in the wake of the civil war. While the Dignas was the first group to publicly challenge its guerrilla allies for the right to be autonomous, it was not the first autonomous feminist organization in the country. That honor belonged to CEMUJER (Centro de Estudios de la Mujer "Norma Virginia Guirola de Herrera"), founded in August 1990. In 1990, nearly two years before the war's end, it was not easy to be independent. Yessica, one of the founders of CEMUJER, explained: "We emerged autonomous, pluralistic, an organization for the human rights of women. We had many problems, even with the women's organizations that had political ties. We had no financing, we had no infrastructure. . . . This is the only women's organization in the country that was really autonomous when it emerged" (interview, August 1, 1994). In 1990 it was hard to be independent since there was hardly any tradition of independent women's organizing, since the partisan women's organizations were wary of independent feminists and since the war continued. In fact, even though CEMUJER was independent from the beginning, like all the other organizations it came into being as much because of the war as despite it.

It is highly unlikely that CEMUJER would have ever been founded by the sisters of Norma Guirola if not for her death in late 1989. Norma Guirola, an intellectual, communist, and feminist, was murdered by the military while at work in the office of IMU (Instituto de Investigación, Capacitación, y Desarrollo de la Mujer), the feminist think tank she had founded in 1986. So even CEMUJER, the only feminist organization that was born independent, was deeply rooted, like all the others, in El Salvador's long history of political violence (on Norma Guirola's life and death see CEMUJER 1992).

Like Yessica, María de los Santos would probably never have become a feminist activist if not for the war. The daughter of peasant farmers,

María de los Santos was born in 1966 in a small town in the province of Cuscatlán. The third of five children and the oldest girl, she found her educational opportunities limited. When she was seven her parents sent her to school but it was hard to combine her duties at home with those at school: "Girls were given a lot of work: the chores, grinding corn, making tortillas, carrying water. Since I was her first daughter [my mother] made me do a lot of household chores. The first year [in school] I didn't pass. The second year I did pass on to second grade. I eventually studied up to sixth grade" (interview, July 12, 1996). But she did not manage to complete sixth grade because "there was already a problem, the famous eighties. . . . My dad was accused of being a guerrilla. They sent him anonymous threats: 'get out of the country.'" At first, her father stopped sleeping at home, to protect himself and his family, until one night soldiers arrived and set their house on fire. So the family fled. María de los Santos ended up in the capital, San Salvador, where she became a market vendor alongside her mother. In the market she met the women of ORMUSA.

ORMUSA (Organización de Mujeres Salvadoreñas) had been founded in 1985 in Costa Rica by Salvadoran women who were affiliated with Democratic Convergence.[4] Originally the new organization was a way "to do something about women's economic needs. At that time there was quite a bit of financing available for those sorts of projects, especially from the Europeans . . . The work was supposed to be for women but the truth is that it was completely partisan" (interview, August 3, 1994).

Like so many other women's groups that sought feminist autonomy in the nineties, ORMUSA was created due to the convergence of two different interests. On the one hand, by the mid-eighties many foreign development agencies and solidarity groups were interested in funding women's projects. On the other hand, the party that founded ORMUSA, an ally (though not a member) of the FMLN, had an interest in receiving funds. Shortly after ORMUSA was founded, "in 1985, the party, which thought it would be beneficial to build bases of support in [El Salvador], had ORMUSA begin to work here under the name of a hair cutting and sewing academy" (interview, August 3, 1994). At that point María de los Santos joined the group, without her family's knowledge.

Around 1990, the women of ORMUSA began to tire of being the women's auxiliary of Democratic Convergence.

> We thought about what we women really wanted and discovered that to an extent we served within the party mainly for logistical support. In 1990 we began to become independent from the party. It was difficult but we did it. We began to have relations with other women's organizations and we started to define ourselves as a feminist organization, though we knew very little about feminism. It was difficult because some people have always tried to give the word *feminism* another meaning. We began to be involved with COM and from there a few differences emerged because we considered ourselves to be more feminist, and that was not acceptable since we Salvadoran women cannot allow ourselves to be influenced by foreign women. Because that is what people of COM would say.[5] (interview, August 3, 1994)

The women of ORMUSA thought that allying with other women's groups, through the alliance known as COM, would help the organization in its attempt to pull away from Democratic Convergence. But, as had been the case for CEMUJER, ORMUSA members found that they faced resistance from many women. If they were breaking their links to Democratic Convergence, did that mean they were replacing those links with new ties to foreign feminists? Was it really possible to be autonomous or was it merely a tradeoff: freedom from Democratic Convergence in exchange for dependence on the foreign feminists? ORMUSA was to resolve the issue, at least temporarily, by leaving the COM and joining a less partisan alliance of women's groups known as Concertación (see endnote 5). In this way the women of ORMUSA were not completely alone as they began new lives as autonomous feminists; Concertación offered them the support of a larger alliance. But the larger issue—what autonomy meant and what it cost—was not so easily resolved.

While all the dilemmas inherent in autonomy were not immediately (or maybe ever) resolved, once a few organizations started demanding autonomy from their guerrilla patrons, nearly all the other women's groups followed close behind. It is no surprise that many different organizations waged their separate battles for autonomy at about the same time. For one thing, the end of the war (obviously) occurred at the same time for everyone; many spent the early nineties rethinking their life's work. Also, in 1991 the autonomous women's coalition known as Concertación was founded; that also facilitated simultaneous autonomy battles within individual organizations. Finally, for many the concern about women's roles within the FMLN and within its constituent parties was not brand new when the war ended; such issues had been addressed by a number of former guerrillas as early as the mid-eighties.

Yamilet's story is a nice illustration of this pattern, of how young women were mobilized into the guerrilla movement for reasons similar to those that motivated their male counterparts but who, over the course of their participation, came to reevaluate their goals, coming to see gender justice as an essential component of social justice. Yamilet was born in San Salvador in 1961 to "a peasant woman who migrated to the city when she was very young to make a living, and a man who was a salesman, who abandoned my mother after she became pregnant with me" (interview, June 26, 1996). While they were poor, Yamilet's mother worked up to four jobs at once to make sure that her daughters could attend high school.

Yamilet was a student at Young Ladies Central (Central de Señoritas), a public institute, in the second half of the seventies, the same time that the urban social movements that had characterized opposition politics in El Salvador throughout the twentieth century were on the upswing (Lungo 1989, 93). While she was not an activist, at least not initially, she could hardly ignore the changes in the world around her: "I think I was a normal girl who studied, had fun, had friends; we would go out together, but there was this special situation, there was a rise in the activism of the student movements. I did not participate directly, except for a few demonstrations that I attended. And also there were church movements in my neighborhood. I taught catechism to children. I distributed the church magazine *Orientación,* and that magazine was persecuted. I belonged to a youth group in my neighborhood: we would get together, we would sing, we held retreats, and we would reflect." Yet even though her volunteer work was largely confined to church groups, that did not protect Yamilet from the growing government violence around her: "I remember that one time a man went to a meeting of a group we belonged to and he was from a group—ORDEN[6]—that was one of the most evil organizations in El Salvador. He was armed and drunk at the meeting. He came into the youth meeting and he started to say incoherent things to us; he showed us his ORDEN membership card that had been authorized by a military officer; he showed us his gun. That is, he did not directly threaten us but just by being there without any reason and talking incoherently. . . . it made us afraid."

Many residents of San Salvador were afraid in the late seventies. Yamilet and her friends all knew something was wrong but nobody spoke of it. Yet the signs were all around them. "For example, we knew that dead bodies would appear on the street, that our fellow students would disappear, that some demonstrations had been repressed—for example, the student demonstration of 1975. I was very close the day of the demonstration and the only reason that I didn't go was because the school closed its doors and did not let anyone leave, and that was how we were saved, really, because that was one of the biggest student massacres. . . . So I had no direct tie with any student movement but reality has a way of getting out." And in her very physical surroundings, her neighborhood in a poor suburb of San Salvador, there was yet another sign: huge shantytowns sprung up on the outskirts of the neighborhood, populated by refugees from the violence in the countryside. Reading all these signs, Yamilet decided that if she wanted to go to college in peace, she would have to leave El Salvador. For despite the hopes of her new neighbors, city dwellers were hardly immune from the government's wrath and students living in the city were at especially high risk.[7]

So when a friend told her of scholarships for study in the Soviet Union, Yamilet rushed to apply. Luckily, applicants did not have to be affiliated with the Communist Party; what mattered was their performance on a series of exams. As she did well on those exams, she was awarded one of the forty or forty-five scholarships offered that year. Shortly afterward, in September 1979, Yamilet left for the Soviet Union with the intention of spending the following four years studying psychology. Instead, Salvadoran politics found her. Shortly after she arrived in the Soviet Union, the civil war between the FMLN guerrillas and the military-dominated government began back home. From a distance she and her fellow students became involved: "We worked within

an organization of Latin American students and of course we were supporting the liberation movements. We would work and send money
through the Communist Party, which was our contact." In 1982 a del-
egate from the party asked "if I would be willing to return to El Salvador to join the armed struggle. I told him yes. . . . It was already 1983
when a telegram arrived . . . saying that I had to be in Moscow in a
week. . . . [From there] we went to Nicaragua. In Nicaragua we received
training for a few months. I was organized within the Communist
Party. All five parties [of the FMLN] were in Nicaragua" (interview,
June 26, 1996). By the end of 1983 she had finished her training and il-
legally returned to El Salvador, by way of Guatemala, where she worked
at the front, following the government's radio communications, and
later as a political organizer for the Communist Party, one of the five
parties of the FMLN, eventually becoming one of the first members of
a women's group—ADEMUSA—that was founded by the Communist
Party in 1988 to support the war effort.

From the beginning Yamilet participated in ADEMUSA, ceasing to
participate only during the months she spent in prison in 1989 and
1990. But unlike some of other women's movement activists, Yamilet
was very reluctant to rebel against the party. In the last days of the war
and the first days of peace, she was optimistic that she could successfully carry out what is called double militancy, working both within
the party and within the women's movement. Yet as long as her group,
ADEMUSA, was beholden to the party, it was very hard to fully ad-
vocate for women's rights: "They always put off our activities. That
was a process at the level of the institution but also at a personal level.
I stopped insisting on promoting the women's movement within the
party because I felt that it wasn't possible. . . . It was not a priority."
Yamilet as an individual and ADEMUSA as an organization tried to
keep their feet in the worlds of both the party and the women's organizations longer than some. But when Yamilet became the director
of ADEMUSA, in June 1993, it was finally time to cut all organizational ties with the Communist Party: "We decided that we were not
going to go around dressed in party colors. . . . [But there were] costs
for us. They said that we were looking for a fight. . . . [In one] press
conference they said that I was a traitor. That was really something"
(interview, June 27, 1996).

In reacting to ADEMUSA's request for independence by calling Yamilet a traitor, the leaders of the Communist Party inadvertently helped consolidate the autonomous feminist movement. Had she been treated differently, Yamilet probably would not have broken her personal ties to the party. But when her announcement that ADEMUSA sought autonomy was equated with treason, she decided to devote herself exclusively to the women's movement. While it was initially hard to break with the past, the benefits of autonomy were soon apparent. Yamilet was one of many newly independent women who participated in the Women 94 coalition, a project that would have been impossible only a few years earlier, when most groups were still controlled from above by the parties.

With Autonomy in Hand: Feminist Activism in the 1990s

In the early to mid-nineties, Salvadoran women's rights activists participated in a series of feminist events or gatherings (*encuentros feministas*), both in El Salvador and elsewhere in Latin America.[8] The gatherings could be considered both a cause and a product of the autonomy battles. They were one of the causes in the sense that they provided many women with a framework within which to place the misgivings they had already been feeling. They helped many to realize that they were not alone; rebellion of any sort is always easier in a group than in isolation. But to some extent the gatherings were also a result of previous autonomy struggles. The agendas at those meetings reflected the gendered concerns of the women who participated in them, in contrast to the women's meetings held during the war years, in which the agendas were typically shaped by the concerns of the male-dominated sponsoring organizations. The later gatherings were like ropes dropped by the autonomy pioneers, allowing other women to be pulled up to meet them. Without those ropes a few groups would have sought autonomy anyway, but the majority in all likelihood would have continued following the organizational patterns of the war into the postwar period.

Of all the gatherings of the early postwar period, none had the impact of the sixth Latin American feminist gathering in 1993, which converted the town of Costa del Sol, El Salvador, into the central site of

Latin American feminism, at least for a few days. The arrival of international feminism was met by responses that were loud and sometimes threatening. Many partisans of the Salvadoran right understood the feminist gathering through the framework that had shaped their actions during the war, accusing the organizers of the conference of lesbianism, of inflicting AIDS upon El Salvador, and of being controlled by a U.S.-based organization, the Committee in Solidarity with the People of El Salvador (CISPES). All these accusations were consistent with right's analysis of the war as a foreign imposition, the result of a worldwide communist conspiracy, rather than seeing it as a response to generations of authoritarianism and inequality.

The accusations were also consistent with a view of Salvadoran women as subservient to the interests of outsiders: of U.S. solidarity activists, of lesbians (assumed not to be Salvadoran), and of feminists (also assumed not to be Salvadoran). But when death threats were issued repeatedly against five of the Salvadoran women who organized the feminist encuentro, it seemed that right-wing activists did not completely believe their own rhetorical claims that feminism was just a foreign contagion. In the end, despite the rhetoric, despite the death threats, and despite the pressures on Salvadoran businesses to refuse service to the feminists, over fifteen hundred women participated in the feminist gathering in October and November 1993 (Blandón 1994; Stephen 1997, 17–20). The Latin American feminist gathering, and all the debates it engendered, could have never happened during the war. Arguably it could not have happened before the war either. This is not to understate the horror of that conflict but merely to note that the war unsettled what had been a tightly controlled society, unleashing demands that most would have feared making in the prewar years.

In 1993, the same year as the international feminist gathering, the new political rights that were a product of the peace process served to advance women's organizing in various ways. In January of that year, between twenty-eight and forty women's organizations joined forces so as to gain a voice in national politics.[9] The result was a coalition known as Women 94, which sought to play a feminist role in the campaign leading up to the "election of the century,"[10] held in March 1994. As is always the case when different people look back at the same events, there were disagreements about what really happened in the development of the Women 94 coalition. But there was remarkable agreement over its origins. Every activist who discussed those origins with me noted that leaders of the most autonomous, and most radically feminist, coalition (Concertación de Mujeres por la Paz, la Dignidad, y la Igualdad) were responsible for initiating the effort. So Women 94 was perhaps the most significant fruit of the autonomy battles of the early nineties. In its accomplishments and its limits, it illustrated how much gender relations and relations between the parties and civil society had been transformed.

Over the first eight months of the coalition's existence (January to August 1993), activists developed their platform through working groups on women and violence, health, education, environment, work, legislation, development, land, and political parties. About fifty women were involved in the groups, which were mainly comprised of women who felt the direct impact of policies in these areas (for instance, most of the members of the working group on land and credit were peasants). For many who participated in Women 94, the whole process was remarkable. Juana, a member of the MAM, explained that "for the first time we could breath in a space where there was democracy. Nobody told us, do this. . . . That filled us with immense joy" (public talk, March 1994). While it was hardly her first experience in politics, Juana explained that it was the first time that she had been part of a structure that was not organized hierarchically, in which there were no president or vice-president and no party officials. In fact, instead of taking orders from the leaders of the parties, the members of Women 94 soon tried to advise those party leaders.

In August 1993 the platform was officially presented to the political parties in a ceremony that began with a march of five or six thousand women and ended in a fancy hotel in San Salvador. But only two major candidates attended, both from the leftist coalition: presidential candidate Rubén Zamora, and Shafik Handal, a candidate for mayor of San Salvador. Individual women from ARENA and secondary representatives from the Christian Democrats (PDC) also attended the presentation of the platform.

There were fourteen demands in the main version of the platform.[11] Of those, nine could be considered feminist,[12] as they represented a direct challenge to power dynamics between men and women. Those points included demands for "comprehensive sex education without prejudice," "free and voluntary motherhood,"[13] and "fifty percent of leadership positions for women." Another three of the fourteen demands could be called feminine, for they addressed women's interests within the gender division of labor in El Salvador, but without directly challenging male power. These included a call for "stabilization of food prices" and "more and better public hospitals." The final two demands could be either feminist or feminine, depending on the interpretation. The parties were left to consider these demands until the beginning of the new year, when they were called to a public debate. Partisan response to that debate, like the response to the initial presentation, was lukewarm. Once again, the leftist coalition and the PDC were the only parties to send official representatives. Finally, the parties were asked to commit to the platform, in a signing ceremony held on March 8 (International Women's Day). This time, the PDC did not send an official representative but ARENA did. So the final version of the platform was signed by Rubén Zamora, of the leftist coalition, and Gloria Salguero Gross,[14] of the right-wing ARENA party.

While it is undeniable that the partisan response to the platform was less than ecstatic, the two parties that endorsed the platform were the two top vote getters. Between the two, the coalition and ARENA won nearly three-quarters of the votes cast in the election of March 1994. The two parties then faced off in a run-off election held in April, which ARENA won easily (Spence 1994, 37). Arguably, Women 94 achieved its partisan goals by gaining the endorsement of the two biggest parties in the country. And yet that begs the question of what endorsement actually meant. In the case of ARENA, the answer seems to be "not much," at least in the short term. One week after Gloria Salguero Gross signed the platform in the name of ARENA (and four days before the election), ARENA celebrated the "grand closing" of the "women's crusade." At this "very important event," the wives of the presidential and vice presidential candidates presented a document that contained "the principal necessities and aspirations of the Salvadoran woman" (advertisement, *El Diario de Hoy,* March 15, 1994).

ARENA's document on women was presented by women whose status within the party was that of wife, rather than by any of ARENA's female candidates. The symbolism of this choice is fairly straightforward.

That symbolism was reinforced by ARENA's platform, which mentions women only three times. Women were promised subsidies to "mother-infant programs," implementation of a new family code so as to "protect women, children, and old people," and nutritious rations for "pregnant mothers and children" (Soro et al. 1994, 31–32). Feminist activists who studied the platforms concluded that the "analysis that we have done of ARENA's platform, both in its general proposals for society, and its specific proposals for women, demonstrates a profound opposition to all that is demanded in the Women 94 platform" (80).

The impact of the Women 94 platform on ARENA's platform was quite limited at best. Still, it would have been too much to expect a far-right party like ARENA to give a strong endorsement to a feminist platform. In fact, personal animosity between most members of the women's movement and ARENA that had built up during the war could have led ARENA to conduct an antifeminist campaign like that of Violeta Chamorro in Nicaragua (see chapter 1). That ARENA conducted a fairly gender-neutral campaign and that it signed the Women 94 platform represented a small step forward in feminist influence within right-wing party politics in El Salvador.

But what of feminists' relationship with the leftist coalition, and especially the largest coalition member, the FMLN? To what extent did feminists have an impact on the coalition's campaign? The official platforms of the parties that made up the coalition were almost all more feminist friendly than ARENA's platform. Those platforms referred to women more frequently than did ARENA's and, most important, the platforms of the three members of the leftist coalition (and that of the Christian Democrats) explicitly addressed the problem of discrimination against women, which ARENA's platform did not (Soro et al. 1994, 42).

Given that these platforms were not widely read, a better measure of feminist success may be what occurred at public events during the campaign. Women 94 was a very visible presence at some of the Coalition's rallies through booths in which information was provided and Women 94 T-shirts were sold. Furthermore, the leaflets distributed by the FMLN at these rallies promised to fulfill many of the feminist's demands. In one pamphlet, entitled "Now Is the Time for Real Solutions," ten promises were made that included combating delinquency, increasing employment, stabilizing prices, improving health and education, and promoting "the rights and participation of women." Another pamphlet was focused directly at women. Entitled "First Our Demands: Woman, Vote for Yourself, Vote FMLN," the pamphlet outlined seven ways in which the FMLN would improve women's lives, all of which could have been taken directly from the Women 94 platform.

Most important, given the high levels of illiteracy in El Salvador, both pamphlets were illustrated with progressive images of gender relations, including a little boy standing on a box to cook, two women working as carpenters, women and men receiving land, and a female member of the new National Civilian Police stopping a knife-wielding delinquent. Through both words and images, members of the leftist coalition (and especially the FMLN) seemed willing to identify themselves with organized feminism by the mid-nineties. By the late nineties, in El Salvador as in Nicaragua, women's activists who had emerged from left-wing organizations were able to forge successful alliances with right-wing women around a number of issues: opposition to domestic violence, quotas for women in political parties, strengthening of child support laws (Hipsher 2001; Ready 2001). There were significant limits to those alliances: in 1997 the Congress of El Salvador tightened the law that already banned abortion by passing one of the most extreme antiabortion laws in the hemisphere, severely penalizing the procedure under any circumstances, even to save the pregnant woman's life. Most organizations within the women's movement were unwilling to take a public stand in favor of abortion rights; those few that were willing were not nearly as well organized as were right-wing forces (Hipsher 2001). Yet while the alliances were quite limited it is remarkable that, with autonomy in hand, it was possible to build any sort of left-right alliance shortly after such a brutal civil war.

Lorena Peña, a former guerrilla commander, cofounder of the Mélida Anaya Montes women's movement (MAM), and congresswoman (representing the FMLN), discussed her experiences working with Gloria Salguero Gross, president of the Legislative Assembly, where she represented the ARENA party, the same party that had been responsible for most of the bloodshed of the eighties. Peña noted that Salguero Gross had changed in the course of working on legislation alongside her former enemies. "And Gloria is not the only one who has changed.

I, Lorena Peña, who was a guerrilla, who wanted to kill those from ARENA a thousand times over, I find myself in solidarity with her, that woman. It is shocking to me" (interview, August 1, 1994). Quite a bit had changed—both in her own life and in the life of her country—since the prewar days when fifteen-year-old Lorena Peña began her career as a social activist, teaching literacy to poor rural dwellers as part of the liberation theology movement. But the remarkable twists and turns of life in El Salvador are more than good stories. Those stories can help us better understand a number of theoretical puzzles: what difference it makes if guerrillas overthrow the state, what the consequences are if they fail to seize state power, where political ideas come from, how social movements emerge, and why they change. I now turn to these puzzles.

Viewing El Salvador in Nicaragua's Light

The differences and even greater similarities between the recent histories of El Salvador and Nicaragua make them particularly well suited for comparison. And academic observers are not the only people who think so; Salvadorans and Nicaraguans themselves often view happenings in the other country as a model (or a warning) for themselves. So when the Somoza dictatorship was overthrown in Nicaragua in 1979, the right in El Salvador (and in Washington) panicked, seeking to consolidate the power of the military by increasing the rate of political murder. And they were right to panic, for many Salvadorans believed that the guerrillas would soon overthrow the military dictatorship that had ruled since 1932, thinking that Nicaragua provided a script that El Salvador would follow. According to the slogan that was shouted in Managua and elsewhere in the eighties, if Nicaragua triumphed, El Salvador will triumph.[15] Of course, slogans are not necessarily true and this one was not. The war was not quickly won by the guerrillas; instead it dragged on for more than a decade. When it finally ended in a negotiated settlement in 1992, the political party that held power was ARENA, the party of the old oligarchy and the new capitalist elite, the same party that was responsible for most of the human rights violations committed during the war. ARENA continued to govern El Salvador into the next century.

So one could argue that the men and women of the FMLN had failed in their attempt to end dictatorial rule in El Salvador. Four years after the peace accords were signed, elements of the old dictatorship were alive and well. "The death squads have assassinated more than one hundred leftist leaders since the peace accord was signed, and they continue without being investigated or taken apart" (Vázquez, Ibáñez, and Murguialday 1996, 50). The women's groups that sought autonomy from the former guerrilla organizations were not able to gain freedom from the threats of the death squads either. So the death threats against the autonomous feminists who sought to host the encuentro in El Salvador in 1993 were not necessarily idle. "On May 20th of this year the organization's office was ransacked. The carpet was almost burned and they set fire to the office and they killed the off-duty officer of the PNC [the civilian police] who was guarding the place" (member of the MSM, interview, August 2, 1994).

The sporadic violence that characterized life in postwar El Salvador, aimed especially at those who sought to contest social inequality, suggests that perhaps the guerrillas were right. The continuation of violence after the war suggests that it is extremely difficult, though not necessarily impossible, for transformational projects, like that of the feminist movement, to occur without destroying the old state. This is especially true if that state rests on a military that sees democracy as a threat to national security.[16] A comparison between El Salvador and Nicaragua suggests that the nature of the state matters a great deal for social movement activists, even for activists in new social movements like the feminist movements.

In that sense, the traditional approach to the study of revolutionary movements, with its intense focus on the state, has some merit. Despite all the limitations the Sandinista leadership placed on the emerging women's movement in the eighties, the overthrow of the Somoza dictatorship by the Sandinistas in 1979 (and the destruction of the authoritarian military) was a critical prerequisite that allowed for the Nicaraguan women's movements' considerable accomplishments. This might give pause to those partisans of new social movement theory and postmodernism who would downplay the state as an arena for organizing, instead retreating to identity and body politics (e.g., Laclau and Mouffe 1985; Slater 1994). An intense focus on personal politics to the detriment of national politics is a luxury that citizens of the wealthy established democracies may afford. But for the majority of the world's citizens, who live in places that are much more like Nicaragua and El Salvador than like the United States and Europe, the possibility for identity politics continues to be shaped in important ways by the state and the class structure.

So there is some basis to the claim that the revolutionaries failed in El Salvador because they did not seize the state. But that claim is far from completely true. Real life is too complicated to be stuffed into two boxes: either failure or success. It is true that the guerrillas did not overthrow the authoritarian state and that the continuation of authoritarian political practices after the war constrains the actions of the feminists and others who challenge social inequality. Yet the guerrillas did transform life in El Salvador in many ways and that, after all, was one of their original goals.

After the war, the left finally had the right to participate in electoral politics. The former guerrillas had (albeit often against their own wills) been responsible for the creation of a vast network of autonomous social organizations. They had transformed the lives of tens of thousands of women who participated in the guerrilla movement and its affiliated revolutionary organizations. After the war, many of those women refused to return to their old lives. If the case of El Salvador tells social scientists anything, it is that the term *failed revolution* should be used with extreme caution, if at all. No social movement as massive and long-lived as the Salvadoran guerrilla movement ever truly fails, though it may often lead to unexpected changes.

The case of El Salvador, viewed in comparison with Nicaragua, illustrates the importance of the state in shaping opportunities for social movements, feminist and otherwise. At the same time, it should point us away from the state centrism that has often plagued political science. Measuring the transformation of power relations in El Salvador by focusing exclusively on the state would miss many of the most interesting political changes of the postwar period.

The Salvadoran stories that are told in this chapter also show that political ideas, and the social movements that promote those ideas, invariably grow out of soil that is both domestic and international. The many factors that eventually led feminist groups to form—family traditions, preexisting networks, the transformation of the Catholic Church, women's mobilization within the revolutionary coalition, and the guerrillas' sponsorship of women's organizations—were largely national in scope.[17] But they were not completely national. It is no coincidence that second-wave feminist movements emerged across the region—and across the globe—at roughly the same time, that is, during the last quarter of the twentieth century. The stories of guerrilla struggle and feminism show that movements in one country can have significant influence on those in another, especially when those countries share as much common history and culture as do El Salvador and Nicaragua.

During the early nineties, autonomous feminist movements emerged in El Salvador and Nicaragua, in both cases largely led by women who had been first politicized through the revolutionary movements.[18] As the decade wore on, women's organizations in both countries would form broad coalitions to try to influence electoral politics (Women '94 in El Salvador and the National Women's Coalition in Nicaragua in 1996) and to fight manifestations of gender inequality like domestic violence and paternal irresponsibility. In both countries these coalitions sometimes united women who had been on opposite sides during the wars of the eighties. In El Salvador, as in Nicaragua, lesbian and gay rights organizations were founded in the nineties, very tentatively in the case of El Salvador and more significantly in Nicaragua.[19] In large part the movements developed in such similar ways because citizens of each country had lived through similar histories. But communication between activists in the two countries also played a role. And while there certainly was some reciprocal influence, overall, that influence moved in one direction: from Nicaragua to El Salvador.[20]

Through feminism, then, Nicaragua played the role of regional vanguard in the nineties, a role in which the FSLN leadership saw itself in the eighties. One of the reasons for the influence of Nicaraguan feminism within the region is no doubt because the feminist movement emerged and grew in that country faster than elsewhere in Central

America,[21] in large part because of the mobilization that happened during the decade of the revolution (despite all its contradictions). Ironically enough, the Central American vanguard at the close of the century was led by Nicaraguan feminists who vehemently rejected the whole notion of vanguardism.[22]

Over the course of the eighties and nineties feminism in Nicaragua shaped feminism in El Salvador in multiple ways. While the main work of the autonomy struggle was carried out by Salvadorans for Salvadorans, one can reasonably argue that the autonomous feminist movement would not have emerged when it did (or possibly not at all) if not for the catalytic influence of feminists from Nicaragua and elsewhere. That influence could be seen by considering the early autonomy struggle in El Salvador, the politics of abortion, the role of feminism within the labor union movements, and the impact of travel between the two countries. The following analysis of the impact of feminism in Nicaragua on feminism in El Salvador could be seen as a case study of a larger phenomenon, what Sonia Alvarez (1998) calls the "transnationalization" of Latin American feminism in the nineties.

One of the influential foreign feminists, Catia, explained her role in the Dignas' decision to seek autonomy from the guerrillas, a decision that would set off a wave of autonomy declarations. The oldest of four children, Catia was born in 1953 in a small town in Spain's Basque country. When she was a young girl she and her family moved to Bilbao, where her father worked in a factory, her mother sewed, and Catia combined care for her siblings with her studies, first at a Catholic high school and then at the University of Bilbao. In 1975 she was twenty-two years old and finishing her degree in economics when the Franco dictatorship, a dictatorship almost as long-lived as those of Nicaragua and El Salvador, finally ended with the death of Francisco Franco. With the dictator gone, politics opened up a bit and the next year Catia helped to found the first feminist group in Bilbao with a campaign to defend eleven women who were threatened with prison sentences for having had abortions. Among the women I interviewed, Catia was highly unusual for initiating her political life as a feminist: "practically since 1976 I have always been a feminist activist" (interview, July 17, 1996).

Before the decade had ended, in July 1979, the Sandinistas overthrew the Somoza dictatorship in faraway Nicaragua. When the Sandinistas called for foreigners with professional credentials to help re-build the country and construct the revolution, Catia answered the call. She lived in Nicaragua during most of the eighties and early nineties, working for various government agencies and volunteering with the Sandinista-affiliated women's organization AMNLAE. "Later AMN-LAE threw me out because I was a feminist. I had a lot of trouble with the [female] Cuban advisers and with the party" (interview, July 17, 1996). No matter, it was not the first time she had been thrown out of an organization for attempting to integrate her feminism with the rest of her leftist politics.

In 1991 she was working for Puntos de Encuentro, one of the au-tonomous feminist organizations in Nicaragua, and visiting El Salvador regularly. That was when she, along with her partner Nina, facilitated the Dignas' first intense feminist seminar: a week on sexuality followed by a week of feminist theory. As she prepared for the two-week work-shop, some of the eighty-four Dignas who participated "spoke with fear in very low voices, [saying] that the party wanted to know what we were going to do in a workshop about sexuality." But their voices soon grew less fearful: "During that meeting I won their hearts. I understood them as party activists, I understood them in their struggle for auton-omy. I wouldn't have been able to pull the topic of autonomy like a rab-bit from a hat. I did not make them autonomous" (interview, July 17, 1996).

Another factor that led the Dignas to seek feminist autonomy was that one of the founding members, Magdalena, had spent time abroad—most important, at the 1990 Latin American feminist gather-ing in Argentina. Catia described what happened at the encuentro: "That was where I met her. I said to her, Who are the Dignas? She said that we were born five months ago and we do not want to be like all the other women's groups in El Salvador. Without a woman like [Mag-dalena] one cannot understand the feminism of the Dignas. But it also can't be explained without [Nina] and me. It was a meeting of hunger with the desire to eat" (interview, July 17 1996).[23]

Even after gaining autonomy from the former guerrillas, the Dignas organization of El Salvador maintained its ties to the Nicaraguan fem-inist movement. That link sometimes highlighted the differences be-tween the two movements. For instance, one of the presentations at the

Dignas' sixth anniversary celebration in July 1996 was a play, performed by the Nicaraguan Colectivo de Mujeres de Matagalpa, on the death of a woman as the result of an illegal abortion.[24] After the play, one of the actors explained that they normally followed each performance with a debate but that it seemed like such debates did not take place in El Salvador. Despite her challenge to the crowd to prove her wrong, there was no debate at that event either. The festive nature of the Dignas' anniversary celebration might have explained the reluctance of the crowd to engage in such a serious discussion. But the fact that the Nicaraguan feminist actress consistently found Salvadorans unwilling to discuss the consequences of the abortion ban, testified to the state of feminism in El Salvador, or to the continuing level of fear years after the war ended (or perhaps to both). Yet despite that contrast, it would be wrong to exaggerate the differences between late-twentieth-century abortion politics in El Salvador and Nicaragua. In both Nicaragua and El Salvador, abortion was illegal, though theoretically Nicaraguan law permitted therapeutic abortion to save the life of the pregnant woman while Salvadoran law did not permit abortion under any circumstances. The difference was not in the laws, then, as much as in the response to those laws.

In Nicaragua, as early as 1991, some women's organizations performed safe (though clandestine) abortions. According to insiders in the women's movement in 1996, no Salvadoran organization engaged in such civil disobedience over the abortion issue. Differences in degree of caution regarding the abortion issue also extended to the public positions that organizations took in the mid-nineties. While the twenty-five member organizations of the Nicaraguan National Feminist Committee publicly supported abortion rights, only a handful of Salvadoran organizations were willing to take such a stand, though many of their leaders offered to me that they personally support legalizing or decriminalizing abortion.

In postwar El Salvador, few feminists were as publicly open as their Nicaraguan counterparts regarding their views on abortion rights, and no wonder, given the nature of public discussions of the topic. In the summer of 1996 a group of five women's organizations (the Dignas, MAM, IMU, MSM, and the Asociación de Madres Demandantes) sent out a press release calling on the Ministry of Health to initiate a public debate around the issue of abortion.[25] In response, the minister of health, Eduardo Interiano, "said that it appears that those ladies have their cables crossed, asking that abortion be depenalized and permitted. . . . he said that he would like to make a space for them in the psychiatric hospital so as to give them an 'electroshock'" (*Prensa Gráfica* 1996, 3). In response, four groups (the original groups except for the MSM) signed a paid advertisement noting that threatening electroshock therapy in response to their request for dialogue both insulted people who suffered from mental illness and, "coming from an authority of the health ministry like you, it reflects a lack of awareness of the new time in which our society lives," an allusion to the government's frequent wartime practice of using electricity to torture people who were suspected of sympathizing with the left (Asociación et al. 1996, 43A).

In 1997 the issue of abortion came before the Legislative Assembly. Bill 137 would have allowed abortion in cases of danger to the pregnant woman's life, if the pregnancy resulted from a rape, or if the fetus was gravely damaged. Three organizations (the Dignas, MAM, and CEMUJER) along with one women's coalition (COM) supported the bill. But the proposal was defeated, and in its place antiabortion laws were tightened, banning the procedure under all circumstances (Hipsher 2001, 156–58). In addition to abortion politics, labor union politics in the nineties provided an illustration of the differences between the two movements and the influence of foreigners on the Salvadoran movement. Remember that in Nicaragua organized feminism first emerged through the women's secretariats of the labor unions, especially the Association of Rural Workers, the ATC (see chapter 1). In this respect, the story of feminism in Nicaragua is unusual; feminism is usually an urban phenomenon that then gets extended to the countryside.

The experience of feminism in El Salvador followed the more typical model: from the cities to the countryside. Also, more typically, all female groups, rather than women's secretariats within the unions, were the first to demand independence from the male-dominated organizations that first founded them. Many union activists in El Salvador were aware of these differences; at a roundtable discussion on women and union politics, the example of Nicaragua came up more than once. One group had been visited by a psychologist from the Nicaraguan organization Puntos de Encuentro, a man who had successfully spoken of masculinity to their male colleagues (who had been unwilling to discuss those issues with their female coworkers). Another Nicaraguan NGO, CANTERA, was soon to help them develop a new program. Thinking about these experiences, one of the participants in the discussion observed that they had a great deal to learn from union activists in Nicaragua who were really "more advanced" in their feminist organizing (Women and Labor Unions, forum sponsored by the Dignas, July 20, 1996).

A final factor that illustrated the relationship between feminism in the two countries was travel, or specifically, the meaning that activists gave to travel to the other country, meaning that differed depending on one's country of origin. In the nineties many Nicaraguan residents traveled to El Salvador to spread the good news of feminism, some of whom have already been mentioned: Catia's workshops for the Dignas, the performance by the Colectivo de Mujeres de Matagalpa, the visits to labor union organizations by activists from Puntos de Encuentro and CANTERA. In 1998 the Nicaraguan feminist magazine *La Boletina*[26] reported that its representatives had traveled to El Salvador at the invitation of the Network of Salvadoran Women for Unity and Development (Red de Mujeres Salvadoreñas por la Unidad y el Desarrollo) to give advice on how to initiate a similar feminist publication in El Salvador (1998, 71–72).[27]

Nicaraguans traveled to El Salvador primarily to teach some aspect of how to organize, though no doubt they also learned through their contacts with Salvadorans. In contrast, the Salvadoran activists often mentioned the role that visits to Nicaragua played in their own development as feminists. During the eighties large numbers of Salvadorans spent time in Nicaragua since revolutionary Nicaragua was a place where refugees from the death squads, or activists within the revolutionary coalition, could find shelter. In Nicaragua they sometimes had experiences that could not have happened back in El Salvador. For instance, the authors of a study of female former guerrillas noted that whether they were from the countryside or the city, all the women they interviewed had been raised in households where the topic of sex was taboo. Moreover, the schools in El Salvador did nothing to lift the silence that surrounded sexuality. But those who had attended public school in Sandinista Nicaragua had different experiences. "In

Nicaragua things were very open. I remember when I was in seventh, eighth, and ninth grade, they gave talks on sex education once a week. We also took classes from another compañera, she taught classes to the young people of the party" (Elvira, quoted in Vázquez, Ibáñez, and Murguialday 1996, 141).

In the nineties, once the war had ended, many Salvadorans continued to visit Nicaragua periodically. Lorena Peña, a former guerrilla commander, explained that she and another leader of the women's group she had helped found (MAM) had taken a trip to Nicaragua in 1983 to collect information about feminism in that country. She listed the groups they visited—Puntos de Encuentro, Mujer y Cambio, Ixchen, CANTERA, the ATC, Mujeres de Matagalpa—and concluded that "we went around there being inspired." Yet she was careful to add, "but we're not married to them, we are independent." Given the FMLN's historic ties to the FSLN of Nicaragua and given that, of all the women's groups, AMNLAE continued to be the closest to the FSLN, it was surprising that she, an FMLN congressional representative, had not visited with anyone from AMNLAE. Thinking perhaps she had forgotten to mention that visit, I asked about AMNLAE. "No, not with AMNLAE; we didn't have enough time or interest. But it's not that we have anything against AMNLAE" (interview, August 1, 1994). That comment spoke volumes about the evolution, by the nineties, of Central American feminism away from its roots in the guerrilla organizations and their closest allies, like AMNLAE. Only a few years earlier, the AMNLAE office would have been the first stop for an FMLN leader like Lorena Peña.

International development projects were the one international influence on Salvadoran women's organizing in the nineties that had nothing to do with Nicaragua, for Nicaragua was at least as impoverished as El Salvador. As noted earlier, in the eighties, foreign funding for women's projects had played an important role in encouraging parties within the FMLN to set up separate women's organizations. So while the influence of outside funders was nothing new in the postwar years, there was one dramatic change in the politics of foreign development projects during the nineties. That change was in the role of the U.S. Agency for International Development (USAID).

During the war, the government of the United States had been solidly on the side of the Salvadoran military in its war against the revolutionaries, providing $3.6 billion in aid for the war effort, a level of economic support unprecedented in the history of U.S.–Latin American relations (McClintock 1998, 221). So the U.S. government was hardly a neutral observer of Salvadoran politics. Knowing that history, I was amazed to learn that many of the women's organizations that had been founded by the guerrillas of the eighties were recipients of large grants from the U.S. government in the nineties—that is, from their historic enemy.

Why was the Salvadoran office of USAID willing to extend funds for social services in a politically neutral way, that is, without penalizing groups for having roots on the "wrong" side of the war divide? Certainly the transition from the Reagan and Bush administrations (both of which had promoted the Salvadoran military) to the Clinton administration (which had not been implicated in the politics of the war) could be part of the explanation. The end of the cold war that had justified funding the Salvadoran military certainly was another factor. But in Nicaragua at that time (the early to mid-nineties) there were no similar cases of USAID office funds being granted to women's organizations with revolutionary roots, according to women's movement activists and AID officials I interviewed. Though the cold war had ended in both Nicaragua and El Salvador by the early to mid-nineties, the U.S. government had won more decisively in El Salvador than Nicaragua (since the Salvadoran guerrillas had never taken power, as had the Nicaraguan guerrillas). Logically, U.S. officials would be less threatened by women's organizations with roots in the guerrilla struggle in El Salvador than in Nicaragua. A final difference may be one of personality, that the AID officials stationed in El Salvador were more technocratic and less ideological than those stationed in Nicaragua.

Whatever the explanation for USAID's granting of funds to Salvadoran women's organizations, those grants had a significant impact on the movement, mainly because they were so large. María de los Santos of ORMUSA told me that AID gave them $10,000 a month for carrying out a health project (health services for mothers and infants along with family planning) to serve ten thousand residents in ten rural communities.[28] At the same time as they provided services, the women of ORMUSA tried to do consciousness-raising work with the recipients of those services. "Within that program, health care is always accom-

panied by gender analysis" (interview, August 3, 1994). This combination of service provision and feminist organizing seemed to be acceptable to the providers of the funds for those services, at least as long as
the main focus was on service provision. AID funds for the project were
channeled through an umbrella group called the Mother and Child
Health Program (Programa Salud Materna Infantil, or PROSAMI), a
group that included some fifty NGOs. According to María de los Santos, "PROSAMI is very demanding with respect to finances but politically we haven't had any problems" (interview, August 3, 1994).

While agreeing with María de los Santos's assessment that AID did
not place direct political pressures on grant recipients,[29] Xochitl thought
that the development agency's grants had definitely had a political impact on the women's movement, a negative one in her assessment. One
effect was that AID grants tended to lead to greater hierarchy within organizations, as the evaluation process was not amenable to the sort of
group decision making that had been more common before large
grants were widely available. Another effect had to do with the nature
of the grants themselves: what they funded and, more to the point, did
not fund. While her organization, ADEMUSA, had originally sought
funding for an organizing project, the end result was the opposite of
what they had sought. "One of AID's requirements is that the grassroots work has to be exclusively devoted to service provision: maternal
health and infant survival . . . [they require] extremely high numerical
goals. That doesn't give you any chance to do workshops with women,
or to think things through. . . . That was where we had a lot of problems—if we were going to be an NGO or if we were going to be a
women's organization. [Yamilet], all by herself, decided that ADE-
MUSA was going to be defined as an NGO" (interview, July 30, 1996).

Xochitl's complaints about the transformation of power relations
within ADEMUSA and the new emphasis on service provision rather
than consciousness raising may have led to the decision to have her and
four others fired. "[The administration] fired us in March 1996. We
were fired by the administrator in charge while [Yamilet] was away on
a trip. We were given a week. . . . That is something I don't understand.
[Yamilet] feels a lot of resentment toward the [Communist] Party and
with good reason, but she doesn't know how to channel her resentment. [Yamilet] no longer is the same person who began this whole

process. The system took her over. And we had trusted her. Her resentment led her to look for other options. One of the options that she found was . . . AID. AID is promoting her hard. . . . Of those of us who founded ADEMUSA the only one who is left is [Yamilet]. That's a problem that all the NGOs are having now" (interview, July 30, 1996).[30] Xochitl's observations seem to once again confirm the adage that money corrupts. Perhaps they also point to the need for a new adage, that money depoliticizes. And yet, despite those problems, what were the directors of women's organizations to do? Refusing to taint their hands with AID money could mean that thousands could go without the health services those organizations could otherwise provide. Or it could mean that those services would be provided by more conservative NGOs that did not even try to address power inequalities between the sexes. And under some circumstances, accepting development grants did not lead to the demobilization of feminist efforts.

In the case of the Federation of Cooperative Associations (Confederación de Asociaciones Cooperativas or COASES), women's positions within the union movement were promoted rather than compromised through foreign grants, allowing for the creation of the Coop Woman (Mujer Cooperatista) project in 1993. Adela explained how that came about as a result of cooperation between foreign funders and women within the federation: "A very strong organization from Norway finances us. If an organization has no women's program, they do not give it a grant. If there are no women in leadership positions, they do not give it a grant. For our part, we have taken care of developing women's programs. The pressure comes from outside but it would be easy for them to say that they had kept their promise without actually keeping it. But we make sure that things get done. We women have an independent account: $14,000 per year" (interview, July 15, 1996). Without the pressure of foreign funders, many male cooperative members would have hesitated to share power with women. And yet if grant makers rigidly defined the numbers of direct services to be provided, as was the case for the AID grants, the new women's programs might have left women where they began, in a position of providing services to others. Ultimately, the politics of international development after the cold war was as complicated as ever: a great deal depended on the nature of the strings attached to the grants.

After the Cold War

Both Nicaragua and El Salvador found themselves serving as cold war battlefields, suffering over a hundred thousand deaths between them in the eighties alone. In the years following the fall of the Soviet Union, patterns of political behavior and ideologies that were forged through the violence of the cold war years were not easily transformed. And yet, on occasion, they did change. Certainly the fact that the Salvadoran office of USAID would grant money to former enemies to provide health services was an indicator of one such transformed relationship. The Central American left also found itself reevaluating its role in the world in the years following the conclusion of the wars, both cold and hot. The story of the feminist movements that broke away from the guerrilla organizations and larger revolutionary coalitions is one result of that process of reevaluation. Without any doubt, the feminists of the nineties had traveled quite a way from the revolutionary organizations of their youths. Yet for all their travels, they still carried vestiges of their original ideological road maps, vestiges that gave Central American feminism a distinct character. In other words, they were still recognizable as Latin American leftists.

"During the second half of the twentieth century, partisans of the Latin American Left stressed change over continuity; democracy and human rights over domestic security; and national identity and sovereignty over national security. . . . In economic and social matters, the left tends to emphasize social justice over economic performance . . . income distribution over well-functioning markets, reducing inequalities over competitiveness, social spending over controlling inflation" (Castañeda 1994, 18). This set of social values was sometimes used to justify ignoring personal politics—issues like domestic violence, sexual freedom, equality between men and women—which supposedly would be addressed after the triumph of the revolution. But those social values also gave Central American feminism what feminists often called a *global* quality, a term that may be loosely translated as "holistic." A *global* project, in the Central American sense, is one that is all-encompassing or big picture–oriented or macro. When Central American feminists explained their vision of feminism as a global project, a project aimed at transforming society as a whole, one could hear the echoes of their revolutionary histories. The legacy of the revolutionary struggle for Central American feminism was this radical, holistic vision, along with a deep-seated optimism and fearlessness in the face of daunting odds.

Of course, Salvadoran feminists did not challenge those odds completely on their own. Instead, they enjoyed a somewhat favorable international context. International factors played an important role in the emergence and expansion of the Salvadoran feminist movement following the conclusion of the civil war in 1992. Those international factors included the emergence of regular conferences in which women's rights activists could exchange ideas, most important, the feminist gatherings, one of which was held in El Salvador. More important in numerical terms, many of the women who founded the feminist movement in the eighties had spent time in exile in countries such as Nicaragua, Mexico, Australia, and the United States. When they returned to El Salvador at the close of the war, they brought ideas from social movements in those countries.

Another way in which migration influenced the movement was through individual feminists from northern countries who spent time in El Salvador as part of their solidarity work. While most visited only briefly, a few influential foreign women, like Catia, spent years in El Salvador. During her years in El Salvador, Catia shared the experiences of her early years as a feminist activist in her native Basque country (in Spain) and more important, she was a living link to the feminist movement in Nicaragua, where she had also lived for years. The final critical role that feminists from wealthy northern countries played was as providers of money, either directly through international feminist foundations, or indirectly through pressure on agencies such as the United Nations and USAID.

Without the exchange of ideas across borders through short-term or long-term travel, without the critical grants for women's projects that became increasingly available starting in the late eighties, Salvadoran feminists would have been less successful. But the impact of feminists from elsewhere did not mean that they copied feminists of the north. Instead they used the opportunities created through travel and small grants to create a feminism that was very Salvadoran, a feminist movement that was notable for its roots in the Salvadoran left and that looked quite different from northern feminism.

In the post–cold war world it was often fashionable for northern feminists, especially academic feminists, to give up on the big picture, to instead retreat into transgressive personal actions in the hopes that deconstructing Madonna or piercing one's tongue might challenge social inequality. Yet despite the real influence of feminism from the north, some of the more personalistic elements of that movement had little impact on Central American feminism. No doubt that was at least partly because of the Central American's roots in a tradition of struggle for holistic, revolutionary change, roots that remained alive even as feminists tried to challenge the vanguardism and sectarianism that was also inherent in the guerrilla tradition.

The FSLN of Nicaragua and the FMLN of El Salvador were eminently cold war movements, both fitting comfortably into the framework identified by Castañeda. The feminist movements that broke away from those organizations could also be seen as a response to that cold war tradition. In contrast, the EZLN of southern Mexico, a movement whose initial public appearance was years after the end of the cold war, was the first major guerrilla movement in the region to act without the constraints and resources that shaped guerrilla movements throughout much of the twentieth century. It is to the future of revolution in the twenty-first century that I now turn.

Chapter 4

Conquering the Space That Is Ours

Women, Civil Society, and the Zapatista Rebellion

EARLIER LATIN AMERICAN guerrilla movements, like the Sandinistas of Nicaragua and the FMLN of El Salvador, took a long time to incorporate the struggle for gender equality into their revolutionary agendas. But the Zapatista Army of National Liberation (Ejército Zapatista de Liberación Nacional, or EZLN), was different from the very moment when it first publicly emerged, in the early hours of the new year of 1994. Lisa, an activist in the Zapatista Front for National Liberation (Frente Zapatista de Liberación Nacional, or FZLN), a group linked to the EZLN, explained: "This struggle has different implications than the others because it is very complete from the beginning. I think it has learned from the earlier processes and it has gone beyond them. Obviously as a woman I am very interested in taking on women's struggles. [In FZLN meetings] we have begun to talk about the fact that one cannot be a Zapatista and an oppressor. And it is incongruent to be a revolutionary and to block women's liberation" (interview, June 26, 1997). Even if Lisa might have exaggerated in claiming that the Zapatistas were born complete, that they incorporated a demand for fully equal gender relations into the revolutionary agenda without hesitation, it is certain that they were more complete than their predecessors.

On January 1, 1994, the first day of the rebellion, the Zapatistas distributed copies of a twenty-page booklet called *El despertador mexicano*

(The Mexican alarm clock).[1] Pages seventeen and eighteen of the book-let were devoted to a list of women's demands, known as the Revolu-tionary Women's Law,[2] in sharp contrast to the original agendas of earlier guerrilla groups in Latin America, which barely mentioned gender is-sues, if at all.[3] That the women's demands were listed near the end of the booklet is also telling, of course. Women's demands rarely were at the top of the Zapatista agenda during the first years of the public rebellion. Yet those demands never disappeared completely either, and they were to fuel a dramatic increase in the numbers of organized women, and the co-herence of the women's movement, in Chiapas and in Mexico as a whole.

The first sentence of the Revolutionary Women's Law read much like so many earlier declarations of independence, inviting women to join a universal struggle against oppression without specific reference to gender inequality: "[T]he EZLN incorporates women into the revolu-tionary struggle without concern for their race, creed, color or political affiliation, the only requirement is to take up the demands of exploited people and to commit to obey and enforce the laws and regulations of the revolution." But at that point the similarity ended, for the Zapatista document went on to list ten specific women's demands. The list in-cluded demands that were directed at the government, as is typical of guerrilla demands, insisting on women's right to primary health care and education. But some of the demands were made to a different au-dience, addressing fellow guerrillas and fellow indigenous people: in-sisting on women's right to participate in the decisions made in their communities, to choose how many children to have and when to have them, to avoid forced matrimony, to live free from violence both in or out of their homes. In the long history of guerrilla politics in Latin America, the personal had never been analyzed in such explicitly polit-ical terms.

According to Zapatista spokesperson Subcomandante Marcos, the Revolutionary Women's Law came out of a series of meetings with in-digenous women in dozens of communities in the months leading up to March 1993. In that month, according to Marcos, the "first upris-ing of the EZLN" occurred when Comandante Susana read the law to an audience of "nervous" men and "singing" women (Marcos 1994, 69; Rovira 1997, 110–17). The women's movement activists I interviewed thought this was what had happened, although several suggested that the impact of the Revolutionary Women's Law was greatly limited by the fact that some women who entered the Zapatista forces after the law was presented did not even know of its existence. Paloma, an activist in the Women's Group of San Cristóbal (Grupo de Mujeres de San Cristóbal),[4] had a rather ambivalent answer to my question about the meaning of the Revolutionary Women's Law:

> What I think is that the EZLN is not a feminist movement but rather a movement that is military, hierarchical, and authoritarian. Not all of them have gender consciousness but some of them do. The EZLN is not against working with women but I think that it has been a little careless about work with women. The topic of women always is treated as less important than other topics. But it does try to break with a patriarchal system. We had an interview with some of the commanders about unjust punishment in the case of women who had been raped who did not get to participate in the decisions. And they told us that they recognized their faults, they promised to work so that women's situation would change. The fact that an indigenous woman, with a military rank, can wear pants and take up arms is an incredible accomplishment. One female commander told us that it was not hard, that life in the communities was harder. (interview, December 4, 1995)

While it would be wrong to exaggerate the feminist elements within the EZLN agenda—it was, after all, a military organization dominated by men—it would be equally wrong to dismiss those elements out of hand. The apparent openness of the organization to criticism by external feminists was just one measure of the difference between this guerrilla uprising and the many uprisings that preceded it.

Why did the EZLN differ, with regard to gender issues, from the guerrilla movements that preceded it? Quite simply because the EZLN began life in a different world than that of earlier movements, like those in Nicaragua and El Salvador. That world was shaped, on the one hand, by the indigenous communities that had been transformed over the decades that preceded the rebellion through migration, the transformation of the Church, and the rise of new organizations for both men and women (Kampwirth 2002, 89–106). On the other hand, by the nineties the EZLN acted within a new international order, a post–cold war order in which international feminism was an important player. Those factors meant that the EZLN leaders faced local and international pressures to incorporate gender issues into their agenda, right from the beginning.

What were the Zapatista positions on gender issues? What impact did the emergence of the EZLN have on the shape of civil society in general and the women's movement in particular? What role did indigenous women play in the new civil society? The EZLN was partially the product of a generation of gender changes in Chiapas; in turn, it was the catalyst for a series of new changes in gender relations in Chiapas during its first years.

But Zapatismo was not the only force that acted on the emerging women's movement during the nineties. A number of sometimes coordinated forces sought to crush the Zapatista movement and, with it, the demands for equity and democracy that the movement represented. Anti-Zapatista forces acting through white guards (private armies), paramilitary groups, local police forces, national military forces, and sometimes even through the social welfare agencies that were the public face of the state, tended to focus their attention on the unarmed and growing civil society that supported the Zapatistas' demands rather than on the Zapatistas themselves, who, after all, were far more difficult targets, armed and hidden deep in the Lacandón jungle. Utilizing the carrot-and-stick strategy that had served the PRI well for seven decades, organizations within the growing civil society were alternately co-opted or attacked.

In 1994 the Zapatistas took up arms against the Mexican government for a mere ten days before they began what was to be years of negotiations with that government.[5] So the Zapatista story was in sharp contrast with the peace process in El Salvador, a process that took more than ten years to begin. It was in even sharper contrast with the peace process in neighboring Guatemala, which took place only after thirty years of civil war. Early negotiations were yet one more indicator of the difference between the Zapatistas and earlier Latin American guerrillas; it also illustrated the difference between the PRI's Mexico and the states that earlier guerrillas sought to overthrow.

The Expansion of Civil Society

If Zapatista successes in the first years of the rebellion are to be measured in terms of their interactions with the representatives of official

Mexico (i.e., the government), then the Zapatistas were miserably un-successful: their territory seized, their supporters raped and murdered, their calls for reform unmet. But the Zapatista agenda went beyond the reformation of the government. If one looks at civil society it becomes clear that life in Chiapas changed in significant ways during the rebellion.

The civil society promoted by the Zapatistas contrasted sharply with the popular organizations promoted by the FSLN of Nicaragua and the FMLN of El Salvador. Indeed, many of the differences between the Mexican model of guerrilla struggle in the post–cold war era and the Central American model of guerrilla struggle during the cold war were captured in the contrast between civil society and popular organiza-tions. Civil society has been called the "arena where citizens can play a role in . . . associational life" (Waylen 1998, 14; also see Alvarez, Dagnino, and Escobar 1998; Jaquette and Wolchik 1998; Keane 1988). Civil society has little meaning without effective autonomy, especially from the state, though autonomy from political parties is also often written into definitions of civil society. Though the civil society litera-ture typically does not address guerrilla armies, logically an effective civil society would need autonomy from guerrillas as well.

Autonomy, then, was a key concept separating the Marxist-Leninist tradition that shaped the FSLN and the FMLN during their guerrilla years from the radical democratic tradition that the EZLN had em-braced by the first day of its public life. The same autonomy that was won only after long battles between women's movement activists and the guerrillas (or former guerrillas) in Central America was encouraged at the beginning of the rebellion by the new guerrillas of Chiapas, the EZLN. While autonomy was illegitimate within the theory of the van-guard (the knowing vanguard party that guides the actions of popular organizations), it held a place of honor within the theory of civil society, the same civil society that the leaders of the EZLN publicly embraced.[6]

But of course theory is one thing, practice often quite another. To what extent did the EZLN live up to its own ideals in convoking a truly autonomous civil society? Or was that a contradiction in terms? Could civil society be called to action by the EZLN and still be civil society? Or would civil society become a new set of popular organizations, directed by a new vanguard? In June 1994 the EZLN called on civil society to participate in the first Democratic National Convention

(Convención Nacional Democrática) to be held in August. While hardly written in classic Marxist-Leninist language, one could hear echoes of the language of early guerrilla movements in the declaration that called for the convention:

> We are not proposing a new world, but only something very prior to that: the waiting room of the new Mexico. In this sense this revolution will not end in a new class, or class fraction, or group in power, but in a free and democratic "space" of political struggle. This free and democratic "space" will be born on the stinking cadaver of the State-party system and presidentialism. A new political relationship will be born. . . . The EZLN's political maturity, its maturity as representative of the sense of a part of the Nation, is in the fact that it does not want to impose this conception on the country. The EZLN claims what is evident to itself: Mexico's maturity and its right to decide, freely and democratically, the path it is to take. From this historic waiting room not only will a better and more just Mexico emerge, but also a new Mexican. (quoted in Womack 1999, 283)

By promising that it did not seek to impose a correct line, and that it did not fight for a particular class, the EZLN made it clear that it had evolved far from the days of its origins as the FLN, a traditional Latin American guerrilla group (Womack 1999, 190–97). While calling for a revolution, that revolution seemed to be much more like the 1989 revolutions of Eastern Europe than the prior revolutions of Latin America. Yet its vision of democracy seemed to be far less institutional, more revolutionary perhaps, than the Eastern European sort of democracy, rejecting presidentialism without specifying the mechanisms that would replace it, other than "civil society" (identified as "sovereign" elsewhere in the document) and the "new Mexican" (words that evoked Che Guevara's "new man," a concept that would have been familiar to Mexican readers).[7]

The Democratic National Convention was to be a gathering in which the Zapatistas participated without leading. To some extent that promise was fulfilled. One observer called the role of the Zapatistas "peripheral," observing that "only 20 delegates among the 6000" were from the EZLN. Yet at that same convention a Zapatista leader, Major

Tacho, "read the names of the 100 people chosen by the Zapatistas to head the Convention" (Stephen 1994b, 7; 1994c, 5; 1995). Carla, an anthropologist and adviser to the Center for Research and Action for Latin American Women (Centro de Investigaciones y Acción para la Mujer Latinoamericana, or CIAM), was one of those people called to leadership (of the second Democratic National Convention, held in Tuxtla Gutiérrez two months later). She was less than pleased about this naming from above: "The problem is that [Marcos] wrote a letter suggesting the names of the people that he wanted in the ruling council, and this tore apart the whole process of representation. . . . They named me without even asking me. When they announced my name I didn't know if I should go up [to the stage] or not. I ended up going up because it was an opportunity to represent women" (interview, February 1995). Carla later wrote Marcos to complain that "everything he says becomes an order and that ends up reproducing machista structures. . . . He didn't really answer me, he just wrote saying that I was right."

The Zapatistas' initial efforts to promote without directing civil society, their efforts to reject the politics of the vanguard, were not perfectly successful. That illustrated the difficulty of making a transition from a revolutionary model in which popular organizations would be led by a vanguard, to a revolutionary model based on civil society. It also illustrated a basic truth about civil society, a truth that enthusiasts of social movement politics often tried to ignore: civil society was a product of the society within which it emerged, with all the contradictions that implied. Far from being "one homogeneous happy family or 'global village,'" civil society was "also a terrain of struggle mined by sometimes undemocratic power relations and the enduring problems of racism, hetero/sexism, environmental destruction, and other forms of exclusion" (Alvarez, Dagnino, and Escobar 1998, 17). Inequality within civil society itself was a problem that the growing women's and indigenous rights movements would have to face.

Women's Organizing during the Rebellion

While women's organizations were not invented by the EZLN, and in fact some of those groups helped lay the organizational groundwork for the emergence of the guerrillas, a qualitative change in women's organizing occurred beginning in 1994. In response to the opportunities and problems created by the EZLN, groups that had worked in isolation began to identify with each other. On the eve of the rebellion there were already two important currents of women's organizing in the state of Chiapas—predominantly mestiza groups in the cities and predominantly indigenous groups in the countryside—that had roots going back a decade in the case of the former and four decades in the case of the latter. Together, these two sets of women's groups mobilized thousands but their influence was restricted since they remained largely separate until after the Zapatista uprising. A few organizers, like Amalia, a mestiza woman who was unusual for having feet in both currents, tried to bring them together. She told me about attending a feminist conference with indigenous women who worked with her in a handicrafts cooperative: "I invited the other women in the cooperative to go with me so that they would know that there were other women's organizations. We did participate but it ended up being sort of a failure. At that time—it was in '93—the majority of the feminists did not do work with indigenous women; they either worked with popular groups or in elections" (interview, January 1995).

But the inclusiveness of the Zapatista agenda drew women from both currents into new coalitions. One reflection of that transformation was the beginning of a series of statewide women's conferences. The first meeting of the statewide women's coalition, the Chiapas State Women's Convention (Convención Estatal de Mujeres Chiapanecas), was held in late July 1994, six months after the Zapatistas first went public. Representatives of twenty-four organizations attended that conference, representing a wide array of women, including indigenous women's artisan cooperatives, women who worked in coed indigenous, peasant, and worker's rights groups, church women, as well as women who worked in predominantly mestiza organizations that were explicitly feminist in their agendas.

Not only did women's organizers within Chiapas start to speak to each other but the state convention provided an opportunity to create links with women's organizations in Mexico City for the first time, in the case of most of the predominantly indigenous groups, or to strengthen ties for the mestizas who had often lived in Mexico City at some point before migrating to Chiapas. A bit more than two months later, in early October 1994, a second Chiapas State Women's Convention was held. This time, four times as many organizations were represented (from twenty-four to one hundred). Then, in February of the following year, just days before President Ernesto Zedillo's decision to break the ceasefire with the Zapatistas, the first National Women's Convention (Convención Nacional de Mujeres) was held in the state of Querétaro, with the participation of more than three hundred women from fourteen states (Rojas 1995a, 3; Rovira 1997, 229; Stephen 1995, 97).

The women's conventions, which began in 1994 and continued to meet throughout the nineties, were explicitly linked to the broader political transformation that was set off by the appearance of the EZLN; they responded to both the Zapatista agenda and to the increased political violence within the state. Furthermore, they had ties with an array of civil groups within the unarmed Zapatista coalition, including the Democratic National Convention, that have already been discussed, and with the rebel government in transition, which I will discuss shortly.

The political turning points that arose in rapid succession after January 1994 forced the isolated women's organizations into a coalition; they gave some unorganized women the courage or desperation to join groups, and they facilitated the formation of women's groups within mixed indigenous and peasant rights groups. The reaction to Zapatismo and militarization meant that it was finally meaningful to talk about a women's movement in Chiapas instead of individual women's organizations. But reacting to the agendas of others came at a price, a price that began to be reconsidered by 1997.

In May of that year, the coalition of women's groups met once again, this time with a new name, the State Women's Gathering (Encuentro Estatal de Mujeres). Paloma, a mestiza who had participated in the conventions since their beginning in 1994, told me that the participants in 1997 decided that they had made some mistakes: "as women we've allowed ourselves to be carried along by the political turning points; we are always in a hurry to do things because we are always working at the rhythm of others" (interview, June 25, 1997). And not only were the participants in the women's conventions allowing themselves to be driven by the agendas of others, but within the conventions themselves a bad dynamic had developed, with one group "helping" and another being "helped."

"We advisers are always working with indigenous women and we as mestizas, what about us? We forget ourselves amid the problems of indigenous women" (interview, June 25, 1997). That dynamic had its risks for the indigenous women as well as for the mestizas. So they decided to set up working groups for all the ethnic and linguistic groups in attendance with each table being headed by a woman from that group. That meant that, instead of having the mestizas act as advisers at the working groups for indigenous women, each group had its own working table, headed by a member of that particular group, including a table for mestizas. But a solution for one problem created new problems. One of the big accomplishments of the women's conventions—breaking down the traditional segregation of the women's movement—might be lost through the creation of separate working groups. So the participants decided to try working together, without divisions by ethnic or language group. Instead, they would be "all mixed up." And so they were when the next statewide gathering was held in June 1997. According to Paloma, many of the indigenous women were surprised to realize that, despite the class and linguistic advantages enjoyed by the mestizas, they also had problems, a reality that had been obscured by the adviser-advisee relationship that was a legacy of the older paternalistic model of organizing, predominant before 1994.

Another legacy of the old way of doing politics that the participants in the women's gatherings tried to address in 1997 was the tendency to make general demands that were very hard to disagree with but that were also very hard to meet. Instead of making only the most general demands, such as condemning violence, war, or discrimination, they decided to try building from the ground up, starting with small, concrete demands. For instance, instead of demanding education in general, the women's gathering resolved to request "that in the churches they say that women have a right to an education" (interview, June 25, 1997).

By the late nineties, the state women's conventions had made enormous strides: they were attended by a wide range of organizations and ethnic groups, they were better integrated into the national and international women's movement, and they were increasingly sophisticated in their political analysis. The gatherings had made such strides in a relatively short time in part because of the decades of organizing that preceded the rebellion. They also benefited from the parallel organizing in other branches of civil society. One of the most important new forces in civil society was a national indigenous rights movement in which women were significant players.

Indigenous Rights and the Struggle for Autonomy

The Zapatistas' promotion of indigenous rights is a central difference between the EZLN and other Latin American guerrilla movements. Those earlier movements defined social justice as mainly or entirely a question of class justice, often dismissing concerns over ethnic or gender inequality as a distraction from the real struggle. In contrast, the EZLN was an indigenous rights movement from the very beginning. At least that is how many remember those beginnings. In fact, the EZLN traced its roots to the FLN, a group that, like most other Latin American guerrilla organizations, identified its mission as primarily one of class justice. And as late as January 1994, when the EZLN made its first public appearance, indigenous rights played a very minimal role on the EZLN agenda. But in February the EZLN sat down for the first round of negotiations with the federal government and made thirty-four demands, many of which directly related to indigenous people. The Zapatistas' demands included "the creation of an independent indigenous radio station; the mandating of compulsory indigenous languages for primary through university education; respect for indigenous culture and tradition; an end to discrimination against indigenous people; the granting of indigenous autonomy; the administration of their own courts by indigenous communities; the criminalization of forced expulsion from communities by government-backed caciques and allowing the expelled to be able to return; and, finally, the establishment of maternity clinics, day care centers, nutritious food, kitchens, dining facilities, nixtamal and corn mills, and training programs for indigenous women" (Harvey 1998, 203–4). But at that point, indigenous rights were still not central to the Zapatista agenda, according to one leader of the indigenous autonomy movement. When the Zapatistas called for a national referendum in August 1995, indigenous rights activists encouraged them to include a sixth question "about indigenous rights and the EZLN said no. For the EZLN the most important thing has always been democracy. That was true until '96, when the issue [of indigenous rights] was placed on the negotiating table [that led to the San Andrés Accords]" (interview, April 12, 2000). Before the end of the century, the demand for indigenous autonomy had risen to a place of importance on the EZLN agenda that was probably parallel to that of the demand for democracy.

One reading of this shift is that it was an example of the Zapatistas' intellectual flexibility and willingness to let other social groups have input into their agenda. In other words, it could be understood as a manifestation of the shift from the model of popular organizations led by a vanguard party, to the model of an autonomous civil society. At the same time, the shift in the EZLN agenda could be read as the result of successful lobbying by indigenous groups that had already been working on the issue for years. I would argue that it was a combination of the two. Without pressures from indigenous rights activists, the Zapatistas would have had little reason to transform their agenda shortly after the beginning of the rebellion, but if the Zapatistas had been more doctrinaire and vanguardist they would have been unwilling to consider the concerns of the indigenous rights activists, no matter how compelling their arguments and no matter how long they had organized for those goals.

In 1986, nearly a decade before the public emergence of the EZLN, the first "autonomous region" had been declared in the eastern part of the state (Ruiz and Burguete 1998, 30). In 1990, Margarito Ruiz Hernández, an indigenous rights organizer and congressman from the PRD, proposed an amendment to the Constitution that would create "multiethnic regions" in which residents would have the right "to organize their social, economic, and political life in a way consistent with their own forms of organization and their cultural heritage" (Ruiz Hernández 1999, 22). Yet despite these early attempts at regional autonomy, before the nineties indigenous people tended to organize for rights as peasants (in other words, around class rather than ethnicity). George Collier (2000, 22) suggests the shift from class to ethnicity was a response to changes in the government's economic policies, as well as changes in the international system as a result of the end of the cold war and the rising importance of identity politics within international social movements.[8]

At least in retrospect, it made sense that the leaders of the EZLN, a group that operated in the predominantly indigenous state of Chiapas and that had a membership that was almost entirely indigenous, embraced the issue of indigenous autonomy. Both the indigenous rights organizations and the EZLN benefited from the insertion of the issue of regional autonomy on the Zapatista agenda: the indigenous rights organizations benefited, since the upheaval created by the EZLN allowed them to advance their work for autonomous regions, while the EZLN benefited because supporting regional autonomy helped it consolidate and expand its base of support.

But for all the apparent agreement over the agenda of indigenous autonomy, relations between indigenous rights groups and the EZLN were far from smooth. There were also tensions within the indigenous rights movement: in the years after the EZLN went public, many indigenous women began to demand that autonomy apply to their lives as well, a demand that many men did not expect when they proposed autonomy. Once the issue of indigenous rights was placed on the national agenda, it was not resolved quickly. That was hardly surprising—after all, the issue had been unresolved for some five hundred years.

A Brief Overview of the Indigenous in Mexican History

The indigenous people of Mexico are, of course, descendent from the original people who inhabited what is now Mexico at the time of the Spanish conquest, more than five hundred years ago. In contrast to the United States and some other parts of Latin America, most of the modern-day citizens of Mexico are descended, at least in part, from those original peoples. But many of those descendants of the original peoples are formally considered mestizo, rather than indigenous, even if their genetic makeup is 100 percent indigenous. In Mexico ethnicity is determined, for legal and social purposes, by language. If an individual speaks Spanish but no indigenous language, he is mestizo, even if all his ancestors were indigenous. This greatly reduces the numbers of Mexicans who are counted as indigenous (the same system, if used in the United States, would reduce the official Native American population from 2 million to 350,000). It also leads to logical absurdities: a baby born to two indigenous parents is not legally counted as indigenous until she is old enough to talk. Nonetheless, even despite these official efforts to undercount indigenous Mexicans, Mexico still has the largest and most diverse native population in the western hemisphere, with at least eight million indigenous people (10 percent of the population) who speak ninety-two different languages, according to official government figures (ANIPA n.d., 3). Some social scientists, considering that those who identify as indigenous should be counted as such even when they are not fluent in an indigenous language, estimate that the numbers of indigenous people are much higher: approximately 25 million people (30 percent of the population) who speak more than 230 different languages (Ewen 1994, 28–29, 38).

For a long time Mexicans had a schizophrenic attitude toward the indigenous; at once glorifying the indigenous past and marginalizing the modern-day indigenous population. Reminders of the ancient Aztec and Mayan civilizations were omnipresent—in textbooks, museums, even displays in subway stations—while the real live indigenous were relegated to isolated and impoverished villages. That isolation was reflected in the law until recently. Though the revolutionary constitution of 1917 was quite radical for its time, ultimately incorporating large sectors of the population, especially peasants and urban workers, into the ruling coalition, it did not even mention the existence of millions of indigenous Mexicans. Instead, from the time of the consolidation of the revolution under President Lázaro Cárdenas (1934–40) to the early 1990s, *indigenismo* would be the dominant governing ideology; an ideology that promoted the extension of services to the indigenous communities so that they would be incorporated into the body politic, becoming more like mestizos in the process. "Indigenismo . . . [replaced] the racist notion that native ethnicity was uncivilized and therefore prevented Mexico from becoming a great nation. . . . At the level of government policy, indigenismo encompassed two intertwined goals . . . the incorporation of the Indian into national society without total cultural obliteration; and the improvement of Indian life through education, political and economic organization, and the reform of the larger surrounding society. The revolutionary aspect of indigenismo was the idea that Indian poverty was largely the result of inequities in Mexican society and not simply a consequence of ethnic or racial inferiority" (Benjamin 1996, 202). Then, in 1992, for the first time since the end of Spanish colonialism, the existence of indigenous communities was ac-knowledged in national legislation through the reform of Article 4 of the Constitution. Article 4 recognized that Mexico is multicultural, and it promised to protect the right of indigenous Mexicans to con-tinue existing as indigenous people: "The Mexican nation is multieth-nic, originally based in its indigenous peoples. The law will protect and promote the development of languages, cultures, practices, customs, re-sources and specific sorts of social organization and it will guarantee that members of those groups have effective access to the jurisdiction of the state. In any lawsuits or agrarian proceedings in which [indige-nous people] may take part, their practices and judicial customs will be considered within the framework permitted by law" (quoted in Hernán-dez Navarro 1997, 71). The reform of Article 4 marked the official end of the integrationist policy of indigenismo, but it was not clear how in-digenous people were to put their new rights to self-determination into practice. Moreover, some saw the administration of Carlos Salinas de Gortari (1988–94) as giving with one hand while it took away with the other. At the same time rural indigenous people were finally recognized through the reform of Article 4, they lost their right to make claims to land through the reform of Article 27. Their ethnic identity as indige-nous was acknowledged while their class identity as peasants was disre-garded (Ewen 1994, 33–36; Hernández Navarro 1997, 70–71).

For many indigenous women Article 4 was a mixed blessing. Like indigenous men, they had an interest in the state's defending their eth-nic identities, even if only at a rhetorical level. But unlike most indige-nous men, they had good reason to be wary of a law that protected all indigenous customs without distinction. For gender inequality was a well-entrenched tradition in many indigenous communities, one that had been central to the long-term preservation of those communities. Refusing to allow girls to attend school and to learn Spanish well (or at all) guaranteed that those girls would grow up to raise their own chil-dren in their native language. Harsh punishments for females who were too independent meant that few women dared to leave the confines of their village or to innovate within the village. In some ways, isolation had been a good strategy for the preservation of indigenous culture; it was quite a feat that at least ninety-two languages were still spoken in Mexico, five hundred years after the Spanish conquerors arrived to impose their own language, religion, and culture. But that strategy had a terrible cost, a cost that was paid disproportionately by indigenous girls and women.

> The problem is if the [local] authorities say that land cannot be inherited, according to Article 4 we women are going to be left without land. And if we are widows or have many children we are going to be left without land. (Grupo de Mujeres et al. 1994, 42)
>
> Violence (beatings, rapes) is not good. It is not fair that we are sold for money. Nor is it just when "because of custom" they don't let us be represented, nor to have the right to land. We don't want bad customs. (38)

These two indigenous women expressed the concerns of many when they analyzed Article 4 at a workshop sponsored by a coalition of women's groups in 1994. The problem was how to embrace their culture at the same time as they rejected those elements of tradition—the bad customs—that subordinated them as women. It was a problem that would not be easily resolved by the national indigenous movement that emerged during the first years of the Zapatista rebellion.

Indigenous Rights Activists Respond to the Zapatistas

The story of the rise of a nationwide indigenous rights movement is akin to the story of the women's movement. In both cases, individual groups, many of which had existed for decades, seized the opportunities presented by the Zapatista rebellion to set their local demands in a national and sometimes international context. At the same time the rebellion created a crisis for unarmed indigenous groups as the state was rapidly militarized and as local power holders angrily sought out someone to blame. Responding to the opportunities and crises created by the Zapatista rebellion, indigenous groups formed new coalitions, seized land, and made demands.

Some of those demands were awfully quick in coming. Less than two weeks into the rebellion, on January 13, 1994, a coalition of 150 organizations, the State Coordinator of Indigenous and Peasant Organizations (Coordinadora Estatal de Organizaciones Indígenas y Campesinas, or CEOIC), marched on San Cristóbal to demand that the federal armed forces withdraw from the state of Chiapas. Three weeks into the rebellion, the CEOIC again met in San Cristóbal, this time with the participation of 288 organizations.

While the majority of the organizations were male dominated and men headed the working groups, a number of women's artisan cooperatives and peasant women's groups participated in that meeting, making sure that some of their demands were placed on the agenda: that peasant women would have access to land and credit, that women be given more space to participate politically, that social, cultural, and productive organizations be created for women, that the government grant pensions to widows of the Zapatista war. The coordinating body, CEOIC, was continually reminded of women's demands from that point forward, for a standing women's commission was created. Finally, on the last day of January 1994, the first month of the new political era in Mexico, 280 indigenous and peasant organizations formally pledged their support for the Zapatista rebels (Ceceña, Zaragoza, and Equipo Ch. 1995, 160–62; Hernández Castillo 1994, 37).[9] These rapid responses from Mexican civil society, both within the state and nationwide, were evidence that the Zapatista demands spoke to a widespread sentiment, especially within indigenous Mexico.

Having thrown their lot in with the Zapatistas, the indigenous groups largely stood with the EZLN: through the peace talks of February and March, through the Zapatistas' rejection of the government's offer in June, through the national election in August, and through the first meeting of the National Democratic Convention, also in August, in which they were central participants. During these months, indigenous peasant groups seized land on occasion, but that was not a departure from their strategies prior to 1994. It was not really until October that indigenous groups initiated a strategic shift.

Marking the October 12 anniversary of the Conquest, indigenous groups marched on San Cristóbal. At that rally, they declared that from that point onward, nine municipalities of Chiapas would be autonomous and multiethnic (Ceceña, Zaragoza, and Equipo Ch. 1995, 174–75; Gómez Nuñez 1999, 194). Two months later, in December, the Zapatistas followed the lead of the indigenous coalition by declaring that twenty-nine indigenous municipalities would be autonomous. By the end of the decade, "80 percent of the Indian peoples form[ed] part of one of the autonomous municipalities" (Lomelí 1999, 249).[10]

Those who sought autonomy were not separatists, instead they demanded that residents of predominantly indigenous regions should have greater control over political, economic, and social life within their territory. Indigenous people did not want to cease to be Mexicans, rather they wished to be granted rights as Mexicans in conditions of equality with mestizos. From their perspective, being granted the same rights as nonindigenous Mexicans required acknowledging their differences. To reach effective equality with other Mexicans, indigenous people argued that they had to have the right to use, and be educated in, their own languages (i.e., to have access to bilingual education), the right to control resources within the territories where they lived (especially land), and the right to resolve political and judicial disputes within their communities in accordance with their own customs (Collier 2000; González and Quintanar 1999; Ruiz Hernández 1999; Russo 2000; Stavenhagen 1999).

During the last months of the first year of the public rebellion, the seizure of land and municipalities, which had been ongoing, greatly increased in frequency, and the territory that was controlled by the Zapatistas and their sympathizers spread. Three weeks after the declaration of autonomy, the National Democratic Convention met for the second time. A ruling body was appointed in that meeting, comprised of three representatives of each social sector, except for the indigenous sector, which was represented by eleven people (Ceceña, Zaragoza, and Equipo Ch. 1995, 174–75). So through the declaration of autonomy, and the extra representation for indigenous people at the National Democratic Convention, indigenous people, who had always been the poorest, the most marginalized, the least represented, were at least this once at the political forefront.

The addition of autonomy to the Zapatista agenda was a real strategic shift from the EZLN perspective, though from the perspective of many indigenous rights organizers it was not a new demand. What was

new from their perspective was that the beginning of the rebellion provided the opportunity to put many of their ongoing demands into
practice or to accelerate the pace of their work to regain control over
the state. As part of those efforts to regain control of the state, at the
same time as they declared the first autonomous regions, in October
1994 the indigenous groups that supported the EZLN pledged their
support for Amado Avendaño,[11] pledging to join him in his efforts to
keep the PRI's Eduardo Robledo (elected governor in August under
suspicion of fraud) from being inaugurated in December.

Inaugurating the Rebel Government

The parallel inaugurations of December 1994 would be a symbolic
struggle over legitimate government, over representation, over the role
of the indigenous in Mexico. Did the indigenous belong at the margins
of modern Mexico or were they the most truly Mexican of all Mexicans?
The inaugurations suggested radically different answers to that question.
While in the normal course of events the governor elect would have
been inaugurated in the state congressional chambers, events in 1994
were far from normal, so for security reasons Eduardo Robledo was inaugurated in the city theater. The inauguration site was surrounded by
"[h]undreds of heavily armed federal troops . . . [and] only PRI loyal-
ists, many bused in by the party, were allowed to get anywhere near"
(DePalma 1994). During the ceremony, Robledo, who wore a dark-blue
suit, was surrounded by other dignitaries, including President Zedillo,
all wearing dark-blue suits. One man wearing traditional indigenous
clothing did appear on the stage, in seeming violation of the unspoken
dress code, but his role in the ceremony was peripheral. After taking the
oath of office with his arm straight out and elevated at about forty-five
degrees (a posture that, unintentionally one assumes, resembled a Nazi
salute), the new governor implicitly acknowledged the controversy surrounding his election by promising to resign if that would lead to the
end of hostilities with the Zapatistas "and the return of tranquility to
the people of Chiapas."

The second inauguration held, on the same December day in the
same city (Tuxtla Gutiérrez, the official capital of Chiapas), utilized the

symbols of a different sort of political legitimacy. The official inauguration had been legitimized by the presence of invited guests including
the president of the country, by the presence of the armed forces, and
by swearing to uphold an institutional order that had been forged in
the 1910 revolution. The parallel inauguration was legitimized by the
presence of any who chose to attend the open-air ceremony, by the
presence of thousands of indigenous people from more than three hundred organizations, and by swearing to "govern by obeying," a principle of indigenous politics that dated back many centuries.[12]

The ceremony was both mestizo and indigenous, a blend of ancient
political rituals and modern protest tactics. Wearing a dark-blue suit,
surrounded by indigenous men in white shirts heavily embroidered in
red, Amado Avendaño was inaugurated with the passing of the "indigenous ruling cane" (a short stick tied with ribbon) amid a cloud of in-
cense. The ceremony, which was followed by dancing to live marimba
music, was marred only by the truckloads of soldiers that surrounded
the three to four thousand protesters (Kampwirth 1996b).

Lidia, a participant in the Rebel Government led by Amado Avendaño and a member of its women's commission, explained how her
opposition to the PRI's Robledo came out of her grievances as an indigenous woman, grievances that had been in the making for a long
time: "We don't want Robledo because he doesn't take into account
the indigenous people; that's why we are in struggle now. . . . We want
a government in transition because the government in transition is to
govern, but not to govern all by themselves. If they do not do what the
people want, we can get another government. Robledo says that the
people voted for him but that's a lie. That Robledo lies a lot. In almost
all the communities we voted for Amado, that's why we are at his side
right now. Enough already, as the compañeros say" (interview, February 1995). Lidia made it clear that her objection to what she saw as illegitimate power was not just about the August election of Eduardo
Robledo. Invoking the Zapatista's famous phrase—enough already—
she explained that the Zapatista agenda, including the Rebel Government, was a response to centuries of insults to her people.[13]

While the Rebel Government in transition was inaugurated in Tuxtla
Gutiérrez, a predominantly mestizo city, it presided over offices in San
Cristóbal de las Casas, the unofficial capital of indigenous Chiapas. On

the same day as the inauguration, representatives of the new government were lent the offices of the National Indigenous Institute (INI), offices that had been seized earlier in the day by a coalition of unarmed indigenous groups. Another participant in the Rebel Government, Anita, explained how the groups decided to seize the INI: "All the indigenous communities met on October 12 and they decided they had had enough repression, they had had enough of five hundred years of domination. We want to govern ourselves [they said]. They demanded the buildings; they said this belongs to us and if you want to stay you can, but we can't pay your salaries. So the other people left" (interview, February 1995). Without firing a shot, the Zapatistas were gaining territory and extending their influence in civil society. At the beginning of the new century, indigenous groups still controlled the twenty-six-building INI complex, though the Rebel Government itself lasted little more than a year.

In February 1995, two months after the Rebel Government and a broad coalition of indigenous groups took office in the old INI complex, President Zedillo broke the ceasefire with the Zapatistas and sent troops into the jungle, supposedly to arrest Marcos and other top Zapatistas. But Marcos was not arrested; instead, the army seized most of the nearly 40 percent of the state that had been held by the EZLN (Lomelí 1999, 248) and arrested numerous unarmed social movement activists. Yet the members of the Rebel Government were not arrested. In fact, the indigenous coalition kept their control over the INI complex, complete with electricity, working telephones, fax machines, and keys to the office doors. In the middle of the federal government's most violent response to Zapatismo since the rebellion had formally started, relations with the emerging indigenous rights movement were handled gingerly.

Indigenous Rights on the National Agenda

Later that same year, in October 1995, the Zapatistas began to talk with representatives of the federal government about indigenous rights and culture. That round of negotiations (which would lead to the San Andrés Accords), took place in a very different political context than the first round of negotiations in February 1994. To be sure, there were continuities: the PRI continued to be the dominant party at both the national and state levels, and while different men held the presidency and the governorship than had in 1994, their stance toward negotiations with the Zapatistas was effectively the same. One observer described that stance as being "willing to talk but not to negotiate and certainly not to fulfill promises" (Hernández Navarro 1997, 85). In fact, representatives of the ruling party were not only willing to talk, they were eager to talk with the Zapatistas, for engaging in talks helped preserve the image of the Mexican state as reasonable, as preferring talks to violence, as totally different from the Central American states that had faced guerrilla rebellions a few years earlier.

But if the government's position had changed little, the negotiating position of the EZLN had changed considerably in comparison with 1994. In February 1994 the Zapatistas controlled large portions of the eastern half of the state of Chiapas; from February 1995 onward they controlled very little territory. While in 1994 pro-Zapatista social movements were growing exponentially, by late 1995 the old government strategy of divide and conquer was starting to have a negative effect on those groups. While the Zapatistas wanted to hold the second round of peace talks in Mexico City, to make the point that the reforms they called for were national in scope, the central government vetoed that proposal, threatening to arrest any Zapatista leaders who left the confines of the state of Chiapas. In contrast to 1994, when the talks were held in the spectacular colonial cathedral of San Cristóbal, the 1995 talks were be held in temporary shelters hastily erected on a basketball court in the highland town of San Andrés Larráinzar. Yet with few other options, the Zapatistas had an interest in talking.

So immediately after the Zedillo administration broke the 1994 ceasefire by sending troops into the jungle and calling for the arrest of top Zapatista leaders, the EZLN nonetheless agreed to start a new round of peace talks. The rebels had little choice. While the government might have had more options, it also had an interest in talking, so Congress created the legal framework for new talks by passing the Law for Dialogue, Conciliation, and Peace with Dignity in Chiapas (Ley para el Diálogo, la Conciliación, y la Paz Digna en Chiapas) on March 11, 1995, a mere month after the Zedillo administration had declared war on the

EZLN. The months between March and October were occupied with prenegotiations to agree on the location, the ground rules for the talks, who would participate in the talks, and other such details. Finally, on October 1, 1995, the two sides sat down at what was supposed to be a series of working groups. The first was to address indigenous rights and culture (Hernández Navarro 1997, 74–75).

The end result of the first working table was a set of accords[14] that were signed on February 16, 1996, without the presence of photographers, for the EZLN feared that the image of accords, rather than the reality of accords, was what mattered to government negotiators. Their fears were not unfounded. Following what has been called "an old government tradition of signing promises that are then not carried out" (Hernández Navarro 1997, 81), the federal government simply did not pass the laws that would have been needed to put the promises of the accords into practice. Because of the failure to legislate, along with paramilitary violence in the north of the state and several other problems, the EZLN suspended the negotiation process on September 2, 1996, almost seven months after the accords were signed and one day after President Zedillo failed to even mention the accords in his annual state-of-the-union address (82–83, 85).[15]

From the perspective of the indigenous rights movement, the discussions at San Andrés Larráinzar were an opportunity to follow through on the promise of Article 4, to devise practical ways to guarantee the government's support for indigenous cultures. Had they been ratified by Congress, the San Andrés Accords would have recognized the right of indigenous groups to determine their own fates through a variety of mechanisms, including the autonomy that had been declared in October 1994 by the CEOIC (Hernández Navarro 1997, 71–73). The section of the accords that addressed the indigenous women's situation indicated both how many indigenous women valued autonomy and how their vision of autonomy was not identical to that of men: "We demand the right to land, to have representation in the houses of Congress and in all the branches of government: traditional, communal, state, and federal. [We demand] that traditions and customs 'that do not hurt us' are recognized, to gain autonomy for our peoples in which indigenous women have a place that is equal to that of men with respect for our dignity" (Rojas 1995c, 233). Women's vision of autonomy was more personal than that of men; it was about access to economic resources for themselves as women and for the children they raised and about guaranteeing that they would be respected even as they lived out the customs of their ancestors. Zapatista women wanted political and economic autonomy for their communities, as did their men, but they also wanted guarantees that their own personal autonomy would be enhanced in the process.[16]

These demands for land, autonomy, and respect were made during the first phase of the San Andrés talks, in October 1995. During the second phase, held in November, the government seized on women's desire for land to try to divide the Zapatista coalition. A member of the Zapatista delegation complained that "the government delegation wanted to send us back to fight with our men for 50 percent of the land, when what we demanded was that there should be more land distribution in which women also are included" (quoted in Rojas 1995d, 240). In response, a member of the government delegation insisted that the women had requested that within existing *ejidos,* or collective farms, sections should be redistributed to women.

Whether the Zapatista women had originally requested only that new land reform include women, or that land that was already in collective ownership be redistributed to include women, a delicate issue had been touched upon: disputes over land had divided many a political coalition in the past. When indigenous men called for the end to discrimination against themselves as indigenous people, were they also willing to give up their privileges as men? That question would not have to be addressed directly in the context of the San Andrés Accords, since they were not ratified.

So did anything come out of San Andrés, from the perspective of the Zapatistas and their supporters? After all, the demand for indigenous autonomy was nothing new. But the process of negotiating at San Andrés did more than repeat an earlier demand. "In the heat of the negotiations at San Andrés indigenous issues began to be considered a substantial part of national politics" (Hernández Navarro 1997, 76). The San Andrés negotiations had little long-term impact, if impact is measured in terms of government policy, since the accords that resulted from the negotiations were never ratified. But they had a ground-shaking impact if measured in terms of social movement politics. For the nationwide indigenous rights movement was conceived in San Andrés.

While representatives of the government and the EZLN, along with a host of invited guests, negotiated at San Andrés, indigenous organizations did not silently wait. Instead, forums and debates were held by indigenous groups all over the country to debate the results of the ongoing San Andrés process and to possibly influence that process. During three days in late November and early December the government sponsored National Consulting Forums on Indigenous Rights and Participation (Foros de Consulta Nacional sobre Derechos y Participación Indígena) in twenty-one of the thirty-one states of Mexico. Despite the significant presence of indigenous people who worked in government agencies or belonged to government-sponsored organizations, some of the results of that forum were awfully similar to the demands made by the Zapatistas at San Andrés. And the demands made in the series of forums sponsored by independent groups were even closer to the Zapatista agenda, combining material and cultural demands with proposals for new relations between the state and indigenous peoples (Hernández Navarro 1997, 76).

One of those forums sponsored by independent groups was the fourth convention of the National Pluralistic Indigenous Assembly for Autonomy (Asamblea Nacional Indígena Plural por la Autonomía, or ANIPA), which was held on December 8 and 9, 1995, on the grounds of the former National Indigenous Institute of San Cristóbal. Attended by some five hundred people from twelve states (along with delegations from Guatemala, Chile, Norway, Canada, and the United States), it was one of the biggest national meetings held while the Zapatistas negotiated a few kilometers away in San Andrés. At the ANIPA meeting, which I attended, it was clear that the formerly male dominated indigenous rights movement was changing: the ANIPA meeting was held in conjunction with the First National Meeting of Indigenous Women for Autonomy (Primer Encuentro Nacional de Mujeres Indígenas por la Autonomía), which began a day earlier (December 7) and overlapped by a day so that women could participate in both meetings and so that the women's group could present its demands to the larger indigenous convention. By the second day of the women's gathering, the assembly was told that 252 women were present (Morquecho 1995a, 16; 1995b,

25). A lot had changed in just a year and a half. At ANIPA's first confer-ence, held in April 1994, the male leaders objected to the idea that in-digenous customs that violate the human rights of indigenous women should be changed (Rojas 1995b, vii). In contrast, during the fourth na-tional conference, in December 1995, a banner over the crowd read: "May tradition be women's equality."

The links between the ANIPA agenda and the Zapatista agenda were obvious, at least within the women's gathering. The ongoing talks in San Andrés were taken as a point of departure as those who were delegates to the talks spent some time explaining their demands, emphasizing "that customs that hurt women should be left behind"[17] particularly the customs of domestic violence, forced matrimony, and denying women access to land. Health and reproductive rights was another emphasized area, calling for "respect for women as the ones that give life. And re-spect for the number of children that each woman wants. At times [doc-tors] operate on [women] without getting their consent." The Zapatista delegates had called for bilingual and multicultural education but, as they explained to the women at the ANIPA conference, they were re-jected by the government delegation, which explained, "There already is an official language." Finally, the dominant theme throughout the conference was probably the call for demilitarization. They objected to the military presence because of the physical and economic[18] vio-lence it engendered but also because of violence against their dignity as women. "The soldiers threw condoms in the river; they created a lot of prostitution." It was clear that the participants in the first national indigenous women's gathering identified with the Zapatistas. But they were not submissive partners. One of their final proposals was "to send a letter to the Zapatistas, informing them of the results of our meeting and asking them to open up a space for the women who are present here."

If the national indigenous rights movement was conceived in San Andrés, it was born in the Zapatista-sponsored National Indigenous Forum (Foro Nacional Indígena), held in San Cristóbal on January 3–8, 1996. Nearly five hundred delegates from thirty-two indigenous groups were there, representing 178 different organizations. Much as at the ANIPA conference that had been held a month earlier, autonomy was the "central demand that tied all the proposals together." But autonomy did not mean withdrawal from Mexico, as one of the speakers at the forum was careful to note: "We feel that we are profoundly Mexican, even though the founders of the Mexican state and all the governments that followed them ignored our existence, and even though many Mexican men and women adopted this same attitude against us and even today they continue to deny us.[19] Because of that, in affirming our existence once again, we want to let it be known today that our current struggle for recognition of our differences is not to begin a fratricidal war, much less to separate ourselves from a country that we feel is as much ours as our Indian identity" (Rojas and Gil 1996a). The participants in the forum demanded that they be allowed to maintain their different customs at the same time as they were treated as equals, as they had during the ANIPA gathering. But in contrast with the ANIPA conference, the Zapatista forum was open to all indigenous groups that wished to attend.[20] Partly because of its inclusiveness, the forum opened the possibility of a national indigenous movement with a permanent structure and a clear agenda. That movement demanded rights, rather than charity, for indigenous people (Hernández Navarro 1997, 70).

As at the San Andrés talks and the ANIPA conference, a working table on indigenous women's issues made a series of demands. Many of those demands resembled those made previously: an end to militarization, inquiries into the rape and murder of indigenous women, bans on alcohol and the domestic violence it tends to facilitate. Among the material demands, the women came up with new ideas for access to health care and education: "Proposals were made for the creation of school-day care centers for women where there would be guarantees of primary, secondary, technical, college prep, and university education, this last type through the creation of an indigenous university to which the women would have equal access" (Gil and Rojas 1996). There was no inherent connection between indigenous identity and backwardness; far from rejecting modernity, the women at the forum embraced higher education along with health care and all the rest. But in proposing the indigenous university, they sought an education that would not come at the expense of their ethnic identities.

Yet while there was no reason, in theory, that one could not be indigenous and highly educated, in practice indigenous women usually had limited educations and limited experiences. So ironically, even in the midst of a forum that asserted indigenous rights to self-determination, mestiza "advisers" still were there to counsel the indigenous women. Not surprisingly, that created tensions, leading thirty some indigenous women to pull out of the working table on women to discuss among themselves, "arguing that the mestizas monopolized the right to talk." That disagreement was soon smoothed over as the indigenous women who had objected to the excessive help from the mestizas graciously acknowledged, "we are conscious that our sisters of different cultures are not at fault, instead it is the dominant system that has placed us at a disadvantage" (Rojas and Gil 1996b).

But whether or not the temporary bad feelings had dissipated, the underlying problem had not. How were indigenous people, especially indigenous women, to ever truly determine their own fates if non-indigenous people monopolized the right to speak? And yet, after more than five hundred years of subjugation, how could indigenous women ever gain the skills they needed for autonomy without the help of more privileged outsiders?[21] At the end of the forum, such contradictions were acknowledged but swept under the table as part of a conscious strategy. Rather than risking the sorts of debates that could divide the movement as soon as it was coming into existence, the participants agreed to disagree, at least for a while, as they started preparations for the first National Indigenous Congress (Congreso Nacional Indígena), to be held in the center of national power, Mexico City, and to culminate on one of the most significant days on the indigenous calendar, October 12, which in 1996 was the 504th anniversary of the Spanish conquest of the Americas (Rojas and Gil 1996b).

As part of the preparations for the national congress, a coalition of twenty-two groups (including NGOs, human rights collectives, indigenous women's artisan groups, and one political party—the PRD) met in Mexico City for two days every month from May through September. Coming from all over the country—Chiapas, Oaxaca, Guerrero, Querétaro, Veracruz, San Luis Potosí, Mexico City, Puebla—they joined to analyze Article 4 of the Constitution (which would give new authority to local indigenous leaders), thinking through ways to rework it so that traditions of gender inequality within indigenous communities were not reinforced. While the document that was presented to the first National Indigenous Congress focused on legal and practical strategies to improve the conditions of indigenous women, a more general theme of women's rights was emphasized, attempting to break down the old unequal dynamic between indigenous women and their mestiza helpers. In fact, the seminar participants noted that since 1994 "there has been a new sort of relationship between indigenous and mestizo people" (SEDE-PAC 1996, 2).

The nineteen-page document that came out of the women's meetings in Mexico City was presented to the first indigenous congress when it met in October 1996 with the hope that the autonomy that the movement sought would not be conceived in gender-free terms. But the woman who captured the country's attention during the congress was not any of the participants in the new nationwide women's movement. Instead it was a woman who was widely thought to be dead: Comandante Ramona.

Ramona Breaks the Blockade

Comandante Ramona, a Tzotzil woman who was deathly ill, represented the EZLN at the congress. She was the first to break the blockade with which the government had tried to restrict the EZLN, and their demands, to the periphery of the country.[22] From the very beginning of the Zapatista rebellion, Ramona was a central figure. One of two women on the eleven-member ruling indigenous committee (along with Major Ana María), it was she who presented the Mexican flag, captured on the first of January 1994, at the February peace talks in the cathedral of San Cristóbal. More than any other single Zapatista woman, it was Ramona who captured the imagination of millions. This comment, made at a workshop in 1994, was typical of those I heard during my fieldwork: "How wonderful that Ramona appeared! We think she loves us, that is why she came out to journey; it is like she is pulling us along. She shows us the path we can create, she is a great, wise person" (Grupo de Mujeres et al. 1994, 22).

Ramona was an unlikely guerrilla: small, sickly, unthreatening; dressing not in military fatigues but in the elaborately embroidered clothing that identified her as an indigenous woman from the highlands. Perhaps for those reasons, Ramona was often spoken of in mystical, quasi-religious terms; something I never heard in the case of other Zapatista women. Ramona was said to suffer for women, suffering because she loves us so. She was even said to happily die so that others might live a better, if not eternal, life: "Among the indigenous leaders of the rebellion there is a small woman, even small among the small people. . . . Ramona did not know it well at that time and we didn't either, but she carries in her body a sickness that consumes her life and shuts down her voice and her sight. Ramona laughed when she did not know she was dying. Now that she knows it, she continues laughing. Before nobody knew she existed; now she exists, she is a woman, an indigenous person, and a rebel. Now she lives, Ramona, a woman of that race that has to die in order to live" (Marcos, quoted in NCDM 1996b, 5). Tens of thousands greeted this rebel woman when she arrived in Mexico City (Hernández Navarro 1997, 87). Sending Ramona to the indigenous congress was a brilliant move; a move that made the Mexican government out to be a Goliath losing in battle to a female David, at least this time.

After breaking the government blockade on the Zapatistas and receiving lifesaving medical attention in Mexico City,[23] Ramona was ready to provide the symbolic leadership for a new national movement for indigenous women's rights. Nearly a year after the first National Indigenous Congress, indigenous women celebrated their first national conference in August 1997 in the capital of the state of Oaxaca. Comandante Ramona inaugurated the first National Gathering of Indigenous Women (Encuentro Nacional de la Mujer Indígena), a gathering attended by more than four hundred women from twenty-three indigenous regions. Telling the crowd about how she and others worked to create the Revolutionary Women's Laws in 1993, she suggested, "All of us should ask ourselves if Zapatismo would be what it is without women. Would indigenous civil society and that of nonindigenous people, who have helped us so much, be the same without its women? Can one imagine the new rebel Mexico that we want to create without new rebel women?" (NCDM 1997a, 3). As the first four years of the public phase of the Zapatista rebellion were reaching a close, both the Zapatista movement and the indigenous women's movement that the EZLN had helped advance had changed significantly since the days when Ramona and Susana traveled from village to village, gathering information for the Revolutionary Women's Law.

At the level of the state of Chiapas there was more of a women's movement than there had been before 1994, a movement comprised of indigenous women as well as mestizas. Now there was a coherent indigenous rights movement. Moreover, women and their demands were a visible presence within that movement. Indigenous rights were on the national agenda in a way that they had not been before, partially because of the Zapatista's demands and partially because of the growth of a unified national movement for indigenous rights. That movement, like its counterpart in the state of Chiapas, was a movement in which women's rights were always an issue, albeit an unresolved one. And by 1997 indigenous women had enough organizational resources to hold a national gathering, just for women, to promote their own demands. The presence of Ramona and other Zapatista women at that gathering testified to the importance of the EZLN in making such a development possible. At the same time, the movement had a life of its own that went beyond the EZLN.

The EZLN had also been transformed during the first years of the rebellion. While it did not succeed in getting much more than unkept promises out of the federal government, it nonetheless had an impact on national politics. While events like the 1997 massacre in Acteal[24] made it obvious that it still could not protect its supporters from the violence of the military and paramilitary groups, the EZLN was increasingly capable of directly participating in national politics. Once Ramona had made a crack in the federal government's blockade, the wall did not hold for long. The next time the Zapatistas went to Mexico City, for the founding of the unarmed Zapatista Front (FZLN) in September 1997, it was in massive numbers; more than eleven hundred Zapatistas helped inaugurate the FZLN.

Following the same route Emiliano Zapata had taken when he went to the capital early in the century, 1,111 Zapatistas (one for each of the indigenous communities that support the EZLN), along with supporters they picked up en route, arrived in Mexico City in a caravan of more than one hundred fifty vehicles, mostly buses. More than two thousand delegates representing three hundred committees from every state of the Mexican union were there to greet them and to formally create the new Zapatista group. Like the EZLN, the FZLN opposed war and militarization; it supported democracy. Unlike the EZLN, it would never use armed struggle to promote its goals. Strangely perhaps, for an organization that sought to transform national politics, the FZLN pledged to reject formal politics: members of political parties and those who received salaries from those parties were not allowed to join the Zapatista Front, and the FZLN would not participate in elections. Within its ranks, its members swore to uphold the indigenous principle of "governing by obeying" (Gil 1997; NCDM 1997b, 1; Preston 1997).

Women's issues were part of the FZLN agenda, as was the case for all the national opposition organizations discussed in this chapter that had emerged since 1994. A few months before the official formation of the FZLN, I asked Lisa, a member of one of the nascent FZLN committees, if she thought there was a gap between the Zapatista's discourse on women and the reality of women's lives. She said there was but also thought that "we women can possibly fill in this gap." It helped if the men supported them but, ultimately, it was up to the women of the Zapatista Front to make that happen, as she was trying to do through her work in the promotion committee for the incipient FZLN. "As a woman I emphasize the necessity of promoting a world of equals. That is, we are trying to feminize the struggle. In fact, we are currently working on the question of principles, on the question of women. In the meeting I dared to use the term *women's liberation* and it caused a lot of terror in the men. The goal is that women assume the discussion. Another gain is the fact that we are specifically talking about women's issues. The issue is already up for discussion; there were very aggressive men and we responded to them. . . . There were men who said that women's liberation meant to want to be like the Europeans and take off our bras. I said that to take off one's bra or anything else, one does not ask permission." Asked whether she considered herself a feminist, she answered in the affirmative (something that was unusual in Chiapas): "Yes, I am a feminist, with all that implies. Because even inside the Zapatista Front, to say that I am a feminist implies that I am a radical" (interview, June 26, 1997).

Clientelism, or the Carrot

The transformation of the women's movement and the indigenous rights movement that occurred during the second half of the nineties was shaped by the EZLN and also, in subtle and not so subtle ways, by those who opposed the Zapatistas: the federal government, state government, and a myriad of shadowy forces, including the paramilitary groups, who realized that simply refusing to ratify the accords that were signed with the Zapatistas was hardly enough to make them go away. In fact, the lack of a rapid solution at the level of formal politics probably promoted the massive growth of informal political movements, including the movement for indigenous women's rights.

One way the state and federal governments, under the control of the ruling party, the PRI, responded to the rebellion was by doing what they had always done very effectively: seeking to divide and control civil society through clientelism—the offer of material benefits in implied or overt exchange for political loyalty—also known as co-optation, or the carrot.[25] In his study of the independent teacher's movement, Joe Foweraker describes the Mexican government's use of such clientelistic strategies to create or reinforce divisions within Mexican civil society, a civil society that, if unified, might more effectively challenge the dominance of the ruling party: "The federal government has consistently cultivated this 'compartmentalized' civil society and has sought to restrict the scope of popular movements in order to disarticulate them on a case by case basis" (Foweraker 1993, 11).[26]

Clientelism, a system of controlled inclusion, was the key (much more than coercion or fraud, though they helped too) to the PRI's amazingly long hold on power: seven decades without interruption at the national level.[27] Through clientelistic measures, the federal and state governments threatened the cohesiveness of the Zapatista's base of support over the course of the nineties. One of the most common answers to my question about how things had changed since 1994 was that the government paid more attention to indigenous people and was more interested in funding their organizations. Their perception was consistent with published reports that, after 1994, Chiapas received more federal money for poverty alleviation than any other Mexican state had ever received.[28] Carrots flew all over Chiapas in the second half of the nineties.

I asked Marcelina, a Tzeltal woman who was part of a women's group that received funds from the government, if the federal agency that funded her project imposed any conditions. She replied, "Up until now, no. After the conflict the government paid more attention to indigenous people. Before it didn't give money to indigenous people for cultural projects. [The government] began to arrive in the community but it never did this before" (interview, December 5, 1995). One of the people in charge of overseeing such government grants, María de los Angeles of the National Indigenous Institute (INI), told me that financing for indigenous women's programs in the early nineties was fairly sparse but that it increased significantly in the late nineties, reaching the point that it was more or less the same as the funding for men's programs. While in 1996 the institute funded twelve handicraft projects, in 1997 it funded twenty-five projects in what she called "indigenous cultural preservation" (interview, July 11, 1997). But funding new projects was not necessarily enough to make up for many indigenous people's resentment over the INI's past paternalistic policies, resentment that arguably was among the many roots of the rebellion (Collier 1994, 142–43).

Nearly four years into the rebellion the funding for indigenous people's projects had increased, but the underlying paternalism had not disappeared. While visiting the San Cristóbal office of the INI in July 1997, I noticed a poster on the wall that announced an event with two titles—K'in Maya II, or Maya Party II, in Tojolabal and Segundo Encuentro de Musica y Danza Indígena, or Second Gathering of Indigenous Music and Dance, in Spanish—that had just been held on a cooperative farm, or ejido, in the municipality of Las Margaritas. Having just returned from Las Margaritas (in which the atmosphere was so tense that many people were unwilling to even give me directions, something I had never before experienced in Latin America) I was surprised by the happy-go-lucky tone of the poster.

June 21 and 22, Ejido Saltillo

Municipality of las Margaritas, Chiapas

INI, Cultural Union of the Tojolabal People, Promotion

of Indigenous Culture

Being of one heart, all know that the hour to sing has arrived. The truly united hearts want to raise our voices; they want to say to the whole world, we are joyous and content.

The Spanish-language quote about singing used the sort of vocabulary and grammar that is typical of indigenous people who speak Spanish as a second language, and it was in quotation marks in the poster. Both the vocabulary and the quotes were no doubt meant to suggest that one of the "joyous and content" residents of Margaritas (what many called a war zone) was being quoted.

While such festivals might placate some indigenous people, others were not pacified so easily. As long as the central Zapatista demands—demilitarization, autonomy, democracy—were not met, many indigenous people would continue to express their admiration for the EZLN, even as they accepted government funding for their programs. Thinking back to the beginning of the conflict, Marcelina told me, "I myself was not frightened because I knew [the Zapatistas] were not against us, they were against the government. We are asking for support but we are not involved with any party, in any conflict. We admire the Zapatistas . . . we are allies but perhaps we are independent" (interview, December 5, 1995).

But was it really so simple? Was it possible to be both a Zapatista ally and a recipient of government grants? It is true that there were few overt strings attached to grants; the PRI's version of clientelism was often subtle. Yet government grants were hardly free of political implications. Official carrots played a complicated role in meeting the Zapatista challenge, as illustrated by several cases of government-funded groups that were publicly critical, or even defiant, of that same government.

In May 1994 a two-day workshop entitled "Women's Rights in our Customs and Traditions" was held in San Cristóbal. Forty-seven indigenous women gathered to discuss a series of problems, including discrimination and violence against women and indigenous people, and to consider possible solutions, including the Zapatista Revolutionary Women's Law and the reforms to Article 4 of the Constitution. While the gathering was organized by a number of independent women's organizations,[29] it was held at a facility provided by the INI, which also provided housing for the participants (Grupo de Mujeres et al. 1994, 2). Yet despite the government's monetary support through its agency, the INI, significant criticisms of the government were made at the workshop. In response to the question, Who abuses us? one working group of Tzotzil women came up with this answer: "We are abused by the mestizos, the governor. They do not respect us, they deceive us; they view us with contempt because we are Indian. They do not keep their promises when we ask for things that we have a right to" (Grupo de Mujeres et al. 1994, 9). Similarly, a working group of Tzeltal women had the following reaction to the question of exploitation: "We are abused by the government, the ranchers and the rich because they have power; they have been exploiting indigenous people for more than five hundred years" (11). Not all the groups focused on the government as their primary exploiter; some also mentioned men from their own communities, such as their husbands and brothers. But of the six working groups, five listed government officials among the exploiters of indigenous women.

Of course, the groups that had done the organizing could not control what the participants in the workshop were to say. But they did choose to spend part of the second day analyzing the Zapatistas' Revolutionary Women's Law. After viewing and discussing a film on domestic violence, the workshop participants broke into groups to analyze the law; some of the criticisms of the government that came out of this analysis were striking, given the location of the meeting. For example, "Clinics, better attention, and medicine are all necessary. Treatment should be good; one example: a woman arrived with a dead child, she was pregnant, and they didn't want to see her; they gave her sheets to wash if she wanted to be seen. The bad treatment is mainly in the IMSS-Solidaridad.[30] We want them to give us adequate medicine, not any old pill that gets rid of pain but does not cure. Also, the doctors arrive and they ask us to sign papers where women give permission to have their tubes tied, sometimes without explaining what it means. In the clinics, they treat patients badly, sometimes they ask them to get naked" (Grupo de Mujeres et al. 1994, 29). The appendix to the proceedings of the workshop listed all the names, ages, and home municipalities of the women who participated. A copy of those proceedings were then sent to "the Justice Department of the National Indigenous Institute and the Fifty-Eighth Congress of the State of Chiapas" (43).

Ironically perhaps, an agency of the national government, the INI, provided the money and other resources that made it possible for indigenous women to come together to criticize that same government.

But in a sense, the INI benefited from its grants to the indigenous women in that it got information from them. While the speakers quoted above were not identified by name in the copy of the proceedings that were given out to INI officials and others, the names of all the participants were listed in the back of the proceedings. In exchange for the small grant that made the two-day workshop possible, the government received a list of names of female indigenous leaders, a list that might be handy as the government sought to control the rebels and their supporters in the women's and indigenous rights movements.

The second case of the government funding overtly defiant organizations has to do with the question of autonomy. A more significant case than that of the indigenous women's workshop, since it continued over the course of years, this case of clientelism eventually engendered open battles within the Zapatista coalition. It all began in 1994 when, during a demonstration to mark the 502nd anniversary of the Conquest, a coalition of indigenous rights groups declared that nine municipalities in Chiapas were autonomous. In October, the same month that autonomy was first declared, a booklet was published by one of the movements that had just declared autonomy from the government, the Independent Front of Indian Peoples (Frente Independiente de Pueblos Indios, or FIPI) along with an NGO, the Committee for the Support and Defense of Indian Rights (Comité de Apoyo y Defensa de los Derechos Indios, A.C., or CADDIAC). The forty-seven-page booklet on individual rights within the Constitution was prefaced by FIPI's coordinator general, Margarito Xib Ruiz Hernández, who thanked a government agency, the Secretariat of Social Development (Secretaría de Desarrollo Social, or SEDESOL) for having funded the project (FIPI and CADDIAC 1994, 3). On top of that, while they declared autonomy, the members of FIPI were heavily dependent on another government agency, the National Indigenous Institute. In the back of the booklet, two addresses are listed for FIPI in Chiapas, both within the INI complex, a complex that would not be "liberated" by the indigenous coalition for another two months.

Given this high degree of dependence on government agencies for resources, what exactly did indigenous autonomy mean? As already noted, the meaning of autonomy was debated for years after the first declaration of autonomy. Many thought autonomy meant that they would control their own communities in ways that were consistent with their traditions; it did not mean that the indigenous communities would cease to be part of Mexico nor that they would cease to receive services from the Mexican government. So theoretically it was possible for an organization to be autonomous from the government and at the same time to receive most of its resources, including the buildings in which it met, from the government. But in practice, how meaningful was that sort of autonomy?

Conflicting answers to that question would tear apart the Zapatista coalition only half a year after the autonomous municipalities were first declared. In May 1995, at the same time as the federal government negotiated with the EZLN over the details of what would be the San Andrés talks, government officials made a hard-to-refuse offer to other members of the Zapatista coalition. Dante Delgado, a special commissioner from one of the federal social service agencies, SEDESOL, approached the coalition of indigenous organizations that had pledged their support for autonomy and the Zapatista army. He offered to address their demands but to do so, of course, they would have to be willing to talk to him, to explain their needs. Delgado suggested that they enter into a dialogue around three themes: economic and social development, women, and autonomous regions. These were three of the six themes that were to be addressed during the San Andrés talks, still many months in the future. But the other themes that were to be addressed at San Andrés—democracy, justice, human rights—were not included in Delgado's dialogue (Rodríguez Araujo 1995).

The indigenous coalition was in a bind, a classic clientelistic bind. On the one hand, the members of the indigenous coalition, like the EZLN, wanted to see all the Zapatistas' demands met, the political demands[31] as well as the economic and social demands. On the other hand, a year and a half of struggling to break the constraints of authoritarian politics and impoverishment had only tightened those constraints. The state of Chiapas was far more militarized than ever, and since the low intensity war limited their ability to make a living, most of the indigenous activists were poorer than ever. Delgado offered relief to exhausted people and they, not surprisingly, accepted the offer.

According to one estimate, when it came time to decide whether to support the Democratic State Assembly of the People of Chiapas

(Asamblea Estatal Democrática del Pueblo Chiapaneco, or AEDPCH),[32] which favored negotiating with Delgado, about 97 percent of the members of the indigenous coalitions voted for dialogue with Delgado and only 3 percent opposed it (Aida Hernández Castillo, personal communication, November 30, 1995). Tens of thousands of the EZLN's civilian supporters had chosen the certainty of the old-style politics of clientelism. The EZLN would respond forcefully in a communiqué written by Subcomandante Marcos: "A group of people from the Aedepch and the rebel government in transition . . . have begun negotiations with the supreme government. In meetings with the consul of the central government, Dante Delgado, these people arrived at agreements, in the name of Aedepch, that signified sabotaging the Zapatista position in the dialogue at San Andrés. The position of the EZLN has been clear: the supreme government should talk to and negotiate with the democratizing forces in Chiapas. . . . The government is carrying out a strategy of division, it aims to talk and negotiate with fragmented forces, which creates the possibilities for corruption, disloyalty and treachery" (Marcos 1995a).

Marcos considered why the indigenous groups would have done such a thing, without sympathizing with that choice: "They are discouraged by the recent blows that we have received. They thought that the struggle would be easy, comfortable, filled with photographs, and huge gatherings. They forgot that liberty is won with sacrifice, that setbacks are normal for those that fight, and that victory is not the result of a declaration or a flag, rather the work of organization, the sum of everyone's efforts, of political consequences, and of strong convictions" (Marcos 1995a). At that point, it seemed that the government's plans had worked. Without even resorting to violence, government officials had undermined the Zapatista coalition to such an extent that the EZLN publicly accused its allies of betrayal. At that point, few could have foreseen the massive nationwide indigenous rights movement that later emerged out of the San Andrés talks, a movement that included the vast majority of those who negotiated with Delgado. What happened?

The fundamental error the government made was to fail to realize how many carrots were needed to satisfy those indigenous groups, whose members were far less subservient than they had been before the rebellion. At the end of August 1995, three months into the negotiations with the federal government's representative, Dante Delgado, eighty women from seventeen of the organizations that had participated in the negotiations met to evaluate the results. At the end of that meeting, only five of the organizations voted to accept the government's offer; the other twelve preferred to receive nothing rather than to be insulted, arguing that the offer was "an offense to the dignity of women who are fighting for social change" (quoted in Rojas 1995a, 54). Dante Delgado's team had requested proposals for projects; that request was followed up with a request to prioritize projects (two per organization). Finally, Delgado's team decided that it would fund only one project per organization and that it would decide which of the two was worthy: "The government—the women said—wants to spoon feed us, it wants to seize us any old way; they think that since we are poor we will be content with very little; they think that since we are women it is easy to screw us over" (Morquecho 1995c, 154). The women who rejected the government's offer insisted that, in any case, their main interest was not material: "We are in this for political purposes, we are going forward in a long-term process. . . . We are not looking for a piece of pie. . . . we have important goals like the government in transition" (155).

What does this mean? Were they returning to their original position—the Zapatista position—that meaningful economic reforms were not possible without effective democratization? Or was it the case, as several suggested to me, that many members of the organizations that negotiated with Delgado never realized that the Zapatistas objected to the parallel negotiation? Whether or not the women of the organizations that belonged to the indigenous coalition known as AEDPCH had realized that they were out of the Zapatista coalition for a few months, they were invited back in shortly after their August meeting.

On October 12, 1995, AEDPCH pledged "its total support to the dialogue between the EZLN and the federal government" (Pérez and Henríquez 1995). But, while even while pledging its support for the EZLN in its negotiations with the federal government, AEDPCH was still, formally at least, engaged in a parallel dialogue with Dante Delgado. In late November the dialogue finally broke down, shortly after the AEDPCH denounced that in Chiapas during 1995, more than 860 social activists had been imprisoned, and forty had been assassinated

(Henríquez and Rojas 1995; López, Balboa, and Henríquez 1995). The next month, one male[33] leader of the AEDPCH would tell me about the relationship between his organization and the EZLN: "They are our brothers. They are our peoples. The demands of the EZLN and our demands are the same. They wear ski masks and we do not, but that's the only difference" (interview, November 29, 1995).

So the wound in the Zapatista coalition was closed over, in large part because the members of the AEDPCH realized that negotiating did not protect their members from political violence and that it did not even get them much in the way of material goods. But even as the EZLN did its best to leave this incident in the past, apologizing for calling the members of the AEDPCH traitors, the wound to the Zapatista coalition must have left scars.[34] And while the federal government ultimately failed in its overt attempt to divide the Zapatista coalition, that does not mean that it gave up on clientelism as a strategy. The very physical space where many of the autonomous indigenous groups were housed—the twenty-six-building INI complex in San Cristóbal—was itself a good example of the blurry line between defiance and dependence.

Remember that the complex of the National Indigenous Institute was seized by a coalition of indigenous groups in December 1994 as they declared their autonomy and their allegiance to the Rebel Government in Transition, headed by Amado Avendaño. Originally, this seemed to me to be a clearly defiant act, but that view was complicated when I discovered that the groups that were housed in this "liberated territory" continued to receive most of their funds from various government agencies.

In 1997 four women who were active in different organizations within the old INI complex told me about their funding sources and three of them mentioned government agencies (FONAI, SEDESOL, Solidaridad). Some of them also mentioned aid from international agencies or their own efforts to raise funds. A fifth woman, Carmen, an adviser to the coordinating body of the organizations within the old INI complex, said she thought that the vast majority of funding for their work in favor of autonomy from the government came from government agencies (interviews, July 1997). Carmen disagreed so strongly with other activists about the wisdom of their ties to government agencies that she left the indigenous coalition in 1998 (interview, April 4, 2000).

With time, the numbers who actively participated in the coalition of indigenous groups that met in the INI complex had diminished. Originally, when the complex was seized in 1994 (and as late as 1997), twenty-four indigenous groups were active in the coalition. That number had diminished to sixteen by the late nineties.[35] By 2000, only eight continued to work out of the old INI complex in San Cristóbal, according to Magali, an adviser who remained loyal to the Autonomous Multiethnnic Regions (Regiones Autonomas Pluriétnicas, or RAP), the coalition of indigenous groups that met in the INI. As Magali explained, many of the groups no longer met in the old INI complex on a regular basis, because of the difficulties of traveling to San Cristóbal, but continued to be supportive of the RAP's activities. In light of the difficulties of raising funds for travel to political activities (since government agencies would fund cultural but not political activities), the RAP chose to remember Emiliano Zapata with a cultural rather than a political event in April 2000 (interview, April 12, 2000).

I attended the opening ceremony of that cultural event, the First "Maya-Zoque" Gathering of Corn (Primer Encuentro del Maíz Maya-Zoque), held on April 14, 2000. The contrast between that ceremony and the ANIPA conference, an indigenous gathering I had attended in the same location in 1995, was striking. At the corn gathering, nine people (eight men from indigenous organizations and one woman from a government agency, the INI) gave speeches about the importance of corn to the culture of the Mayan peoples. While much of the ANIPA conference in 1995 had been explicitly political, referring to the ongoing San Andrés talks between the EZLN and the government, no political issues were mentioned by those who spoke in 2000. Instead, they repeatedly called for unity, as kernels of corn are unified on a cob. According to the posters advertising the event, the gathering was sponsored by seven groups, including the INI (the government indigenous institute) and the RAP (the autonomous indigenous coalition).

Working toward autonomy with funding from the state turned out to be difficult, to say the least. Not only were most of the indigenous groups with the words *independent* or *autonomous* in their titles funded by government agencies, but it turned out that it was not even clear if the indigenous groups actually controlled the INI complex, despite their claims. In 1997 numerous people who worked in the old INI complex assured me that the complex had been legally theirs since early that year and that they had papers to prove it. Yet María de los Angeles of the INI had a different explanation for the papers; they did not give the indigenous groups legal title, they merely loaned the complex to those groups. She said that this was common, that the INI would loan property for various periods of time, sometimes up to a hundred years. "There is no point in fighting. [Better to] be equal, to negotiate it without conflicts" (interview, July 11, 1997).

The Other Side of Clientelism, or the Stick

The strategies for putting down the rebellion were not limited to carrots. Some organizations were too loud in their support for the EZLN or in their condemnation of military and paramilitary violence. Such groups were typically unwilling to accept the clientelistic offer of carrots, with its concomitant government oversight. Other groups, like the Bees (las Abejas), that attempted to stay out of the conflict, may have been threatening precisely for their neutrality: war required that people take sides. Members of those organizations were often the victims of violence during the first years of the Zapatista rebellion.

During those years, the most infamous incident of political violence was the massacre of forty-five unarmed members of the Bees—mostly women and children, mostly shot in the back—on December 22, 1997. While the state of Chiapas was heavily militarized by that point, the massacre was not committed by the military. Instead, it was the work of one of the many paramilitary groups that had been formed following the military offensive of February 1995 with significant support from local politicians from the ruling party. One of the most notorious of the groups, ironically named Peace and Justice (Paz y Justicia), was "openly led by local PRI deputy Samuel Sánchez" (CIACH 1997b, 2). And just weeks before the massacre at Acteal, Peace and Justice received a grant of $575,000 from Julio César Ruiz Ferro, the governor of Chiapas (Preston 1998a).

Paramilitary groups were most active in contested areas of the north and central highlands, where support for the Zapatistas was high but where the Zapatista army could offer less protection than it could in the isolation of the jungle. In contrast to the Lacandón jungle region, the stronghold of the EZLN, where government services were minimal, the north and central highlands had traditionally seen a high degree of government penetration. So while the jungle was united in its anger at the government's indifference, the north and central highlands were deeply divided. Some of the indigenous residents of those regions were threatened by the Zapatista agenda, since they had something to lose if the PRI's hegemony were to be loosened.

Moreover, these regions were ripe for the mobilization of pro-PRI paramilitary groups. A study in the municipality of Chenalhó, where the town of Acteal is located, found 246 paramilitary group members. Drawn from the same communities they terrorized, they were all land-less young men who had no legal way to make a living and no right to participate in the formal mechanisms of politics in their communities, since representation was based on membership in a local ejido, or coop-erative farm. Under such dismal circumstances, mobilization in a para-military group had its appeals, offering them a way to make a living (by collecting "war taxes" from passersby) and offering them the power and prestige that came from carrying arms that were supplied by the organ-izers of the groups. Not only did these individuals gain something from joining a paramilitary group, they had little to lose, as they were already alienated from their communities. "They never had the edu-cation which is offered in periodic assemblies in which the common destiny of the town, colony or municipality is decided and they escaped all community responsibilities. Because of that 'the paramilitary soldiers' have no social or political project of any sort" (Aubrey and Inda 1998).

The strategy of organizing and funding paramilitary groups had one great advantage, from the perspective of the ruling party, over sending in the military or police forces. That advantage was plausible deniabil-ity. The semi-independence of the paramilitary forces allowed their fun-ders to denounce paramilitary violence in a way that would not have been possible had the same acts been carried out by the military or po-lice. But the semi-independence of the paramilitary groups was also the worst thing about them. If the members of a paramilitary group decided to kill many people at once, as they did in the massacre in Acteal, in-stead of killing a few people at a time,[36] there was little that the state or federal authorities could do about it.

The massacre in Acteal created a real public relations problem for the state and federal governments. While Chiapas had disappeared from the international press after the peace process came to a halt in early 1996, it was once again in the world headlines at the end of 1997. The image of shooting at fleeing men, women, and children was not consistent with the new democratic Mexico that had been proclaimed during the midterm election in July of that year, as opposition parties took control of Congress and the capital city for the first time ever. Yet that public relations problem was apparently outweighed by the usefulness of the paramilitary forces, for they were not dismantled in the years following Acteal, even though the paramilitary forces operated in those regions where the Mexican army had a strong presence. Presumably it would have been possible to dismantle those forces had there been an official interest in doing so.[37]

In the city of San Cristóbal, where most of the indigenous rights groups and NGOs had their offices, the stick was also felt during the second half of the nineties, though in a somewhat more subtle way, possibly because foreign tourists were always present in San Cristóbal. Of those NGOs, one of the most prominent defenders of indigenous people's rights, and also one the most consistent targets of violence, was a coalition, the Coordinator of Nongovernmental Organizations for Peace (Coordinación de Organismos No Gubermentales por la Paz, or CONPAZ). The coalition was founded during the first days of the rebellion, in January 1994, by seventy-three NGOs, all of which had been working with indigenous communities for years and sometimes decades (CONPAZ 1994, 2).

Throughout the four years that CONPAZ existed, its member organizations continued the work that they had always done in the indigenous communities (providing, among other things, medical care, agricultural support, popular education), work that was more critical than ever as the militarization of the state aggravated already precarious situations. At the beginning of the rebellion, two other goals were emphasized: denouncing human rights abuses that had already occurred and advocating for an expansion of rights in the future. Human rights were understood by the members of CONPAZ in a broad sense; they included negative rights such as freedom from physical violence and positive rights such as the right to health care and education and the right to live in a democratic country. Since the Zapatistas' demands were so much like their own, some members of CONPAZ participated in the peace talks with the government, as guests of the Zapatistas, and they also supported the Rebel Government in Transition (Bellinghausen 1997; CONPAZ 1994).

While none of these actions made them different from tens of thousands of other people in Chiapas, there were some things that differentiated them. The members of CONPAZ tended to be educated and foreign—that is, not from Chiapas—though nearly all were Mexican citizens. Though most were mestizos, they were mestizos who allied themselves with the Indians, which made them traitors in the eyes of many. Moreover, they had the resources (telephones, fax machines, e-mail) that gave them access to the national and international media. For all those reasons they were a serious threat to those who opposed the Zapatista agenda and they paid for their actions. On multiple occasions, people broke into their office and set it on fire. Computer disks and files were stolen, along with food and blankets that were destined for the residents of the indigenous communities in which they worked. The members of CONPAZ regularly received death threats over the phone, threats that were particularly unnerving since they often targeted the activists' children. On one occasion, an administrator at CONPAZ was kidnaped along with his wife and two children. Two days later they were freed, some sixty miles from the place where they had been seized, after their kidnappers had tortured the administrator, raped and tortured his wife, and cut off their daughter's hair (interviews 1995; action alerts received by e-mail from the Fray Bartolomé de las Casas Center for Human Rights; Henríquez 1996).

The federal government was relatively uninterested in investigating these actions, if their response to my letters is any indication. While they generally did not respond at all, on one occasion I received a reply from President Zedillo's office that referred to the "supposed attacks against the office of CONPAZ." The letter concluded with the exclamation "Effective suffrage, no reelection,"[38] a reminder that this government—which claimed that human rights activists set fire to their own offices—was forged in an earlier revolution (Lic. Francisco Madrazo Granados to author, November 11, 1996).

The violence against CONPAZ was part of a larger pattern of violence against defenders of human rights, according to Amnesty International (cited in Concha 1996). To a large extent, it had its intended effect. Claudia, an activist in one of the NGOs that formed CONPAZ, told me that lots of people had left because they felt threatened or because (due to the tension that was the inevitable result of working under siege) internal disagreements blew out of proportion: "With the low intensity war, we beat ourselves" (interview, July 2, 1997). A few months after that interview, Claudia's words rang true again, as CONPAZ announced that it would be closing down at the end of the year, citing internal disputes (Bellinghausen 1997; CIACH 1997a, 4).

Another organization whose members felt the stick during the years of the rebellion was J'Pas Joloviletik (Women Who Weave), an indigenous women's weaving cooperative founded in 1984 by the National Indigenous Institute. By 1994, 870 women from twenty-four different communities belonged to the cooperative. In December of that year J'Pas Joloviletik declared its independence from the INI, along with many other indigenous people's organizations. But unlike the vast majority of those organizations, J'Pas Joloviletik refused to participate in the parallel dialogue with Dante Delgado six months later. Perhaps because of that defiance, the cooperative was threatened in a number of ways in 1995, according to Helena: "Men arrived there to bother us. To threaten us. They also called us on the phone. One day they came to kill us too. . . . One day the police came asking for me by name. They knew my whole name perfectly—who knows how" (interview, July 15, 1997). On November 29, 1995, that series of harassing visits and calls was followed up with a robbery. That day the cooperative members lost photographs, negatives, handicrafts, sewing machines, and money. Additionally, one of their phones was blocked, another was stolen, and their files were destroyed (Castro and Palomo 1995, 71). The robbery had its intended effect: to frighten the members of J'Pas Joloviletik enough so that they would stop advocating for the rights of indigenous women. In December the cooperative broke up, with about half returning to their old relationship with the INI, while the other half went off to form a new organization that would continue its organizational work at the same time as it tried to sell handicrafts.

A year and a half after the breakup, in June 1997, I visited J'Pas Joloviletik (the half of the organization that kept the name and reestablished ties to the state indigenous institute, the INI). As I paid for a vest, I told the indigenous woman who was taking my money that I was doing a study of the women's movement and that I would like to talk to her about the work of J'Pas Joloviletik. She mumbled no and motioned toward a woman, who was apparently a mestiza, repeating "this lady." That woman told me that she had been there for only five months and didn't know anything. "I just sell." She told me that the ladies who had been there longer were not in, but when I asked when they would be in, she said never, that they lived in their communities. Handing me a one-page history (that was sitting on the counter), she told me that everything I needed to know was there. If the women of J'Pas Joloviletik needed to buy peace with silence, with political acquiescence, then they would pay that price.

Helena was one of those who did not want to give up her work for indigenous women's rights. So she left to join the new cooperative, which met in a less public location. Perhaps because they were harder to find there, they enjoyed a year of peace. Then, in January 1997, the harassment began again: "We were out at about seven in the evening; two men came up to us who acted like they were drunk, but they were not drunk. They were going to touch us but instead they grabbed us, they kicked us. They kicked me in the ribs, they were going to pull off my blouse." A week later Helena and a friend were walking home once again, this time about five in the afternoon, when they passed a parked car filled with men; men they did not know.

A man yelled at us: "Girls, where are you going?" He opened the door, two young men got out, they followed us as we walked, they started running after us and told us, "We already know you. I'm going to take you in the truck until I've destroyed your ass," and like that they began to say ugly things. He grabbed my shawl, he was going to take my bag, he hugged me very hard and wanted to kiss me but he couldn't. [He said,] "Since you always go out in the street, you two are already women of the street, you're already whores." People stood there watching us. A taxi driver came by and said, "Don't hug the girl in the street, take her wherever you want." . . . He followed me again. "You Zapatistas think there are a lot of you. But there are also a lot of us. If you want, we can do it right now." I didn't say anything and he went back to where they were parked.

I felt like I would pass out, I was so scared. Then they came by with the car; there were around seven people and they were going to pull me into the car. When I lifted a rock they left and turned around and waited. They stayed there screaming, "We're never going to leave you alone until we try you out." That day both of us were really frightened.

Helena's aunt was threatened in the market a few days later by a man with a knife, and at that point they decided to move, which ended the harassment, at least temporarily. Helena speculated about why she was attacked by these men she didn't even know: "I think people don't like to see that we women are participating. They don't want women to be able to defend ourselves. They want women to stay low. They don't want there to be meetings, marches. . . . What we think is that we shouldn't be afraid. We should show them that we women are capable" (interview, July 15, 1997).

Is Mexico Salvadorizing?

Shortly after members of a paramilitary group massacred forty-five un-armed indigenous people in the town of Acteal, the daily newspaper *La Jornada* asked its readers that question in thick black letters on the upper corner of the back page. The question was meant to be ominous, and indeed it was. To become like El Salvador was to shift to a more vi-olent and exclusionary politics. Salvadorizing was settling in for a long nasty civil war, a war in which even babies, the most blameless inno-cents, could become massacre victims. But to Salvadorize could mean something else as well, something the editors of *La Jornada* surely did not have in mind. Chiapas, and with it the rest of Mexico, was also Sal-vadorizing in the sense that some of its formally marginalized women were becoming more organized, more empowered, more autonomous. Claudia from CONPAZ thought that Mexico had been transformed by the Zapatista rebellion: "It's a much more politicized society than be-fore, anybody has the nerve to talk about politics much more than be-fore. It's like a wave. With the ERP [People's Revolutionary Army, a group that emerged after the EZLN] people began to realize that what the EZLN was saying was true, that guerrillas were going to emerge all over the country, that the situation was very serious. It had a very national impact, I think, in changing consciousness." But that did not mean that the members of the EZLN or their closest followers were better off than they had been before the rebellion. The Zapatista slogan "Everything for everybody, nothing for ourselves" had turned out to be far too true, Claudia said. "The truth is that they have not gained anything. If anything has won it's been the country" (interview, July 2, 1997).

Of course, to say that many had come to think differently after years of rebellion does not mean that indigenous people were fully respected as Mexican citizens or that indigenous women were fully autonomous within their communities. One of the most striking indicators of how far indigenous women, even organized indigenous women, were from enjoying the basic rights that their male counterparts enjoyed was the way they often responded to my request for an interview. Most of the indigenous women I approached for interviews told me that, first, they had to get permission from their husband, or from the director, or from some other male authority figure. None of the hundreds of other women I spoke to over the course of my fieldwork ever suggested that they had to get permission before they could talk.

Life was changing slowly for indigenous women, but for many of them, it was changing. Marcos discussed some of the innovations within Zapatista communities during the first year of the rebellion that affected women most directly:[39]

When we governed, alcoholism rates went down to zero and that's because the women here became ferocious and they said that booze only makes men hit women and children and carry out awful things, and so they gave the order that there would be no more booze, and so, no more booze, and we did not let the booze get through and the ones who benefited most were children and women and the ones who were hurt most were the businessmen and the government. . . . The women began to see that the laws they had imposed on the men were enforced,[40] and a third of our fighting forces are women and they are very ferocious and, well, they are armed and they "convinced" us to accept their laws, and they also participate in the civil and military leadership in our struggle and we don't say anything about it, and what could we say? (quoted in Rojas 1995a, 21–22).

Marcos painted an image of gender relations in transformation under very unusual and unstable circumstances. The EZLN governed the jungle communities for only about a year, until President Zedillo broke the ceasefire in February 1995 by sending troops to reclaim the jungle. The Zapatistas were still learning, according to Marcos, when "the tanks and helicopters and airplanes and many thousands of soldiers arrived and they said that they came to defend the national sovereignty. . . . And behind the government's war tanks, once again there arrived prostitution, booze, robberies, drugs, destruction, death, corruption, sickness, poverty. And people from the government came and said that finally legality had been restored in the lands of Chiapas" (22). February 1995 was a significant turning point in the Zapatista story, for it was then that the Mexican government regained control of the jungle that the Zapatistas had governed. It was at that point that the paramilitary groups were formed in the northern and central highlands. That was the point, many expected, when the old rules of political life should have taken hold. But the deepening presence of the military and paramilitary forces could not completely crush the rebellions, including the gender rebellions, that had begun.[41]

Those gender rebellions were probably most dramatic in the case of armed Zapatista combatants, but their effects were felt throughout the state, at least among organized women. Juana, a member of an indigenous women's theater troop, told me about how many women had changed since the beginning of 1994: "When they saw that the Zapatista women fought, they said, why don't we do that? There are many women who no longer allow themselves to be dominated. . . . Women have already seen reality, they have had workshops, talks. Before when there were marches, they were comprised almost completely of men. Now there are almost a greater number of women. They are fighting for their own rights" (interview, July 19, 1997).

I asked Juana if anyone ever reacted negatively to their work in the theater collective. She replied, "Men get mad because they say that we are making the women change. That makes the men mad . . . [they say,] before I hit you and you didn't do anything" (interview, July 19, 1997).

The men asked their women why they complain about domestic violence now, and the women explained that now they know they have rights.

Other indigenous activists offered similar accounts of conflicts over gender relations within indigenous communities. In resisting women's demands for the sorts of rights that were claimed in the Revolutionary Women's Law (such as freedom from domestic violence and forced marriage, or freedom to participate politically), men made the claim that women were trying to change the old rules of life; that they had always accepted gender inequality in the past. Women, on the other hand, claimed that far from changing the rules they were trying to reclaim old values that had been forgotten. Using an egalitarian discourse, they insisted that what had changed is that they had become aware of rights that had existed all along.

The language of the Zapatistas is quite egalitarian, so it is not surprising that women's claims for rights during the rebellion would be couched in such terms. The Catholic Church's discourse on women's rights, which also tends to be very egalitarian (at least within the liberation theology branch of the Church) has also had a long-term effect on many women's views of themselves. This is not to suggest that the Church, even those currents within the Church most influenced by liberation theology, has been always supportive of women's rights. As one observer suggested, "the Church's work with women is very progressive at the level of social participation, but anything that has to do with the body, such as abortion and contraception, that is simply not acceptable" (interview, January 1995). Nonetheless, the egalitarian language of human rights used by the Church in general, and by many church activists working with indigenous women, in particular, may help explain many indigenous women's new demands, demands that have informed the Zapatista agenda. Sister Josefa talked about her work with indigenous women: "When they learn about human rights it's like the heavens opening up: 'I did not know that, that I have rights'" (interview, July 19, 1997).

As many indigenous women became more and more demanding of their rights upon discovering them, the men of their communities often became defensive. Indigenous men were not the only ones who were threatened: the very foundations of clientelistic politics were shaken by such demands. "[A]ny notion of rights as universal and equal auto-matically challenges traditional patterns of *caciquismo* and clientelistic control, which, by definition, are personal, particularistic, and arbitrary" (Foweraker 1993, 25). And yet, despite their profound ambivalence in the face of such demands, the men who supported the Zapatista cause were caught in a dilemma. They themselves made egalitarian demands, insisting on the same rights and privileges that all Mexicans enjoyed. Speaking to an international audience, they employed a language of human rights including their right to preserve their particular identities as indigenous people, to speak their own languages, and to carry out their own customs.

What about those Zapatista women who also spoke the language of human rights? Were men ready to allow the transformation of their particular customs so that their women could enjoy the rights that they had recently discovered? Comandante Hortensia had one answer: "We Zapatista women have made the decision to fight so as to conquer the space that belongs to us as women and as people" (EZLN 1996, 19). Hortensia did not request that space, she insisted that it already be-longed to her and that, like it or not, others would have to make way.

Chapter 5

Feminism and Revolutionary Movements in Comparative Perspective

THIS BOOK HAS illustrated one of the fundamental truths of politics: political movements often evolve in ways that are unexpected—and uncontrolled—by the founders of those movements. In the three cases considered here, women were mobilized by the thousands in order to promote revolutionary agendas that had little to do with increasing gender equality. And yet, in all three cases, many of the women who were mobilized for one agenda came to rethink those political goals, and the best way to carry them out, after the original crisis had passed. In both Nicaragua and El Salvador vibrant autonomous feminist movements emerged after the wars. In Chiapas, before the war had even ended, women's rights activities grew and consolidated both in women's organizations and within the nationwide indigenous rights movement.

The cases of Nicaragua, El Salvador, and Chiapas could be read as suggesting that there is some sort of natural affinity between revolutionary values and feminist values, that strong feminist movements emerge automatically in the wake of revolutionary wars. But reviewing gender politics in two other countries that have recently experienced revolutionary upheaval—Iran and Poland—makes it clear that there is nothing natural or automatic about the relationship between revolution and feminism. Iran and Poland are good test cases since, although large numbers of women participated in the revolutionary movements that brought down dictatorships—the fall of the shah in 1979 and the fall of the communists in 1989—the end result of both movements was greater gender inequality. Explaining why women lost rights as a result of the revolutions in Iran and Poland should highlight the factors that allowed for feminist gains in Central America and Mexico.

Finally, I will assess the future of gender politics in Cuba in the postrevolutionary era, considering that future in the light of my findings regarding the roots of feminism in Nicaragua, El Salvador, and Chiapas, and the challenges faced by feminists in those places. In a number of ways, these cases share similarities with Cuba and may be useful guides to what lies ahead. Nonetheless, it is far from clear that Cubans will follow the path laid out by their fellow Latin American revolutionaries. The cases of Iran and Poland suggest reasons to believe that antifeminism, as well as feminism, may play a role in a future Cuba.

Iran: Defending the Martyrs by Veiling Women

The revolution in Iran shares a number of commonalities with the Latin American cases considered in this book, especially that of Nicaragua. As in Nicaragua, a personalistic dictator—the shah—was overthrown in 1979 by a nationalist coalition with a broad class base that benefited from a world systemic opening[1] shaped by the Carter administration. As in Nicaragua, El Salvador, and Chiapas, radical organizing was informed and consolidated through religion: liberation theology in the Latin American cases, highly politicized Shia Islam in the Iranian case (Farhi 1990; Foran 1994). But from a feminist perspective, the long-term impact of the revolutionary movements could hardly differ more. In the Latin American cases, the revolutionary movements created opportunities for women that eventually led to the emergence of autonomous feminist movements. Those opportunities were not exactly gifts from the guerrilla leaders but they were nonetheless part and parcel of the revolutionary processes in which egalitarianism and mobilization were central values.

In Iran, in contrast, the revolutionary leadership successfully defined gender inequality as a revolutionary value. And not only was gender inequality part of the revolutionary agenda, it was a high priority. "[A]mong the first 'revolutionary' actions taken by the new regime was the reveiling of women, nullifying of the Family Protection Act that had abolished man's unilateral right to divorce, and banning women from the judicial profession" (Moghissi 1996, 14). Eventually women were banned from a series of pursuits: from most college majors, from any sports in which they might be seen by men, and from traveling, owning a passport, or even leaving the house without their husband's permission (Hughes 1998; Moghissi 1996, 50; Saadatmand 1995).

By the close of the first two decades of the revolution, gender relations had shifted, the legal restrictions on women's lives were less onerous, and a sort of feminism within the revolution had even emerged, in a softly veiled way (Afary 1996, 45–46; 1997, 104–8; Moghadam 1999, 172–73, 184–91; Wright 2000, 133–59).[2] But that softening of the equation of revolution and gender inequality was just that: a softening. At least at the level of public discourse, many of the most powerful revolutionary leaders remained committed to the idea that men and women were to be treated differently and unequally; the real change was that good revolutionaries could sometimes debate the nature of those differences.

Why was the beginning of the Iranian revolution so different from the beginning of the Nicaraguan one, from a feminist perspective, even though it was similar to the Nicaraguan revolution from a state-centric perspective? The nature of the old regime is one source of clues. In Nicaragua, the Somoza regime was not particularly associated with women's emancipation. It is true that the second generation of the Somoza family granted the vote to women, in 1955, but that was late by Latin American standards,[3] and the vote was not especially meaningful for the majority of Nicaraguans, given the frequency of electoral fraud. It is also worth noting that some women found opportunities to contest traditional gender roles through their participation in the Somoza administration and its associated women's organization (González 2001), but those women were a minority. Overall, the Somoza dictatorship was not associated with feminism in the minds of most Nicaraguans, and, as a result, for most people opposition to the dictatorship did not have any overt gendered meaning.

The dynasty of the Iranian shahs—Reza Shah Pahlavi (1925–41) and his son Mohammad Reza Pahlavi (1941–79)—spanned two generations, coming to an end in 1979, as did the Somoza dynasty in Nicaragua. But the shahs' political project, unlike that of the Somozas, was overtly rooted in the transformation of women's roles. For the shahs, consolidating power and promoting capitalist modernization required confronting the Islamic clergy, and that in turn required challenging traditional gender relations. Under the rule of the shahs, control over family law shifted from the clergy to the state. Many women were mobilized into governmental organizations, formally headed by the shahs' sisters and daughters, to put the new gender reforms into practice, providing literacy classes, job training, legal counseling, and day care services. According to the woman who directed the official women's organization in the 1970s, policies carried out by the women's organization were all approved by the shah himself, "whose national role was the essence and symbol of patriarchy" (quoted in Afary 1996, 39; also 31–41).

While it is true that reforms in family law were often limited and mostly meaningful to middle- and upper-class women who had the resources which made it possible to take advantage of their new rights, such as the right to seek divorce and the right to go to college, it is also true that those reforms were infuriating to the clergy. For the clergy correctly saw them as attempts to diminish its sphere of influence and to increase that of the state. Moreover, the heavy-handed way in which gender reforms were implemented meant that few people saw women's emancipation as particularly liberating. Forced unveiling was probably the clearest example of the brutality of emancipation under the shahs. Since women dressed from head to toe in black chadors were inconsistent with the modernizing image the shahs wished to project and were symbolic of the power of the clergy over everyday life, the chador was banned, and conservatively dressed women sometimes had their veils ripped off in the street. Fear of being unveiled led some women to hide at home. In the end, forced emancipation limited their mobility more than ever (Moghissi 1996, 36–53).

Other women did not have the option of hiding from the shahs' gender reforms because they worked outside of their homes. Since the shahs' macroeconomic policies had led to increases in male unemployment at the same time as those policies opened up opportunities for women in the workforce, many working-class women found themselves supporting their families economically at the same time as they retained all their domestic duties. Women who gained new economic responsibilities without new domestic power did not find liberation very appealing either. "As a result, the advocates of domesticity for women found large support among the poor and working classes, both male and female" (Afshar 1985, 257). When, in the minds of most Iranians, the dictatorship in Iran became associated with women's emancipation, to oppose the dictatorship meant to oppose gender equality.

Another explanation for the differences in the gendered outcomes of the Nicaraguan and Iranian revolutions lies in religion. For many of the Nicaraguan women who went on to become women's rights activists, participation in the liberation theology movement within the Catholic Church was their first political experience. Liberation theology in Nicaragua (and elsewhere) was a radically egalitarian project that generally extended to gender relations. Through the liberation theology movement, women were encouraged to leave their houses, to learn to read, to work side by side with men, and to denounce government abuses of human rights, sometimes at the risk of their lives. They were, in many ways, called to live as equals.

This is not to deny the limits to the gender egalitarianism of the liberation theology movement. The same liberation theologians who were quick to break with Rome around economic issues usually saw eye to eye with the hierarchy in the Vatican regarding issues of sexuality and the family. This was a serious limit to the egalitarianism of the liberation theology project, for how could women live out lives as equals to men if they, but not men, could have their futures undermined by an unplanned pregnancy? Nonetheless, for all its internal contradictions, the religious underpinnings of the Nicaraguan revolution had far more egalitarian gender implications than those of the Iranian revolution.

Shia Islam in Iran, like Catholicism in Latin America, was not always a vehicle for political mobilization. But under the rule of the shahs, it became a means to reject all that the shahs represented: Westernization, economic modernization, political dictatorship. The Ayatollah Khomeini, leader of the Shia movement that seized power in 1979, saw women's emancipation as part of this blasphemous Western project. In his words, encouraging women to participate in public life would only get in the way of their "sacred natural function of raising pious children." Giving women the right to vote was the equivalent of "trampling

on the Quran and exigent Islamic decrees and encouraging prostitution" (quoted in Moghissi 1996, 61). While it would be wrong to explain the fate of women in revolutionary Iran simply in terms of Islam
(for that would make it impossible to explain the variation in women's
positions in Muslim societies), religion goes quite a way in explaining
the differences between revolution in Iran and Latin America.

But the two factors identified so far—the reaction against the shahs'
gender reforms and the power of Shia Islam—do not entirely explain the
success of the ayatollah and his followers in institutionalizing such a profoundly inegalitarian revolution. The third and final factor that sealed the
fate of Iranian women was the role of secular nationalists and socialists in
the revolutionary coalition. Nationalists and socialists—in Iran, as elsewhere, nurtured in the universities—were important, though junior,
partners in the revolutionary movement that toppled the shah in 1979.
Being part of the coalition did not mean that they shared all the same
goals, of course: neither the nationalists nor the socialists supported the
Islamists' positions on questions of gender politics such as the vote, education, and paid employment. The socialists in particular strongly
supported women's emancipation, at least in theory, for that was consistent with the socialist tradition, rooted in the writings of Marx and
Engels. In that sense, secular socialists in Iran were much like secular
socialists in Latin America. And just as in Latin America, the leaders of
the Iranian left encouraged their female followers to patiently put aside
their demands for equality until after what they saw as more important
goals were accomplished (Moghissi 1996, 72–74; Sanasarian 1983,
97–105). Could they have promoted gender equality and still remained
in the revolutionary coalition? Perhaps not. Was remaining in the coalition at any price a good idea? The answer to that question is clearly no,
for once the Islamists came to power they turned on their junior partners, consolidating the revolution by executing, exiling, or otherwise si-
lencing the secular revolutionaries.

But the fate of the nationalists and socialists had not yet been sealed
at the moment when the revolutionary coalition took power. Less than
a month after the overthrow of the shah, there was a last opportunity
to shift the course of the revolution, an opportunity that was missed.
March 8, International Women's Day, could have been the day when
secular women seized some control over the course of the revolution for

themselves and their male counterparts. The day before the March 8 demonstration, the Ayatollah Khomeini, observing that government offices were filled with "naked" women, had ordered that women had to wear the *hejab,* or headscarf, if they wished to continue working. That same week he had announced that the Family Protection Act (which gave women the right to seek divorce and work as lawyers) would be abolished. Violence against secular women increased as many of the ayatollah's followers began harassing women who had not complied with the new dress code.

It was in that context that the demonstration was held, a demonstration that was expected to attract only a small crowd since it was not officially endorsed by any national party, nor by their women's organizations. Instead, thousands marched in the streets in the first public challenge to Khomeini's authority. A demonstration that was supposed to last a few hours stretched to nearly a week. Instead of the original commemoration of international women's history, the demonstration became focused on highly local issues, on a demand that the revolution shift course. The manifesto that came out of the demonstration called for legal, social, political, and economic equality between men and women. It insisted that women's clothing should be chosen by women themselves and that the Family Protection Act should not be eliminated but instead extended to better guarantee gender equality.

THE SIZE AND duration of the demonstration, despite silence from the media and (at best) indifference from the leftist parties, startled the revolutionary leaders. They responded by backpedaling, claiming that Khomeini had not ordered women to wear the hejab, he had merely recommended it. Besides, by the hejab, they argued, he had not meant that they should wear full chadors, or long veils, merely that they should dress in a "respectable" way. The ayatollah also denounced violence against women in his name, though threats and violence from some of his followers in the Hizbullah continued (Moghadam 1994, 201; Moghissi 1996, 139–43; Sanasarian 1983, 99–100).

But in the wake of the demonstration that proved that the ayatollah's government could be influenced through organized resistance, leftist and nationalist women did not manage to extract more concessions from the revolutionary government. Instead, the left-wing political parties sought to mobilize women for goals that were more important, from their perspective. In fact, Janet Afary argues that despite all their political differences, the Iranian leftists and the Ayatollah Khomeini largely coincided in their contempt for feminism. "[T]he lectures of Khomeini, which advocated a politicized 'anti-imperialist' concept of Islam, were not so far from the left's view that feminism was 'decadent.' In both views feminists were either naive or they were outright 'tools' of the imperialist powers" (1996, 44).

Arguably, organized women were more effective in March 1979 than they would be later on precisely because at that moment they enjoyed autonomy from the parties. Once they were reincorporated into the parties it was only a matter of time until they were forced into exile— or worse—alongside their male counterparts. For all the difficulties that revolutionary feminists faced in Latin America, they pale in comparison with those of Iranian feminists in the early days of the revolution. The nature of the old regime, the religion that informed mass mobilization, and the indifference of the left-wing parties to gender issues all helped explain this outcome. In Poland, those same factors were woven into a story that—from a feminist perspective—had more in common with Iran than with Latin America, despite the support of the Polish revolutionaries for liberal democracy and despite the fact that they shared a religious heritage with their Latin American counterparts.

Poland: Rejecting Communism, Promoting the Motherland

One of the last explosions heard at the close of the twentieth century was—in one of those wonderful ironies of history—a series of revolutions against self-identified revolutionary governments. Between 1989 and 1991 communist states across Europe fell in response to some combination of economic crisis, elite divisions, and mass movements from below. The revolutionaries that came to power replaced socialism with capitalism, authoritarianism with electoral democracy, and a Marxist-inspired model of women's emancipation with a version of traditional gender inequality.

In Poland, as in Nicaragua and Iran (and most, if not all, other successful twentieth-century revolutions), the mass movement that eventually toppled the authoritarian socialist[4] state was highly nationalist. Nationalism is always a useful ideology, from the perspective of those who wish to build revolutionary coalitions, since it is one of the few ideologies that may unite people who would otherwise be divided along the lines of class, race, gender, religion, and partisan affiliation. But nationalist movements against the state may only be forged under certain circumstances. The best circumstances for forging such a movement are when the authoritarian state is perceived to be linked to powerful foreigners, whether it was founded by a foreign power, propped up by that power, or, in the most explosive of cases, both founded and propped up by outsiders. That was certainly true in Poland, where the authoritarian socialist state was seen by the vast majority of Poles as a foreign imposition, as imposed by the Soviet Union.[5]

So one factor that Poland shared with many other twentieth-century revolutions was a nationalist movement that sought to overthrow an authoritarian state with historically strong support from one of the superpowers. One of the factors that allowed that movement to succeed was a world systemic opening, much like the opening that allowed for the overthrow of the shah of Iran, and of Anastasio Somoza of Nicaragua. In the Polish case, the world systemic opening was largely caused by Mikhail Gorbachev of the Soviet Union, who, much like Jimmy Carter of the United States a decade earlier, chose not to intervene to prop up his country's client states.

A final similarity between the revolutionary movement in Poland and in many other places is the role of religion as a mobilizing ideology. As in Latin America, that religion was Catholicism. Given that similarity, it would be reasonable to guess that since, in Latin America, an unintended outcome of movements that were rooted in politicized Catholicism was the rise of large feminist movements, the same would have happened in Poland. But that guess would be completely wrong. In the aftermath of the collapse of authoritarian socialism in Poland, feminism has been discredited, even denigrated, even though Poland never had much of an independent feminist movement to reject (Hauser, Heyns, and Mansbridge 1993; Long 1996; Waylen 1994). Why did so many Polish women return to their homes after the collapse of authoritarianism? One of the answers lies in the religion that had helped make that collapse possible.

Catholicism, like all major religions, is something of a big tent. All who fall under the tent must position themselves in relation to the center of power at the Vatican, but the way in which they position themselves varies. Those who identified with the liberation theology movement tended to position themselves in tension with, and sometimes in opposition to, the center of power. While not completely ignoring Rome's edicts regarding gender roles, the liberation theologians, as members of a reform movement, felt somewhat free to reinterpret societal roles in the light of their reading of the bible. In contrast, Catholics in Poland, especially during the years of the authoritarian socialist state, positioned themselves in alliance with the Vatican. This is not to say that liberation theology was political and Polish Catholicism was not. Both were movements with political implications, as indeed is probably true of all world religions. And Polish Catholicism was no less oppositional than Latin American Catholicism. In fact, a key turning point that led to the fall of authoritarian socialism was the visit of Polish-born Pope John Paul II in 1987. But though both were politicized and both sought democratization, their implications for women's roles differed significantly.

For the Solidarity movement, identifying as it did with the center of power in Rome, women played critical if subordinate roles. At the symbolic level, men often were portrayed in heroic leadership roles, while "women appear[ed] in the iconography of Solidarity overwhelmingly in support roles defined by images of motherhood, especially of Mary, the grieving mother of God" (Long 1996, 93). Yet the reality of women's participation in opposition politics did not match this symbolic absence; at its height, in 1980, women comprised half of Solidarity's ten million members (Siemienska 1998, 125, 133).

While the number of participants was apparently inconsistent with the symbolism that surrounded activism, the nature of women's participation was more consistent with that symbolism. With rare exceptions, women did not play leadership roles in Solidarity, instead supporting the opposition movement through extensions of maternal roles, such as providing food to strikers. Most women had to participate in this way, for they carried much heavier burdens than their male counterparts: paid employment, followed by a second shift at home. Logically, they tended toward opposition work that might be combined with their domestic duties, like one woman who ran an underground lending library out of her home, doing her part to undermine the communist government's attempt to control access to information (Long 1996, 60–62).

As in Latin America, women often managed to slip through the grasp of the authorities. Transporting illegal books for the underground press, they were overlooked because women (unlike men) typically had to lug heavy shopping bags and because the authorities tended to see women as less inherently political than men. One woman noted, "During martial law . . . they controlled young people but they didn't control women" (quoted in Long 1996, 62–63). The unseen nature of women's opposition activities came to haunt many of those women in the postcommunist period as the leadership of Solidarity was dominated by men who had played public roles. Women were pushed back to their kitchens after the fall of the authoritarian socialist state for a variety of reasons, including the role of women in Polish Catholicism and in Solidarity. But it is not completely accurate to claim that women were just pushed back; many of them were happy to be pushed. The explanation for that choice lies in the nature of the old regime.

The authoritarian socialist state in Poland, like that of the shah in Iran, was interested in emancipating women as a tool for national development, though there were differences in their models of emancipation. While the shahs' model was rooted in modernization theory (with its assumption that traditional culture is a break on economic development and must be transformed), the emancipation of communist Poland was rooted in the writings of Marx and Engels (with their assumption that sexual inequality would wither away as soon as women, like men, enjoyed the power that would come from having access to their own incomes). Of the two, the shahs' model of women's emancipation potentially required a far greater disruption of family life than the communist model. But both models shared important traits: they were both organized from the top down (assuming that emancipation could be imposed), and they were both eminently public, adding to women's public burden without doing much to address their domestic burden.

In Poland a few legal changes did ease the burden of the new public responsibilities: abortion was legalized, paid maternity leave was required, day care centers were created (Long 1996, 135–36). But at the same time, contraception was often unavailable, shopping lines were long, and men typically remained unwilling to do their share of the housework and child care. So, as in Iran, many women did not experience forced emancipation as liberating. During the time of the authoritarian socialist state in Poland, opposition activists tended to celebrate the private, seeing the family as the realm of freedom for both men and women, the one space where the government could not effectively regulate life (Long 1996, 146–48; Waylen 1994, 345; Verdery 1994, 232). Logically enough, once they were no longer required to work for wages, many women were happy to retreat to the realm of freedom—the home—where they could fulfill the traditional roles promoted by Polish nationalists and by the Catholic Church.

Finally, those few who sought to promote women's rights in the aftermath of communism found themselves confronting the hostility of the leaders of Solidarity, the very organization that had originally nurtured their politicization. That hostility was to quickly destroy the Solidarity women's section. Founded in 1989 with the economic aid of the International Federation of Trade Unions,[6] the women's section was never exactly supported by the union's leadership. But grudging acceptance turned to outright opposition when, in 1990, the members of the women's section crossed an unspoken boundary: from helping carry out the interests of Solidarity's leadership to confronting that leadership and attempting to defend what they saw as women's interests. In response to the women's section's public opposition to a bill that would ban both abortion and contraception,[7] the women's section was shut down under a barrage of accusations: accusations of politicking, of opposing conception, of being anti-Polish (Long 1996, 171).

The story of the rise and rapid fall of the Solidarity women's section is much like some of the other stories in this book. In Iran, Nicaragua, and El Salvador, feminists within the revolutionary coalitions also met resistance from revolutionary leaders. In fact, hostility to feminism by leaders of male-dominated movements has been so common that it seems to be a historic constant (e.g., Berkin and Lovett 1980; González and Kampwirth 2001; Kruks, Rapp, and Young 1989; Tétreault 1994). What distinguished Nicaragua and El Salvador, on the one hand, from Iran and Poland, on the other, was the degree of hostility. That degree depended on whether revolutionary leaders defined the revolution as a project that embraced women's emancipation or as a project that opposed it. Revolutionary men in Central America defined their projects as encompassing women's emancipation (though they consistently prioritized class concerns over gender concerns), while revolutionary men in Iran and Poland rejected women's emancipation, even in theory, as a remnant of the hated old regime.

Still, opposition to feminism cannot completely explain the failure of the attempt to extend Solidarity's agenda of democratization to include gender relations. After all, Solidarity's leaders did initially accept the formation of a women's section. Why did many Latin American feminists overcome the obstacle of resistance from men within their own political coalitions, while feminists in Iran and Poland were stopped in their tracks when confronted with a similar obstacle? Clearly the means used to express hostility is a key factor. In Iran, the willingness of the Islamic government to use violence, even the death penalty, against dissidents was an important factor that shut down the early attempts to organize for gender equality within the revolution. But in Central America and Poland the leaders of the revolutionary coalition rarely used violence or even the threat of violence in opposing feminist activism.[8] So why didn't feminists ignore or confront Solidarity's hostility, just as feminists had challenged the hostility of the FSLN of Nicaragua and the FMLN of El Salvador?

Arguably, the reasons are located in the conditions that shaped the lives of would-be feminist activists, conditions that have already been noted: the nature of Polish Catholicism, the previous role of women within the Solidarity movement, and the legacy of the authoritarian socialist regime. When confronted with hostility, Polish feminists (like feminists elsewhere) had two main choices: to give up or to seek autonomy. Since the pursuit of autonomy is far harder than giving up, it only happens when some women enter the autonomy battle with considerable resources. Those resources include funding (often from foreign sources), which both Polish and Latin American women had, to some extent. But even more important than funding are resources like self-confidence, organizing skills, preexisting networks, and rebelliousness—resources that were the legacy of the guerrilla wars in Central America but that were in shorter supply in Poland, where women had played a more limited and traditional role in the struggle against dictatorial rule.

Feminism after the Fall?

Comparing the gendered outcomes of the revolutionary movements in Nicaragua, El Salvador, Chiapas, Iran, and Poland clarifies the relationship between revolution and feminism. Certain factors can be identified that were important in shaping the gendered outcomes of those conflicts and in explaining why, after the fall of the old regimes, feminists were far more successful in some countries than others. That certain factors shaped outcomes is not to say that they determined outcomes. Even when all conditions favored the rise of feminism, movements never emerged without a lot of hard work on the part of the women who founded them. But those factors did make particular outcomes more or less likely, as illustrated in the following table.

Atmosphere for Feminists Following the Revolutionary Movements

	Nica.	ES	Chiapas	Iran	Poland
1. Gender legacy of the old regime	+	+	+	-	-
2. Religion that informed movement	+	+	+	-	-
3. Revolution socially egalitarian	+	+	+	-	?
4. Role of female revolutionaries	+	+	+?	-?	-?
5. Resources available to feminists	+	+	+?	?	?
6. International feminism	+	+	+	-	?
Autonomous feminism likely	+	+	+?	-?	-?

The arguments expressed in this table were influenced by the work of Valentine Moghadam, who in a wide-ranging comparative work "classified revolutions in terms of gender outcomes: one group of revolutions is modernizing and egalitarian, with women's emancipation a specific goal; another group is patriarchal, tying women to the family and stressing gender differences rather than equality" (1997, 137). What Moghadam calls modernizing and egalitarian is roughly equivalent to what I call a feminist outcome; what she calls patriarchal is roughly equivalent to my antifeminist outcome. Our analysis differs in that Moghadam focuses on the policies carried out by the revolutionary governments, while I am concerned with the opportunities for feminist movements within civil society in the aftermath of the revolutionary movements. But they are intertwined concerns, for the nature of the state always has some impact on the opportunities for autonomous feminism.

Moghadam (1997, 142) found examples of bourgeois revolutions that promoted women's emancipation, as well as those that promoted gender differences; similarly, she found socialist revolutions in which women's emancipation was promoted, as well as socialist revolutions in which gender differences were emphasized. So the type of revolution did not seem to be causal, instead, she argued that factors that dated from before the revolutionaries' rise to power—the previous gender system, the nature and goals of the revolutionary coalition, and the role of women in the guerrilla period—were the main shapers of women's fates (138–39). The factors Moghadam identified are roughly equivalent to my factors 1 (gender legacy of the old regime), 3 (revolution socially egalitarian), and 4 (role of female revolutionaries). Where I build on her work is by adding consideration of the religious tradition that supported the revolutionary movement (factor 2), the resources available to feminists (factor 5), and the impact of international feminism on the revolutionary movements and the social movements they engendered (factor 6).[9] In what follows, I will explain the table with historical examples from the five cases analyzed so far and then will apply those findings to the future of Cuba.

In Nicaragua and El Salvador a whole string of factors combined to allow for the rise of vibrant autonomous feminist movements. First, in both cases the revolutionaries challenged dictatorships that, for most people, were not associated with feminism. In other words, feminism had not been tainted by association with a dictatorship. Second, the Catholic Church, specifically the liberation theology movement within the Church, set the stage for the rise of feminism in the aftermath of the revolutionary movements, a factor I discussed in detail in my previous book, *Women and Guerrilla Movements* (Kampwirth 2002, 8–9, 28–32, 42, 68–69, 71–73, 96–98, 125–27). Liberation theology provided the theological underpinnings for women's direct participation the revolutionary movements in both Central American countries for liberation theologians promoted the idea that men and women were equal in the eyes of God, and encouraged women to organize.

Third, in Nicaragua as in El Salvador, the guerrillas promoted values that were socially egalitarian, informed by some mix of Marxism, nationalism, and liberation theology. In both cases, those egalitarian values extended to gender relations, in theory if not always in practice. Fourth, in the two Central American cases, many women played non-traditional roles in the guerrilla coalitions (and during the revolution, in the case of Nicaragua), roles through which thousands of women were politicized, learning organizing skills, and gaining self-confidence. Fifth, those skills and self-confidence were internal resources that could be drawn upon later by feminists as they struggled for autonomy. Finally, in Nicaragua and especially in El Salvador, international feminism was an external resource that budding autonomous feminists could draw upon as a source of moral support, as a source of ideas, and as a source of material resources.

The case of Chiapas is far more like the revolutionary movements in Central America than those of either Iran or Poland. As in Central America, the gender legacy of the regime that was challenged by the guerrillas was positive from a feminist perspective (that is, the discredited old regime had generally not tried to legitimize itself through feminism from above). As in Central America, liberation theology was the religious tradition that set the stage for the guerrilla war, a tradition that was quite compatible with a movement toward gender equality. The EZLN, even more than the FSLN and the FMLN (during their guerrilla phases), was highly egalitarian in its rhetoric regarding women. The two points in this table in which Chiapas was not the same as Nicaragua and El Salvador were point 4, on role of women in the guerrilla coalition, and point 5, on the resources available to feminists in the post-Zapatista period. Both of those points are marked as probably positive (thus the question mark following the plus sign) in their implications for future feminism, rather than as clearly positive, because we do not yet have complete information. According to the Zapatista leaders' own reports, women play a wide variety of prestigious roles within the EZLN, and there is much greater egalitarianism within Zapatista communities than before the rebellion. If that is true, then many former Zapatista women will be equipped with the resources that will permit them to push for feminist reforms, if they so choose. But prudence requires that we be cautious in accepting this account of life within the Zapatista communities. After the war, once it is possible to do extensive interviews with the women of the EZLN, then it may be possible to remove the question marks from the above table.

The sixth factor on the table—international feminism—is a resource that will be available to those former Zapatistas who choose to promote feminism. In fact, to a large extent, it already is. The EZLN has been notable for its ability to draw on international support networks through its use of technology like the Internet and through its convocation of well-attended international gatherings on multiple continents. Moreover, by the beginning of the twenty-first century, the influence of feminism from Central America, Mexico City, and elsewhere was already notable within some indigenous women's groups in Chiapas.

In contrast to their Latin American counterparts, autonomous feminists were not terribly successful after the overthrow of the old regime in Iran and Poland. As the table summarizes, the circumstances that Iranian and Polish feminists faced differed substantially from those faced by the Latin Americans. On the first point, the nature of the discredited old regime, feminists in Iran and Poland had to confront a memory of emancipation from above, of regimes that used the rhetoric of women's emancipation to legitimize themselves. In the minds of many who opposed the dictatorships, if the dictators had promoted feminism, then those who opposed the dictatorships should promote antifeminism, or a return to an idealized past of gender inequality. Second, in both Iran and Poland, the particular religious traditions that informed the revolutionary movements promoted hierarchical visions of proper gender roles. Neither Catholicism nor Shia Islam were inherently based on gender inequality; like all major religions they were open to multiple interpretations, as illustrated by liberation theology and by Iranian feminist interpretations of scripture. But as it turned out, the particular religious interpretations that informed the revolutions in Iran and Poland were inegalitarian ones.

And so, with regard to the third point in my table, the revolutions fought in defense of those religious values were necessarily also fought in defense of gender inequality. While the Latin American guerrillas might not have always been sincere in their use of the rhetoric of egalitarianism, including gender equality, feminists could try to hold them to their word, an option that was not open to feminists in Poland and

Iran, where the rhetoric of revolution was hardly egalitarian. But while social egalitarianism in the Iranian revolution is marked with a minus sign, the legacy of the Polish revolution was somewhat more ambivalent, since the liberal democratic tradition championed by revolutionary leaders certainly contained egalitarian elements, elements that were at cross-purposes with other schools of thought that informed the revolutionary movement in Poland.

The fourth point in the table refers to the roles that women played in the revolutionary coalitions, and whether those roles either stretched traditional gender roles, or reinforced those roles. In both Iran and Poland, women participated in the revolutionary coalitions in significant numbers. But the symbolism that surrounded that participation (the suffering Virgin Mary in the Polish case, the heavily veiled protester in the Iranian case) was to undercut the reality of women's contribution to the overthrow of the dictators. This forgotten participation is represented as a largely, but not entirely, negative factor with regard to future feminist efforts. But if the memory of that participation were to be reinterpreted, its implications for feminist organizing could change.

The symbolism that surrounded women's participation did not make the reality of participation go away; it just veiled it, forcing it out of official history, into the realm of private memory. So at the fifth position of the table, the internal resources that women might draw on in a struggle for feminist autonomy, is marked as ambivalent. In all likelihood, mobilizing in the role of supportive wife and mother reinforced traditional gender roles. But it does seem, that on occasion, some women in both Iran and Poland mustered the internal resources to challenge gender inequality: during the March 8, 1979, protests in Iran and the emergence of Iranian feminism over a decade later, or during the protests against restrictions on abortion and in the effort to form a women's section in Solidarity. While the revolutions in Iran and Poland did not provide women in those countries with the sort of internal resources that the Latin American activists enjoyed, they may have provided some internal resources, enough so that it is worth leaving this as an open question.

With regard to the sixth and final point of the table—the influence of international feminism—the cases of Iran and Poland diverge. The

Iranian revolution was fought and is still defended in the name of religious values and against the sort of secular values typically associated with international feminism. For that reason, Iranian feminists must take great care to highlight their religious credentials. International feminists, who tend to promote secular values, will find it difficult to support Iranian feminists without undermining the position of those women within Iran. Because of that situation the possible influence of international feminism in Iran is identified with a minus sign.

One might think the same would be true for Poland—after all, the hierarchy of the Catholic Church has found willing allies in the leaders of fundamentalist Islamic countries against the international feminist movement, even to the extreme of opposing the use of the word *gender*.[10] The Polish revolutionaries, tightly allied with the Church in Rome, might be expected to be equally opposed to any international feminist influence. But the Poles are caught between the Vatican and the rest of Western Europe. While the Iranians looked to Western Europe as a model of decadence to be rejected, the Poles looked to Western Europe as a model to be embraced, at least in its economic aspects. That Solidarity accepted foreign feminist funding for its women's section (which was shortly shut down) suggests more ambivalence toward secular international feminism in Poland than in Iran. So the possible influence of international feminism on women's organizing in Poland is represented with a question mark.

In this chapter I have outlined the main factors that explain how autonomous feminism came to flourish in Nicaragua and El Salvador, why it will probably do well in Chiapas after the war has ended, and why its future is far cloudier in Poland and especially Iran. What implications can be drawn for Cuba, site of the only Latin American revolution that held power into the twenty-first century?

Cuba: After the Revolution

The future of autonomous feminism in Cuba will be shaped largely by gender politics there over the course of more than four decades of revolution, starting in 1959. If the quality of women's lives is measured in terms of access to opportunities and the material necessities of life, then life got better for most women during those years. The two most obvious and easily measurable ways in which women gained with the revolution were in the areas of education and health care. Education was prioritized early in the revolution through the literacy campaign, much like the literacy campaign that followed two decades later in Sandinista Nicaragua. By the close of 1961, "seven hundred thousand Cubans, more than half of them women, had learned to read and write" (Smith and Padula 1996, 83–84). That commitment to expanding educational opportunities was institutionalized in the decades that followed. Education at all levels was free (including a stipend to cover expenses) and the numbers of students expanded greatly. In the early nineties there were ten times as many teachers and ten times as many university students as during the last years of the Batista dictatorship. Over half of those who graduated from college were women (Leiner 1994, 64; Smith and Padula 1996, 48–49, 82, 89).

Along with the expansion of educational opportunities, the improvement in health care was the other most significant gain of the Cuban revolution. Two generations into the revolution, Cuba resembled the wealthy countries of the world much more than it resembled its fellow Latin American countries, at least in medical terms. The typical maladies of the poor—cholera, malaria, dengue fever, infant diarrhea, death in childbirth—largely disappeared and the maladies of the rich—heart disease and cancer—took over as the leading causes of death. Expanding medical services into the countryside, and improving them in the cities, benefited women both as recipients of medical care and as providers. "Between 1953 and 1992 the number of doctors in Cuba grew by a factor of eight to nearly 50,000 and the number of nurses increased more than fifteen times to some 70,000. . . . From 1953 to 1990 women's representation among doctors grew from 6 to 48 percent and among dentists from 18 to 69 percent" (Smith and Padula 1996, 57). The collapse of the Soviet Union in 1991, and the loss of its economic support, did significant damage to the Cuban economy. After 1991 the difficulty of daily life generally increased as basic necessities, especially petroleum, were in short supply. Nonetheless, the Cuban government maintained its commitment to providing health care to all. So life expectancies continued to be very high in the wake of the collapse of the Soviet Union, in sharp contrast to the situation in the former Soviet Union itself, where the transition to electoral democracy and capitalism was accompanied by a drop in average life expectancy.[11]

Access to education and good health care, including reproductive health care, were basic necessities that provided for the possibility of gender equality. But the Cuban government understood those basic necessities as just a beginning, in keeping with the Marxist tradition of identifying economic inequality as the root cause of gender inequality. For Cuban officials, paid work for women was the force that would create gender equality. By the early nineties, the labor force was nearly 40 percent female; nearly 45 percent of the women of working age had jobs. These figures represented a dramatic change considering that Cuban women had been less likely to work for wages than other Latin American women before the revolution: in 1953, only 13 percent of them were recognized as part of the economically active population. However, women continued to earn much less than men, although they typically were more educated than their male counterparts (Lutjens 1995, 104; Luzón 1987, 190; Pérez-Stable 1993, 32, 95, 141).

To some extent the Cuban government attempted to provide social services to make it possible for women to work outside the home, even if men did not take over their share of household responsibilities, which was typically the case.[12] As more and more women took on paid jobs, the state built numerous child care centers. Between 1975 and 1986, for instance, 196 new centers were opened. But those public centers did not come near to meeting the demand for child care: throughout the eighties and nineties day care centers had enough room for only one child for every ten working women (Smith and Padula 1996, 133). Grandmothers, rather than day care centers or fathers, were the solution for most employed mothers.

Access to consumer goods was a mixed bag for Cuban women. On the one hand, poor women had greater access to food, clothing, and goods like household appliances than did their mothers and grandmothers. On the other hand, "Cuba's rationing system . . . involved waiting in long lines for poor-quality products" (Smith and Padula 1996, 136). Many women left work early so as to get a place in those lines, and as a result their managers often thought that women were more "undisciplined" than men. Though the revolutionary government formally opposed domestic work as inherently exploitative, women continued to hire other women to take over some of the housework. Even Vilma Espín—hero of the guerrilla era and national director of the Cuban Women's Federation—"admitted that she could not have managed her own career without maids and nannies to help out with her children" (137).

Overall, the revolution brought improvements to the lives of most women including the opportunity to attend college, to receive free and high-quality health care, and to pursue a career. But those gains were mitigated by the scarcity of public childcare, the length of lines, and the continued unwillingness of men to carry out their share of domestic work. With the collapse of the Soviet Union and the fuel shortages that followed, those burdens only worsened: lines at bus stops became out-rageously long and many women found themselves commuting long distances on bicycles in the tropical heat.

The mixed record of gender relations during the revolution could be attributed to a number of factors, both international and domestic. One of the most significant was the role of the Federation of Cuban Women (Federación de Mujeres Cubanas, or FMC). The state-affiliated women's organization was founded early in the revolution, in 1960, to mobilize women to promote gender equality and to promote the revo-lution, a dual agenda that sometimes proved problematic, as was also true for Nicaragua's AMNLAE (see chapter 1). Eventually, the vast majority of Cuban women belonged to the FMC; no other women's organization in the hemisphere came close to rivaling it in size. Over the decades of the revolution, the FMC played a central role in many efforts to improve women's lives, including job-training programs for peasant girls, maids, and prostitutes in the sixties; promotion of affirmative action programs, sex education, and day care; lobbying for the 1975 Family Code (which called for gender and generational equality within the home); and the creation of a series of women's houses, numbering 155 by 1994, which provided a place for cultural activities, legal advice, and courses in topics like modeling, massage, aerobics, yoga, haircut-ting, and herbal medicine (Leiner 1994, 62–63, 66–73; Lutjens 1995, 110, 112; Maloof 1999, 32; Molyneux 2000, 293–311; Smith and Padula 1996, 33–56). Yet for all its varied accomplishments, there were occa-sions when the federation's recommendations seemed to be ignored. In response to working women's difficulties in shopping for groceries during the short window between the end of their working days and the closing of the stores, the FMC's leaders lobbied for longer or more flexible store hours. After years of efforts, meat and dairy stores were finally added to the Plan Jaba, a program in which working women could place an order before work and pick it up after work. But it took more than two decades of lobbying before beauty salons began to open at night (Smith and Padula 1996, 137).

In those cases when the interests of the party and the FMC coincided, or when the leaders of the FMC succeeded in convincing party leaders that their interests coincided, then the FMC was quite successful. But if it could not convince the leaders that a reform desired by women (like easier access to beauty salons), would help party leaders in promoting their own interests (like improving working women's productivity), then recommendations for changes were pushed aside year after year. And if they were ignored, there was little the leaders of the FMC could do. The women's organization was not a branch of the state and it had no ability to either make policy or to implement it. In fact, it received no funds from the state, depending instead on its dues-paying members. But the FMC was not an independent member of civil society either.[13] The women's federation was a popular organization—as were AMNLAE in Nicaragua and the women's organizations founded by the Salvadoran guerrillas—an organization meant to serve as a transmission belt for a vanguard party at the same time as it served its own constituency. "The FMC was an intensely hierarchical organization. . . . With its top-down lines of command and its use of military terminology, the FMC—like all mass organizations in Cuba—had a certain martial aura" (Smith and Padula 1996, 50; see also Molyneux 2000, 293–97).

What impact did the FMC's close relationship with the party have on its ability to promote gender equality? Sheryl Lutjens suggested that, while the FMC was not autonomous from the state, it often served "as an organization that mediates women's relationship to the state" (1995, 112), and that it did "reflect the changing circumstances of the 1990s" (1997, 30). Other observers were less optimistic. Analysts at the political journal *Envío* noted that the "FMC's official discourse appears terribly flat in the face of [new] developments." To illustrate that claim, they quoted the declaration that was made at the end of "the V Plenary session of the Federation's National Committee, which took place in February 1998." That declaration of top-down emancipation could have been made at any point during the revolution: "After 1959, Fidel gave us women the privilege of being the first to advance. . . . We are now worthy, complete, educated, and free: that is the greatest victory that we have attained through the revolution. . . . In the past we were excluded, subordinated, and oppressed, and our work always went unnoticed, but now we are the visible protagonists of a heroic exploit" (quoted in *Envío* 1998a, 37).

While participating in a delegation in 1998, I raised this issue with Odessa, director of a regional FMC office. Prefacing my question with the comment that disagreements were normal in politics and that presumably they at the FMC had occasional disagreements with politicians and government bureaucrats, I asked her to give an example of such a disagreement and to explain what happened. Her inability, or unwillingness, to mention a concrete example was instructive: "With regard to wanting to attain full equality there is no disagreement. Perhaps in the methods, the paths, the ways in which to achieve it" (meeting with Global Exchange delegation, October 20, 1998). A few minutes later, another member of the delegation said that she thought Odessa had not answered my question, that perhaps she had misunderstood, and so she rephrased the question. Again, Odessa could not, or would not, give a single example of a disagreement between the FMC and the party over the course of four decades.[14]

While the FMC dominated women's organizing over the course of the revolution and remained the only formally recognized women's rights organization at the beginning of the twenty-first century, some people did try to mobilize around gender issues outside the official federation. Magín was the first and only independent women's organization to be formed during the revolution. Founded in 1993, it was "deactivated" in September 1996 "by the decision of the Central Committee of the Communist Party of Cuba in the name of national 'unity'" (*Envío* 1998a, 40).

Magín, whose name derived from the words for "imagination" and "image," was founded by a group of women who worked in communications, in response to their experiences at the First Iberoamerican

"Women and Communication" Congress, which met in Havana in February 1993. When their counterparts at that conference repeatedly referred to gender analysis—and they were not sure what that meant—they decided that it was time to make contact with the feminist currents that flowed through much of the rest of Latin America. Starting with workshops on self-esteem (a radical topic in a revolutionary context where collective concerns were consistently prioritized over individual ones), the founders of Magín eventually mobilized three to four hundred women nationwide around a variety of projects: improving the images of women in the media (including soap operas), initiating public debates on domestic violence, ecology, sexist language, and prostitution, promoting sensitivity to gender issues in health care, and publishing materials, such as the magazine *Magín,* with support from UNICEF, and from specialists from at least ten countries (*Envío* 1998a, 41–42; Hiriart 1995, 9; Lutjens 1997, 33–35).

Magín's members never thought of themselves as dissidents; instead they always informed the party and the FMC of their activities. Even so, perhaps they were too autonomous or too much of a threat to the leaders of the FMC, who might have seen them as rivals, despite their insistence that Magín was to complement the FMC, not compete with it. Or perhaps the problem was the same problem that had curtailed those who had tried to organize independently in the past, that the leaders of the revolution protected themselves against external threats—in this case, the passage of the Helms-Burton law in the United States, which provided funding for Cuban NGOs—by enforcing internal unity. That was the explanation that Magín's members received at the 1996 meeting in which they were told they would not receive recognition as an NGO and would have to disband. They were told that they "recognized our abilities and valued our projects, but used as their argument the danger of the two-track U.S. blockade policy—whose strategy is to make us battle a Trojan horse at home in the form of social organizations rather than them declare all-out war on Cuba. The committee explained to us how many people had been seduced by the enemy, with how many scholarships and how much money. . . . They told us that, although our objective was justifiable, justifiable did not always mean appropriate, and that each of us could continue working in the same way, but within the already existing organizations—in this case, the

Cuban Women's Federation" (*Envío* 1998a, 42–43). Many of the women who had participated in Magín valued the opportunity, however brief, to open an array of public debates. They thought that the fact that the leaders of the FMC no longer spoke of feminism with the same disdain as in the past had been at least partially due to Magín's efforts. But they were generally pessimistic about the possibility of continuing their work within the context of the FMC, noting that it was either too big or too set in its ways. Instead, they expressed the belief and hope "that Magín will return sooner or later" (43; see also Molyneux 2000, 311). Perhaps that would happen after the first generation of the revolution ceased to rule, much like the explosion of independent women's organizing that occurred in the year following the formal end of the Sandinista revolution, in 1990, and following the end of the civil war in El Salvador in 1992.

The other attempt to organize independently around gender-related issues came on July 28, 1994, when a group of at least eighteen gays and lesbians signed a manifesto reviewing the discrimination gays and lesbians had suffered in Cuba and elsewhere, noting that the situation for Cuban gays and lesbians had improved dramatically since the 1960s (when gays were sent to rehabilitation camps) and calling for the freedom to organize and live open lives. The group they founded on that July afternoon was named simply the Gay and Lesbian Association of Cuba. While the organization was not targeted for repression, it had the bad luck of emerging immediately before a series of police raids related to a refugee crisis. In the face of that generalized repression, and the lack of organizing experience of the association's members, the association did not last long. However, some who had been part of the association formed a new organization, the Action Group for Free Expression about Sexual Orientation (Grupo de Acción por la Libertad de Expresión de la Elección Sexual, or GALEES), an organization that sought official recognition (Lumsden 1996, 197–98, 211–14).[15]

According to participants in GALEES, that group did not last long either. Their attempt to march with a rainbow flag in the 1995 May Day parade—a bold move on what may be the most important holiday of the revolutionary year—was a failure. The police stopped the gay and lesbian activists from marching, hit them, seized their flag, and gave each of them a citation. In the wake of the parade they received threatening notes—"We know what you're doing. Stop it"—some of their books and literature were seized and they were accused of antisocial activities like meeting with foreigners to take drugs. Each one was then approached separately and asked to cooperate by informing on the others. Instead they chose to disband (meeting with Global Exchange delegation, October 22, 1998).

While independent organizing was even more difficult for gays and lesbians than for feminists (as is probably the case everywhere), the next time gays and lesbians muster the nerve to organize, it might work. Though the right to organize autonomously had still not been won at the beginning of the twenty-first century, Cuban society had changed dramatically over the course of the revolution. "In several municipalities, the cultural sectors of popular power[16] now include enthusiastically applauded drag shows as part of their presentations. . . . The director of the nighttime radio program *Casa de Cristal* is a lesbian, which everybody knows because she openly says so. 'The revolutionary process has not been static, it has undergone change,' she commented one night. 'It has been demonstrated that the roots of homophobia don't go all that deep in Cuban soil. This also shows that we're ready for change'" (*Envío* 1998a, 34). The question was not if change would come or not. The real question was just what sort of change were Cubans ready for.

Cuba's own history foreshadows the transformation that will likely sweep through the island. The only trick is how to read that history. Using the table that summarizes the factors that had shaped feminism elsewhere as a guide, the first place to look is to the nature of the old regime, that is, the revolutionary regime.[17] Women's emancipation, in one form or another, was on the Cuban agenda throughout the more than four decades that the revolution was in power. In a wide variety of ways, opportunities for women expanded greatly over that period, as explained above, though those opportunities were mitigated to some extent by the difficulties of juggling old private responsibilities and new public responsibilities. Despite two attempts at autonomous organizing in the 1990s, nearly all of those changes in gender relations were promoted from above, apparently by Fidel Castro himself, something that could be called patriarchal feminism.[18]

In Iran and Poland, the old regimes (of the shah and the communists, respectively) were also associated with feminism from above. In the case of Iran, that feminism from above might also be called patri-archal, given its association with a single man. If those who come to power after Fidel are people who reject the revolutionary legacy, then they will almost surely reject patriarchal feminism as well, and perhaps any sort of women's emancipation. Maxine Molyneux alludes to this possible outcome, suggesting why the FMC's efforts to combat sexual inequality had not yielded the hoped-for results: "Although it is un-doubtedly true that the organization could have done more to address these issues, the problem may have been the reverse—namely that *too much* or *the wrong kind* of intervention occurred, that too much energy was expended in its attempts to force a diverse population into con-formity with the party line" (Molyneux 2000, 314; emphasis in original). By the late nineties there were a number of indicators of dissatisfaction with feminism from above: "declining support for the FMC . . . the falling proportion of women in most political institutions . . . young people's boredom with the old rhetoric" (314). All those signs pointed to a reading of Cuban history as leading to a postrevolutionary scenario similar to that of Poland or even Iran.[19] In that scenario, the majority would reject feminism along with authoritarianism and socialism.

But that scenario is just one way to read Cuban history. There are other possible readings. Cuba, of course, was part of Latin America and in many ways always had more in common with places like Nicaragua or El Salvador than with Eastern European countries like Poland. While au-thoritarian socialism was largely imposed from without in Poland, it was the result of a nationalist revolution in Cuba.[20] Perhaps more important, Cubans were more likely to identify with other Latin Americans than with residents of other regions. While the unfavorable economic com-parisons that Poles made with their Western European counterparts probably drove opposition to the authoritarian socialist regime, the largely favorable economic comparisons that Cubans made with their Latin American counterparts, especially between Cuba and countries like Nicaragua and El Salvador, may have informed some feelings of satisfac-tion with the authoritarian socialist regime. So for the second scenario of what could happen to Cuba in the years following the end of the Fidel's reign, the place to look is Latin America, especially to Nicaragua.

The Cuban revolution was not informed by liberation theology, as was the Nicaraguan revolution. In fact, unlike the other five revolutionary movements considered in my table, it was a profoundly secular revolution, and so the second point in the table—the religious tradition that informed the movement—is not relevant in evaluating the Cuban future. But with regard to points 3 and 4—social egalitarianism and women's roles in the revolution—the Cuban revolution was quite similar to that of Nicaragua. As in Nicaragua, the values that informed the revolution were highly egalitarian, a point that would favor the development of autonomous feminism. While fewer women participated prominently in the guerrilla era in Cuba, compared to the guerrilla era in Nicaragua, when one looks at the periods after the revolutionaries came to power, the similarities are striking, especially with regard to the popular organizations that were entrusted with organizing women.

The Luisa Amanda Espinoza Association of Nicaraguan Women, or AMNLAE, was a close relative of the Federation of Cuban Women, or FMC. Both were founded with a dual agenda of promoting women's rights and of promoting their respective revolutions. Both played important roles in promoting women's emancipation and in mobilizing women, in providing them a space where they could think about gender relations and learn organizing skills. Both were constrained by their relationship to their respective parties, parties that often had agendas that required them to limit their demands. In Nicaragua many of the women who were originally politicized and later constrained through AMNLAE (and other revolutionary organizations) broke out on their own after the Sandinista party was voted out of office in 1990. The same thing could happen in Cuba.

So the second scenario is that women's emancipation and mobilization through the revolution could be extended in new directions after the first generation of revolutionary leaders are no longer at the helm. Groups like Magín and GALEES might reemerge, accompanied by a host of new groups that dare to make more explicit demands than did the FMC. In this scenario, the FMC would continue to exist, as has AMNLAE in Nicaragua, but it would lose its dominance in the women's movement. The legacy of the Cuban revolution could be a far more vibrant feminist movement than Cuba has ever known. In fact, in light of the social resources that will be available to feminists—point 5 in my table—as a result of the considerable gender equality (measured in socioeconomic terms) that is the legacy of the Cuban revolution, it is quite possible that Cuba could end up with an even more extensive women's movement than that of Nicaragua.

Another factor in favor of this second scenario is point 6, the role of international feminism. As detailed in chapter 2 with regard to El Salvador, women's mobilization through a revolutionary organization could be furthered by the role of international funders (who are increasingly demanding that their funds go to projects that promote women as well as men) and the example of feminist organizations elsewhere in the world, especially in Latin America. Despite Cuba's relative isolation over the course of the revolution, Cuban women were not completely isolated. By the nineties many international feminist currents had touched upon Cuban shores.

Remember that Magín originally came into being in response to discussions of women's issues that Magín's founders overheard at the First Iberoamerican "Women and Communication" Congress that they attended in Havana in February 1993. Over the course of Magín's three years, the organization received support from UNICEF and from a series of foreign visitors who made presentations or led workshops on topics related to women. Additionally, some Cuban women participated in international forums on gender issues, including gender working groups within the biannual São Paolo Forums (gatherings of Latin American left-wing political parties), at least two of the very non-partisan Latin American Feminist Encuentros,[21] as well as a number of United Nations–sponsored conferences on women.[22] Yet another international influence was direct from the autonomous feminist movement of Nicaragua. In 1999, *La Boletina,* a Nicaraguan feminist magazine, printed a letter from a reader in Holguín, Cuba, saying that the magazine had "caused a sensation" in Cuba and that she would like more copies (*Boletina* 1999, 89). As it turned out, ten different organizations in Cuba subscribed to the magazine,[23] in addition to copies that were distributed through less formal channels (Ana Leonor Paiz, personal communication, September 28, 1999).

The plausibility of the second scenario, that independent Cuban feminism would flourish in the postrevolutionary period, building on women's mobilization during the revolution, was only furthered by this series of international feminist influences. Those influences, already felt softly during the revolution, would almost surely increase in strength after the revolution reached its end. But there were more than two readings of the implications of Cuban history, more than two possible scenarios. The third scenario for gender politics in postrevolutionary Cuba combined elements of the first and second. In that third scenario, those who rejected the legacy of the revolution would also reject patriarchal feminism. From their perspective, defending a project of democratization would require being antifeminist, a scenario like the one that has played out in Poland. At the same time, many who were mobilized and constrained during the revolution, and touched by international feminism, would reject the patriarchal half of patriarchal feminism, while embracing feminism itself, a scenario like the one that has played out in Nicaragua. If the third scenario occurs, and the radical antifeminists promote their version of democratization at the same time as the radical feminists promote a very different version of democratization, the results could be explosive.

Revolutionary Movements and Feminism

This book is about unexpected outcomes, about events that were not anticipated, even by the people who would make them happen. While guerrilla struggle has probably been waged in some form as long as there have been states to challenge, for a long time it was men's work. A few women found their way into guerrilla armies—sometimes disguised as men—but they made up a very small proportion of those hypermasculine organizations until well into the twentieth century. That began to change when the twentieth century entered its final quarter, when the cold war entered its last generation. Starting around the late sixties the numbers of women in guerrilla movements jumped noticeably in a number of places, including Nicaragua, El Salvador, and Chiapas. As I argue elsewhere (Kampwirth 2002), a series of social changes including economic globalization, internal migration, and the rise of liberation theology made it possible for some women—especially those who were already integrated into preexisting networks—to act on their political grievances just like their male counterparts.

But of course they were not just like men. While women often found that they were treated with more respect and equality within the guerrilla movements and other revolutionary organizations than ever before, they were not always treated equally. Moreover, the extraordinary days of revolutionary struggle were to come to an abrupt end once the wars ceased. That contradiction (between their experiences of relative equality during the guerrilla wars and the return to inequality after the wars) was to lead certain women, especially those mid-prestige revolutionaries who had gained organizing skills during the wars, to become feminist activists in the postwar period. But their decision to expand the concept of revolution in new ways came at a price.

Over and over again the women who became feminists as an indirect result of their participation in revolutionary politics had to confront a common set of criticisms. Feminism, it was said, was a foreign import. It was bourgeois, even imperialist, a distraction from the real problems that faced men and women in Latin America. Confronting power inequalities between men and women would only impede the inevitable confrontation between rich and poor, landed and landless, imperialist powers and peripheral nations. A conversation I had with a Peruvian leftist in a cafe in Chiapas was illustrative. He was delighted to learn of my research on guerrilla women, those women who fit all his stereotypes of how Latin American women should be: heroic, self-sacrificing, highly conscious of class inequality. But delight instantly turned to anger when I explained more of the details of that project, about how contradictions within the guerrilla coalitions had eventually engendered vibrant feminist movements in Central America and how the beginnings of such a transformation were notable in Chiapas. "Our women" are not like that, he explained.

There is no doubt that Latin American feminism—just like feminism in all parts of the world—has been influenced by people from other regions. But feminism, like any ideology, only takes root when the local conditions are favorable. Moreover it grows in different shapes, and embraces different demands, depending on those conditions. Just as Marxism and liberation theology—two other foreign ideologies—would have had little meaning for Latin Americans if not for long histories of political and economic violence, so too feminism would not have resonated for so many Latin American women if not for people like my Peruvian friend. Men (and women) who continue to insist that emancipatory political projects have nothing to do with gender relations and personal lives are precisely the people who make feminism likely.

Notes

Introduction

1. Ana María was fourteen, while Laura and Sonia were both seventeen when they formally joined the guerrillas. At that point all three had already been politically active for years. Their names, like those of all the women whom I identify by first names only, are pseudonyms. It would be irresponsible of me to use real names in the case of activists in Chiapas, possibly risky in the case of Salvadoran activists, and perfectly fine to use them in the case of Nicaraguan activists. Nicaraguan feminists are freer in large part because Nicaragua is the only case where the old regime was truly defeated.

For linguistic consistency, I use pseudonyms for everyone with the exceptions of those few women who held positions of high prestige within the revolutionary movements (like guerrilla commander or member of the national directorate) and within civilian life (most of the high prestige guerrillas were elected to Congress after the wars ended). I bend my usual linguistic rule in those cases since a great deal has already been published about those prominent women (some of it inaccurate), and so my interview data is a contribution to that historical record.

2. Revolutionary activism comprises a collection of radical social movement activities that included participation in student groups, radical Catholic groups, labor unions, human rights groups, and economic cooperatives. Participants in the groups that were part of loose revolutionary coalitions were fighting for the end of dictatorships and for the structural transformation of their societies. They shared these goals with the guerrillas and many of their groups were organically linked with the guerrilla movements. Local elites responded with death threats and sometimes murder, indicating they were genuinely threatened by revolutionary activism.

3. In the nineties alone the following works on guerrillas and revolution were published: Byrne 1996; Castañeda 1994; Castro 1999b; Colburn 1994; Collier 1994; Farhi 1990; Foran 1992, 1993, 1994, 1997c; Goldstone, Gurr, and

Moshiri 1991; Grenier 1999; Horton 1998; Kanoussi 1998; Keddie 1995; Legorreta 1998; T. D. Mason 1992; Paige 1997; Schultz and Slater 1990; Selbin 1999; Skocpol 1994; Wickham-Crowley 1992. Very helpful reviews of earlier generations of revolutionary theory may be found in several of the contributions to Goldstone, Gurr, and Moshiri 1991, in Foran 1993 and 1992, and in several of the contributions to Foran 1997c.

4. On gender and revolutionary movements see, for example, Afshar 1985; Barrig 1998; Berkin and Lovett 1980; Castro 1999a; Chinchilla 1990, 1994, 1997; Cock 1994; Flynn 1983; Foran, Klouzal, and Rivera 1997; Goldman 1993; Hunt 1992; Jaquette 1973; Kampwirth 2001; Kirk 1997; Kruks, Rapp, and Young 1989; Lancaster 1992; Lapidus 1978; Lázaro 1990; Luciak 1998, 2001a; Macías 1982; T. D. Mason 1992; Massell 1974; Moghadam 1994, 1997; Moghissi 1996; Molyneux , 1984, 1986, 1988, 2000; Murguialday 1990, 1996a; Nashat 1983; Randall 1992; Reif 1986; Reséndez 1995; Saadatmand 1995; Salas 1990; Stacey 1983; Tétreault 1994; Vázquez, Ibáñez, and Murguialday 1996. Reif (1986) and Tétreault (1994, intro.) provide useful literature reviews.

5. For reviews of the literature on revolution, see contributors to Goldstone, Gurr, and Moshiri 1991; Foran 1993, 1992; contributors to Foran 1997c.

6. On preexisting networks and social movement theory, see Alvarez, Dagnino, and Escobar 1998, 14–16; Alvarez 1990; Freeman 1975, 48–70; McAdam 1982, 43–47; Wickham-Crowley 1992, 33–37, 42–43.

7. For more on the historical similarities and differences between North American and Latin American feminism, see González and Kampwirth 2001, 11–17.

8. Another important reason that an independent feminist movement had not arisen in Cuba by the beginning of the twenty-first century was simply that no organization in Cuba, feminist or otherwise, was permitted to organize independent from the state. I will consider these and other factors that shaped the course of women's roles within the Cuban revolution in chapter 5.

9. In this book I will refer to feminism in the singular, in part because that is how Latin American feminists refer to their movement. Some academics have chosen to refer to Latin American *feminisms* (e.g., Sternbach et al. 1992) in the plural, as a way of highlighting the fact that those who organize for gender equality often disagree with regard to fundamental questions like autonomy, political symbolism, strategy, what should be included in a feminist agenda, or even if there should be any particular agenda. While I agree that analysts need to highlight these differences (as indeed I do in this book), I think it is perfectly possible to discuss disagreements without losing sight of the existence of a movement of organizations and individuals who share the goal of increasing gender equality, despite some disagreements. By analogy, I

think it is equally possible (and equally preferable) to discuss disagreements among Catholics without resorting to awkward terms like *Catholicisms* or *Catholic Churches.*

10. Also see Chinchilla 1997, 216–17; González and Kampwirth 2001, 11–17: Molyneux 1986, 280–302; 2001, 152–57; for criticisms of the concepts of feminine and feminist organizing, see Lind 1992, 136–39; Schirmer 1993, 60–61; Stephen 1997, 10–12.

11. On women's organizations in Nicaragua, see Babb 2001; Blandón 2001; Brenes et al. 1991; Chinchilla 1990, 1994, 1997; Collinson 1990; COOPIBO-Nicaragua 1995; Criquillón 1995, n.d., García and Gomáriz 1989; González 1995, 1996, 2001; Isbester 2001; Jubb 2001; Lancaster 1992; Luciak 1998, 2001a, 2001b; Molyneux 1986, 1988, 2001; Montenegro 1997; Murguialday 1990, 1996a; Padilla, Murguialday, and Criquillón 1987; Randall 1981, 1992, 1993, 1994; I. Rodríguez 1990. On women's organizations in El Salvador, see AMES 1981; CEMUJER 1992; Chinchilla 1997; Dignas 1993, 1995; García and Gomáriz 1989; Gargallo 1987; Guerra 1993; Herrera 1997; Hipsher 2001; Luciak 1998, 2001a, 2001b; Moreno 1997; Murguialday 1996a, 1996b; Navas 1985, 1987; Navas, Orellana, and Domínguez 2000; Ready 2001; Ready, Stephen, and Cosgrove 2001; Stephen 1994d, 1997; Vázquez, Ibáñez, and Murguialday 1996. On women's organizations in Chiapas, see Eber 2002, 1995; Eber and Rosenbaum 1993; Figueroa 1996; Flood 1994; Forbis 2000; Freyermuth and Fernández 1995; Grupo de Mujeres et al. 1994; Gutiérrez and Palomo 1999; Hernández Castillo 1994, 1995, 1998; Morquecho 1995c; Olivera 1994, 1995, 1996; Rojas 1994, 1995a; Rosenbaum 1993; Rovira 1995, 1997.

12. By calling such support workers low-prestige, I am referring to the way they often experienced their work and the way they were perceived, in other words, as women who carried out women's work. Of course, with regard to the viability of the guerrilla forces, providers of food were at least as critical as combatants.

Ilja Luciak found that women in low-prestige categories were sometimes thought of as combatants by other members of the Salvadoran FMLN. Of the 8,506 combatants demobilized by the United Nations in 1992, 2,494 (29.2%) were women. Of the 4,090 FMLN political personnel (also considered guerrillas), 1,453 (35.5%) were women. The demobilized included sixty people who were under thirteen years of age (including two one-year-old babies, a five-year-old girl and a six-year-old girl). Just as surprising was that 170 of the demobilized combatants were over the age of sixty (including five women in their nineties). "[I]n the eyes of the guerrillas themselves, the category of 'combatant' is not limited to the arms-bearing fighter" (Luciak 1995, 3–4). After years of traveling and working with the guerrillas (work that was hardly free from danger), some women in traditionally female support roles insisted that their role should be acknowledged in the demobilization process.

Further evidence of the breadth of the category of guerrilla was provided by another study of 1,100 Salvadoran women who had been demobilized by the United Nations. Of those demobilized guerrillas, 28.8 percent reported that they had worked as cooks, 15 percent had been health workers, 15.2 percent had been combatants, 10.7 percent had been part of the base of support, and 40.3 percent had carried out some other sort of work (Fundación 16 de Enero 1993, 10). Yet another study, based on in-depth interviews with sixty women of the FMLN, included the following within the category of guerrillas: combatants, radio operators, doctors, nurses, rural outreach workers, and financial workers (Vázquez, Ibáñez, and Murguialday 1996, 114). But while they all went under the category of guerrilla, they did not all enjoy the same status. "While being a radio operator was less prestigious than being a combatant, the radio operators felt more important than the nurses and the outreach workers, and they in turn felt more important than the cooks. . . . But even though only a minority of those interviewed were combatants, they were all armed" (115–16).

13. To an extent men also gained a degree of prestige by using arms, but this was more the case for women since they stepped further away from their traditional roles by becoming combatants.

14. The argument that former mid-prestige revolutionary activists were the people who went on to become feminist activists is based on my interviews as well as my reading of the literature on the legacy of revolutionary movements. It is summarized in a chart so as to make all elements of the argument easy to read but not to suggest that my arguments (based as they necessarily are on subjective perception) are somehow objective or quantifiable.

15. I consider San Cristóbal de las Casas to be the cultural capital of indigenous Chiapas and thus the more logical site for a study of Zapatismo than the heavily mestizo city of Tuxtla Gutiérrez, which is the political capital of the state.

16. In October 1998, I participated in a week-long women's delegation to Cuba sponsored by Global Exchange. During the course of that week, I interviewed three women who worked in a regional office of the Federation of Cuban Women and heard talks by more than a dozen women from different walks of life (including an economist, college professors, writers, journalists, health care workers and lesbian feminist artists). My fieldwork in Cuba, obviously, did not compare to that in the other three countries and so my discussion of the Cuban revolution in the final chapter is mostly based on secondary sources.

17. Within the FSLN of Nicaragua, an organization that was formed in 1961 and eventually overthrew the Somoza family dictatorship in 1979, many have estimated that 30 percent of the combatants and many of the top guerrilla leaders,

were women (Collinson 1990, 154; Flynn 1983, 416; Reif 1986, 158), though a study of the records of the Sandinista Social Security Institute found that only 6.6 percent of those killed in the war against Somoza were female (Vilas 1985, 108).

In the southern Mexican state of Chiapas, where a rebellion has been ongoing since the beginning of 1994, women are well integrated into the ongoing movement of the EZLN, comprising about one-third of the combatants (Marcos 1995c; Olivera 1996, 49; Stephen 1994a, 2). Women's participation in the FMLN of El Salvador, founded in 1980, was also quite significant. More important, the data from El Salvador is more reliable than the data from either Nicaragua or Chiapas, given that, at the end of the war in 1992, the United Nations oversaw the demobilization of the FMLN, collecting basic data regarding the guerrillas. Approximately 40 percent of the FMLN membership, 30 percent of the combatants, and 20 percent of the military leadership were women (Luciak 1995, 3; T. D. Mason 1992, 65; Montgomery 1995, 123; Digas 1993, 35; Vázquez, Ibáñez, and Murguialday 1996, 21).

18. During the eighties the Salvadoran government received approximately $3.6 billion from the U.S. government. The Reagan administration's support to the Salvadoran government was unprecedented in the history of El Salvador. That the U.S. government would play such a significant economic role in supporting any Latin American government was also unprecedented. In the mid-eighties, the United States alone funded "between 20 percent and 43 percent of the Salvadoran government's budget" (McClintock 1998, 221).

19. Approximately seventy-five thousand died in the civil war in El Salvador. More than 95 percent of those human rights abuses were carried out by the armed forces and its death squad allies, as was documented by the United Nations (cited in Vilas 1995, 135–36 and Montgomery 1995, 242–43).

20. On vanguard parties, see Selbin 1999, 42–43, 62, 70–71, 80. On the impact of vanguardism on women's organizing, see Kruks, Rapp, and Young 1989, 10–11. On vangardism and women's organizing in Angola, see Scott 1994; in Cuba, see Molyneux 2000; in Mozambique, see Kruks and Wisner 1989; Sheldon 1994; in the Soviet Union, see Buckley 1989. On women's efforts to gain autonomy from vanguard parties, see González and Kampwirth 2001; Hipsher 2001; Luciak 2001a, 2001b.

Chapter 1

1. *Construyendo la patria nueva, hacemos la mujer nueva.*
2. Upon overthrowing the Somoza dictatorship in 1979, the Sandinistas

began the process of institutionalizing a political system that was characterized by many of the standard features of liberal democracy (such as competitive elections, constitutional rule, separation of powers) along with many of the features of participatory democracy (such as popular organizations that were highly involved in national politics, along with land reform, educational reform, and other policies that served to redistribute in favor of the least advantaged). Ironically enough, the greatest proof of the Sandinistas' democratic sincerity came when they peacefully handed power over to the opposition UNO coalition in 1990, after losing the second set of national elections that were held under their watch (see Barton 1988; Jonas and Stein 1989, 1990; Pérez Alemán 1990; Selbin 1999; Vilas 1986).

3. The following vision, expressed by one of the nine members of the (all male) National Directorate, was hardly unique: "Our Revolution does not just transform the backward forces of production of the old system. . . . We aspire and we promise that the transformations that are made should go from the factory to the home, from men to women, from parents to children, from the labor union to the family" (Núñez 1986, 1).

4. The Historic Program of the FSLN, first presented in 1969, promised that the "Sandinista people's revolution . . . [would] establish economic, political, and cultural equality between men and women" (FSLN 1986, 186). It listed seven specific reforms that would engender such equality, including eliminating prostitution, ending discrimination against children born out of wedlock, establishing day care centers and maternity leave, and lifting the "political, cultural, and vocational levels" of women through their incorporation into the revolutionary process (187).

5. The speed with which the FSLN moved to change women's legal status may have reflected the power of some women who had risen to leadership positions during the guerrilla struggle and their interest in such legislation. Or it may have been due to male Sandinistas' perceptions that such legislation would help consolidate the legitimacy of the new revolution in the eyes of women, especially in Nicaragua but also internationally (on international influences on early Sandinista gender policy see Luciak 2000, 17; 2001a, 20). While there is considerable evidence that women within the FSLN actively lobbied for legislative gender reforms when creating the 1987 constitution (which I will discuss later in this chapter), the motivations of policymakers during the first days of the revolution are far less clear.

6. The legal changes of the weeks and months following Somoza's overthrow were decrees, very much in the style of a hierarchical guerrilla organization. But by 1982 that guerrilla organization had transformed itself into a revolutionary party for which legislation was a broadly participatory process.

Over seventy-five hundred women and men participated in more than 170 meetings that led to the Law of Relations between Mothers, Fathers, and Children. Similarly, the Nurturing Law was developed through 120 popular consultations in which around ten thousand participated (Murguialday 1990, 127–28; Stephens 1988, 156). Significantly, the most radical expressions of gender egalitarianism that emerged in the early years of the revolution were not written by a few isolated intellectuals but instead were made by thousands of ordinary women. The fact that feminist proposals could not be easily dismissed as having been made by unrepresentative intellectuals may have made those proposals especially threatening to some Sandinista leaders.

7. Ortega's response to the Nurturing Law was one of many examples of how Sandinista leaders understood social justice to be fundamentally a class project and only rarely a gender project. I will discuss the intellectual and historical roots of this understanding of social justice at the end of this chapter.

8. Every lesson had one key phrase that was broken down into its component phonetic parts, and that phrase also served as a basis for discussion.

9. Under the Somozas the health care system was fragmented, inefficient, and elitist, even by Central American standards. Few had access to even the most basic preventative medicine; for example, in 1974 only 5.7 percent of those at risk received vaccinations for diptheria, tetanus, and whooping cough. Overall, only 28 percent of the population had access to regular health care. The majority did not even have access to clean water. All these factors contributed to a life expectancy of only fifty-three and infant mortality rates between 120 and 146 per thousand live births (Bossert 1985, 350–52; Collinson 1990, 95–97; Garfield and Taboada 1986, 425–26).

10. AMNLAE's Women's Houses (Casas de la Mujer) were built in all the regions of Nicaragua (numbering fifty-two by the early nineties). These houses provided services in health, psychological counseling, and legal counseling, at the same time as they offered workshops in areas such as sexuality, contraception, and job training.

11. As the war neared its end in 1988, fifty-eight thousand people, out of a population of a little over 3 million, had been killed (Vilas 1995). No Nicaraguan was untouched by the war, because of the numbers killed, the devastation it wreaked on the economy, and the brutality of contras' tactics. An American priest described one visit from the FDN branch of the contras in 1983: "In Ocaguas, the FDN freedom fighters murdered two campesinos. One was stabbed and had his eyes dug out before being killed. The other was hung from a beam of his own house. . . . The task force arrived in El Guayabo the next day and killed nine people. One of the victims was a fourteen-year-old girl who was raped by several men and later decapitated. They threw her body into a

brook and placed her head in the road at the entrance to the village. They did the same with the head of another campesino" (138). Two women from Anito whose houses were burned told of how the counterrevolutionaries showed them their new weapons (FALs) while talking about President Reagan's support for the FDN. They also showed large sums of money. One campesino was told that he would be paid 40,000 córdobas if he joined the contras. They stole a Bible from Valentín Velázquez. . . . 'This way, the people around here will see that we are Christians,' the FDN members said" (quoted in Gorman and Walker 1985, 109–10).

The Reagan administration's role in the contra war violated international law, and in fact the International Court at the Hague ruled in favor of Nicaragua in June 1986, ordering the United States to pay indemnity for its undeclared war against the Central American nation. In March 1988 the cost of the indemnity was set at $17 billion (which was how much the war was calculated to have cost Nicaragua). That indemnity was never paid (Larios 1991; INEC 1990, 58).

12. On the contras see Bendaña 1991; Brown 2001; Dickey 1985; Chamorro 1987; Horton 1998; Kampwirth 2001; Morales Carazo 1989; Núñez et al. 1998; Pardo-Maurer 1990; Payne 2000; Walker 1987.

13. The contras did not overtly promote a gender agenda, but women did participate in the contra forces, in roles ranging from cook to combatant. For a discussion of women within the contra movement, see Brown 2001, 109–13; Kampwirth 2001, 79–82, 87–89, 91–104.

14. On Nicaraguan women and agrarian reform see Collinson 1990; Padilla, Murguialday, and Criquillón 1987; Pérez-Alemán 1990.

15. In conjunction with the Center for Research on Agrarian Reform (Centro de Investigacón de la Reforma Agraria) and the Ministry of Labor, the women's secretariat of the ATC conducted a broad-ranging study from 1983 to 1985, including interviews with eight hundred female rural workers at sixty work sites. It was a landmark study for its size and because it was the first major study in Nicaragua that linked questions of pregnancy and other family responsibilities with organizational and productive outcomes (Criquillón n.d., 20).

16. Though such feminist questions were generally not asked during the war, in the nineties researcher Lorraine Bayard de Volo carried out an excellent study of the Matagalpa branch of the Mothers of Heroes and Martyrs and the dynamic relationship between those women and the FSLN. In the course of that study she asked, "Why were there no Fathers of the Heroes and Martyrs?" and found that initially that the question "caught many Mothers off guard. The differences between mothers and fathers seemed so obvious to them" (2001, 59). For their answers see Bayard de Volo 2001, 59–63.

17. Other estimates place the number of Nicaraguan women at the Taxco encuentro at over fifty (Sternbach et al. 1992, 224).

18. The proclamation (*proclama*) was a groundbreaking statement issued by the national directorate of the FSLN in 1987 that, for the first time, acknowledged that sexism continued to exist in Nicaragua, despite the reforms of the revolution. Because of its use of the word *machismo* (which loosely translates as sexism) and because it committed the party to fighting sexual inequality, the proclamation represented a qualitative leap in official Sandinista analysis of gender in the revolution. (The full text of the proclamation is reprinted in Murguialday 1990, 285–98.)

19. According to the Constitution, national elections were to be held every six years. As the 1984 election was held in November, the 1990 election was also scheduled for November, but, as part of an agreement with the contras, the Sandinistas agreed to reschedule the election for February.

20. *Doña* is an honorific placed in front of the first name of an older woman.

21. Doña Violeta was a member of the original revolutionary junta, in her capacity as the widow of the martyred Pedro Joaquín. But she resigned within a year, ostensibly for health reasons, as it became clear that the revolutionary agenda went far beyond the overthrow of Somoza. That was her only direct political experience until she was asked to head the UNO ticket in 1989. Arguably, her limited experience in partisan politics was an asset. Enrique Bolaños (who would be elected vice president in 1996 and president in 2001), her principle rival for the nomination, was too associated with big capital and too loud a critic of the revolution to plausibly portray himself as reconciler. For a discussion of the process of choosing UNO's candidates and the U.S. role in that process, see Robinson 1992, 57–60.

22. Sonia Alvarez explains that, in the days leading up to the 1964 coup in Brazil, hierarchical gender roles served to legitimize hierarchical national politics: "Traditional symbols of feminine piety and spiritual superiority, morality and motherhood were manipulated by the political Right to legitimize their repressive political project. Armed with crucifixes and rosaries, thousands of upper- and middle-class women paraded through the streets of Brazil's major cities, imploring the military to perform its 'manly duty' and restore order and stability to the nation" (1990, 6). The model of family life projected by those women was infused with a particular gender agenda, and a class agenda as well. Michele Mattelart (1980, 288) observes that a similar thing happened in Chile in 1973, where traditional femininity legitimized a brutal military coup. For more on the use of political maternalism within left- and right-wing politics in Latin America, see González and Kampwirth 2001, 23–25.

23. Based on my conversations with voters in the months following the election, and my reading of some of the opinion polls conducted before and after the election, it seems that the electorate divided along lines of age as much as gender. An Univisión poll conducted in October 1989 showed that older voters (those over thirty-five) favored Chamorro over Ortega 41 to 33 percent, while younger voters favored Ortega over Chamorro 44 to 37 percent (1989, 2). Another poll conducted in January 1990 found that 61 percent of young men (between sixteen and twenty-four) thought that Daniel Ortega deserved to be reelected; only 42 percent of older men (over forty) and 41 percent of older women agreed (Greenberg-Lake 1989, 1990). A study based on postelection polls found that 52.4 percent of housewives voted for Chamorro's UNO coalition while 33.2 percent voted for Ortega's FSLN. That same study showed that two sectors in which young people dominated—the military and students—went for the party of the revolution: 71.4 percent of soldiers voted for the FSLN while 14.3 percent voted for the UNO; 50.5 percent of students voted for the FSLN while 34.7 percent voted for the UNO (Oquist 1992, 20–21).

In 1990 the electorate divided in ways that were consistent with the symbolism of campaign, between Chamorro supporters, who supported the old hierarchical model of family relations (generally older people), and Ortega supporters, who benefited from the new, more democratic model (in other words, young people).

24. Engels's writings on the development of family (1975) have shaped much of Marxist thought on the subject. He argued that, with the rise of private property, men's desire for control over women's sexuality started, since men wanted a guarantee that their heirs were their biological children. According to the logic of Engels's argument, the way to emancipate women was to provide them with independent economic resources (by integrating them into paid work). Breaking with economic dependence was all that was necessary, according to Engels, since he explained patriarchal rule exclusively through the logic of private property.

The words of Sandinista commander Carlos Núñez provides a good illustration of the influence of this strain of thought. He explains the disintegrating effect of capitalism on families by citing Engels (1986, 8–9). Núñez goes on to argue, "The flag of feminine liberation that the bourgeoisie raises is more like a struggle against men and not against capitalist exploitation. No! The struggle is not against men, the struggle is against the bourgeois class, as the only condition with which they make the revolution" (13). He ends the article by quoting Lenin on the importance of the complete liberation of women for the liberation of the proletariat (20).

25. The equation of feminist organizing and the middle class has a historical basis in Latin America, but that equation has broken down in recent decades (González and Kampwirth 2001, 13–17). In the history of women's organizing that I have just described, there was no clear correlation between feminine strategies and working-class activists, or between feminist strategies and middle-class activists. In Nicaragua it was the union that represented some of the poorest women (the rural wage workers who belonged to the ATC) that first promoted feminist goals within the revolution. In contrast, the generally middle-class leaders of AMNLAE were those who promoted the mobilization of the mothers of combatants (the Mothers of Heroes and Martyrs) through feminine means.

26. For more on this point, see chapter 5; also Funk and Mueller 1993; Goven 1993; Jaquette and Wolchik 1998; Moghadam 1997.

27. Victoria González (2001) has done very important research on women who benefited from the Somoza governments, either making their careers in the Somoza governments, or participating in social organizations affiliated with the Somoza family's Liberal Party. To a large extent those women saw the Somozas as champions of gender equality, particularly valuing the fact that women were granted the right to vote under the Somozas, in 1955. But those women were a minority and in general Nicaraguans did not associate the Somozas with feminism.

Chapter 2

1. The election of a woman as president should have been good for gender equality. The symbolism of a female president probably did have some positive impact with regard to gender relations. But the symbolism was undercut so often that most of that impact was dissipated. The repeated assertions by doña Violeta and her supporters that she opposed feminist goals and was really just a housewife did not exactly further the idea of the president as capable. Furthermore, the fact that Antonio Lacayo (her chief of staff and son-in-law) appeared to do most of the day-to-day work of the presidency also undercut the positive symbolism of a female president. It probably could have not been otherwise, for doña Violeta was in way over her head when she ran for president: very few people, male or female, could be expected to successfully administer a country without ever having held public office. It is to her credit that she seemed to grow into the position (at least in her public appearances), and was far more comfortable bantering with reporters at the end of her administration than she had been at the beginning.

2. Anna Fernández Poncela cites estimates of joblessness in 1992 ranging from 40 to 58 percent at the national level, and as high as 90 percent within the northern Atlantic Coast region (1996, 51, 63). In contrast, Mario Arana estimates that the unemployment rate, in the same year, was 17.8 percent while the underemployment rate was 38 percent (1997, 83). One reason for this disagreement was probably the sources that the two analysts used: Fernández Poncela cites a government agency, a union federation, a private think tank, and a newspaper, while Arana cites two government agencies. Another explanation could be that joblessness, as used in the sources cited by Fernández Poncela, could very well include both unemployment and underemployment, in which case Arana's combined figure for 1992 of 55.8 percent is not far off her national estimates. Despite the debates, the point of these figures—that economic misery increased for the vast majority during the nineties—is not disputed.

3. One might be tempted to see health, education, and welfare policies as feminine or practical issues that are of little concern to the autonomous feminists. That would be a mistake. Since feminism in Nicaragua emerged out of the guerrilla struggle and the revolution, Nicaraguan feminism always had a strong class content, something that was historically not true for feminism in the northern countries. The conflict with AMNLAE, detailed in chapter 1, was not about whether it made sense to organize around issues related to day-to-day survival; all women's activists agreed that such practical goals mattered a great deal. Instead, the conflict revolved around two issues. The first was whether the women's movement should devote all its energies to feminine issues (basically the position of AMNLAE and the FSLN during the war) or whether it should also devote energy to feminist goals, like sexuality or household power dynamics (the position of those who became the autonomous feminists).

The second point of fundamental conflict was a political point: whether AMNLAE should play the role of vanguard within the women's movement and whether the FSLN should play the role of vanguard within the country as a whole, guiding the actions of popular organizations, including women's organizations. The autonomous feminists rejected both vanguardism and an exclusive focus on feminine goals, instead typically carrying out a mix of feminine and feminist work within the same organization.

4. Neoliberal policies promote the reduction or elimination of state services (with the exception of military spending), under the assumption that the private sector will step in to fill the void and that it will do so more efficiently. In the United States the equivalent of this antistate ideology is often called Reaganomics or trickle-down economics.

5. Nationwide, something in the range of one hundred women's houses operated in the nineties. The sort of health care they typically offered included gynecological exams and other reproductive services.

6. Nicaraguan birth rates were an average of five per woman in the cities, seven per woman in the countryside. In comparison, the average birth rate in the United States was 1.8 children per woman (panel on women's health, Casa Benjamin Linder, March 3, 1991).

7. Abortion was never legalized or even decriminalized under the FSLN, though therapeutic abortions were available in the public women's hospital in cases of physical or (sometimes) economic hardship. When the Chamorro administration took power in 1990, it simply enforced the Somoza era penal code more strictly, typically refusing to make exceptions, even in the most extreme cases. A friend of mine died of heart failure at the age of twenty-seven, even though doctors had told her that carrying her pregnancy to term would probably kill her and even though she wanted an abortion. In the political climate of the nineties, the doctors no doubt preferred to err on the side of letting her die rather than perform an abortion that could get them into trouble.

8. The Plan of Economic Conversion was initiated in March 1991 to reduce the size of the state bureaucracy. State employees were encouraged to quit their jobs in exchange for a cash payment of up to $2,000. Theoretically, these former state workers would then invest their cash payments in small businesses of their own. More than twelve thousand state workers left their positions through the plan, none of whom could be hired in any government agency for the next four years, according to the terms of the plan (interview with the director of budget policy in the Ministry of Finance, July 18, 1991).

9. Although the women who took advantage of the plan had been salaried workers, the budget director described them not as women or workers but as housewives (*amas de casa*), as though all women were fundamentally housewives, even if they worked for wages outside their homes.

10. The name referred to the 52 percent of the Nicaraguan population that was female.

11. On Nicaraguan lesbians and gays, see Adam 1993; Babb 2001; Bolt 1996; Codina 1992; Kampwirth 1994, 1996d, 1998b; Lancaster 1992; Randall 1993, 1994.

12. Under the antigay law, Article 204 (which is part of Law 150), both speech and action are punishable. It reads: "The crime of sodomy is committed by any who induces, promotes, propagandizes, or practices copulation with people of the same sex in a scandalous form. It will be penalized with one to three years' imprisonment" (Nicaragua 1992).

13. I have no way of addressing the question of what would have happened to a non-Sandinista gay or lesbian who tried to organize in the eighties since all the gay and lesbian activists I interviewed identified with the Sandinistas in the eighties.

14. While I have interviewed or engaged in informal conversations with a few gay men, this analysis is mainly based on my interviews with lesbians. It seems quite likely that the experience of gay men differed somewhat, though the fact that the gay and lesbian movement is a united movement in Nicaragua, in contrast to many other countries, indicates that Nicaraguan gays and lesbians also share much in common.

15. Through her research on late-nineteenth- and early-twentieth-century feminist organizing, Victoria González (2001, 1995) has demonstrated that Nicaraguan feminism was hardly invented by the autonomous feminists, or even by their guerrilla predecessors. Nonetheless, the women who led all three branches of the women's movement in the nineties traced their personal and organizational histories back to the sixties and seventies, not to earlier periods. In an overview of the history of women's organizing that was typical of the accounts I read and heard, the National Feminist Committee wrote, "From the middle of the 1930s until the 1970s, feminine activities were characterized by a lack of organizational structure" (Comité Nacional 1994, 5).

16. The National Feminist Committee's work from 1998 to 2000 included training seminars for committee members, acting as a lobbying force in national politics, a campaign to depenalize abortion (carried out through local meetings and radio advertisements, at the same time as it fought efforts promoted by Pro-Vida to eliminate legal abortion under even the limited circumstances permitted in Nicaragua), participation in international campaigns related to women's issues (such as the evaluation of the progress of the Beijing conference promises—the Beijing Plus Five campaign), and attendance at Economic Commission for Latin America (CEPAL) meetings in Lima and New York (Diana, interview, March 30, 2000).

17. The Latin American feminist gatherings, or encuentros, began meeting every two or three years beginning in 1981. So the feminist gathering was nothing new in 1993, what was new was its meeting in Central America. On the encuentros, see González and Kampwirth 2001, 19–20; Sternbach et al. 1992.

18. On the Brazilian women's police stations, see MacDowell Santos 2000; Nelson 2002.

19. The autonomous feminist organizations that helped create the Women's and Children's Police Stations were the Centro de Derechos Constitucionales,

Centro "Mujer y Familia," Colectivo de Mujeres "8 de Marzo," Colectivo "Xochitl," Defensoría de Mujeres Violadas, and Si Mujer.

20. The Instituto Nicaragüense de la Mujer (INIM), the Policía Nacional, Hospital "Berta Calderón," Hospital "Manolo Morales," INSSBI, MINSA, and the Procuraduría de Justicia.

21. The Centro de Salud "Pedro Altamirano."

22. The MRS broke off from the FSLN in 1995. Such notable Sandinista intellectuals as former vice president Sergio Ramírez and former guerrilla commander Dora María Téllez, formed the new party in response to what they saw as three problems: that the FSLN had not unequivocally rejected the possibility of future political violence, that the leadership of the FSLN opposed strategic alliances with parties of the center or right, and that the leadership of the FSLN had failed to give up the vanguard model of governance—that is, it had failed to let the party democratize internally (Smith 1997).

23. Dorotea Wilson, a missionary who became a guerrilla leader and later a member of the FSLN national directorate, was one of the many women who participated in the national coalition. She listed (off the top of her head) a number of different groups—parties, unions, and women's organizations—that were part of the coalition. Here is her list (not including the political parties, since I already discussed them): Colectivo de Masaya, Colectivo Feminista La Malinche, Colectivo de Mujeres Itza, Ixchen, AMNLAE, Secretaría de la Mujer de la ATC, Movimiento de Mujeres Trabajadoras y Desempleadas "María Elena Cuadra," FETSALUD, women from right-wing labor unions, Centro Mujer y Familia, Centro de Derechos Humanos "Carlos Núñez," CENZONTLE, UNE (interview, February 5, 1997). Cristiana, the daughter of the senator from Somoza's Liberal Party who was active in the anti-Somoza movement and later in contra support work, was one of the founders of the national coalition, back when it was an organization of female leaders known as the Women's Forum (Foro de Mujeres). Until the formation of the Women's Forum, she told me, she had never sat around a table with such a diverse group of women (interview, January 30, 1997).

24. The Minimum Agenda was divided into four areas: politics and the state, sociocultural issues, economics, and legal rights and working conditions. A number of specific proposals fell within those categories: "To transform the unequal relations of power between men and women . . . to promote relations of solidarity between women . . . to guarantee women's human rights . . . to elaborate the organic law of the Ministry of women and to elevate INIM [the Women's Institute] to the level of a ministry . . . elaboration of action plans to put the results of the world summits and conferences into practice . . . to promote and develop

housing programs to benefit single mothers . . . to design and carry out policies, programs, and projects to mitigate the effects of structural adjustment on women . . . to promote draft laws that would guarantee nonsexist education that impedes the reproduction of established and stereotypical roles" (*Boletina* 1996a, 27–28).

25. The October 1996 election was seriously marred by electoral fraud. Ballots marked for the FSLN were found in garbage cans; blank ballots, tens of thousands of them, were found in the homes of Liberal activists; results from hundreds of polling places, mainly those run by Liberal Party officials, simply disappeared (Cuadra 1996, 16–17; Fernández Ampié 1996, 7–8; *Envío* 1996–97a, 1996–97b; Spence et al. 1997, 13, 17). Few serious observers thought that the FSLN would have actually won the presidential election without the fraud, but fraud probably did sway a few congressional and mayoral outcomes. Moreover, the appearance of fraud had serious psychological effects, confirming Sandinista beliefs that Alemán really was a Somocista, that he was not a legitimately elected president.

26. Many of the students who read Belli's electoral hints were eligible to vote, since the minimal voting age in Nicaragua is sixteen.

27. As it turned out, Humberto Belli, not Luis González, became the head of the new Ministry of the Family. He was replaced as the minister of education by José Antonio Alvarado (Amy Bank, pers. comm., September 25, 1998).

28. While the law creating the Ministry of the Family was specifically aimed at controlling independent organizations that addressed family issues, another law was broader in scope, limiting the fund-raising capacity of all elements of civil society. The "General Law Regarding Non-Profit Organizations" mandated that NGOs would need the "proper authorization of the government" to seek funding from foreign agencies (*Boletina* 1997b, 5).

29. Mere hours after Zoilamérica (who began to use her biological father's name, Narváez) made her accusation public, Rosario Murillo, her mother and Daniel's wife, denounced her in a press conference, calling the accusation a "blow to our family" that should be treated as "a family affair" (*Envío* 1998b, 6). Daniel stood silently at her side, a silence he would maintain in the following years. Though Zoilamérica was supported in her accusations by her estranged husband, Alejandro Bendaña (another high-level Sandinista), and her aunt Violeta Murillo the cost of coming forward was high: through her accusation, she lost her future in the party, her ability to live in peace (as death threats began), and most of her family. As it turned out, though, the tensions within her family were hardly new—for instance, neither her mother nor her siblings had attended her 1991 wedding to Bendaña; the only immediate family member who had attended was Daniel Ortega himself (Belli 1998, C2).

30. In an open letter to Zoilamérica, Margaret Randall, a U.S. citizen who has written numerous books on revolutionary movements in Latin America, explained, "I write as someone who lived in Nicaragua between 1980 and 1984 and who like many in that small community was aware of the abuse of which you accuse Ortega. We knew about it and we stayed silent because of our desire to support the Sandinista revolution, our fear, and our perception that this is Zoilamérica's story, to be told or not told, by her. I am ashamed of our silence, but perhaps that time and place did not leave any other alternative" (reprinted in Huerta 1998, 69).

31. The Women's Commission of the Sandinista Assembly was an exception to the tendency for women's groups to support Zoilamérica's right to make a claim. The commission "was unwilling to directly listen to Zoilamérica's testimony, despite the fact that she, an active Sandinista and even a member of one of the commissions preparing for the May party congress, had requested it" (*Envío* 1998b, 7).

Chapter 3

1. Of course, women participated in Salvadoran politics long before the seventies. Over the course of the twentieth century many women actively participated in opposition politics both in coed organizations and in women's organizations, starting in 1944 with the founding of the Feminine Democratic Front (Frente Democrático Feminino). But the harsh repression that most of these groups endured meant that they were often short lived. The organizations that are the focus of this chapter—groups that were active in the nineties—had much shorter immediate histories, typically having been founded in the eighties or early nineties.

Unlike most Latin American countries, El Salvador never had a first-wave feminist, or suffrage, movement. In part that was because female political activists were occupied with opposing a long series of military governments, and in part because those governments preempted a women's movement by promoting women's suffrage, in an effort to bolster their own legitimacy. In 1938, President Maximiliano Hernández Martínez, the man responsible for killing tens of thousands in the 1932 *Matanza* (massacre), called a constitutional assembly in which women were granted the vote, making El Salvador the first Central American country to give women the right to vote, at least on paper. That theoretical right was put into practice when the Constitution was reformed in 1950 (Moreno 1997, 11–38; other good sources in Spanish are AMES 1981, 8–11; Dignas 1993, 86–106; García and Gomáriz 1989, 203–29; Gargallo

1987, 58–59; Navas 1987; Soro 1992, 1–19; in English, Hipsher 2001, 135–44 and Stephen 1997, 67–84 are both excellent).

2. For the complete peace accord along with other documents related to the peace process see the website of the Centro de Paz, http://www.cepaz.org.sv/.

3. Initially Kristina's father was involved with unions affiliated with the Christian Democrats and later with the PCN (Partido de Conciliación Nacional), a party that was closely tied to the military.

4. To try to reduce the confusion that is inherent in any discussion of party politics in El Salvador, I oversimplified ORMUSA's history in the text, simply linking the organization to Democratic Convergence. In fact, María de los Santos alternated between referring to ORMUSA as tied to Democratic Convergence and to the Popular Social Christian Movement (Movimiento Popular Social Cristiano, or MPSC). Both are true: Democratic Convergence was an umbrella group that included the MPSC. The MPSC itself was a product of a split in the Christian Democrats. When one wing of the Christian Democratic Party, headed by José Napoleon Duarte, chose to ally with the right in 1980, the party was torn apart. "Duarte won the election, but the progressives walked out and almost immediately reconstituted themselves as the Popular Social Christian Movement (MPSC)" (Montgomery 1995, 111). During the middle years of the war, the MPSC belonged to the Democratic Revolutionary Front (Frente Democrático Revolucionario, or FDR), often considered the political wing of the FMLN. In 1987 the FDR was reformulated as Democratic Convergence (158, 207–8).

5. In 1989 a coalition known as COM (Coordinación de Organismos de Mujeres) was formed, uniting five women's organizations (ADEMUSA, AMS, CONAMUS, MSM, and ORMUSA). By 1996, ORMUSA had left and two other groups, Women's Committee for a Peaceful Culture (Comité de Mujeres por una Cultura de Paz) and Segundo Montes Women's Association (Asociación de Mujeres Segundo Montes), had joined, giving COM a total of seven members. From the very beginning there were tensions in and around COM. As María de los Santos indicated, the women of ORMUSA felt pressured by other COM members to stop being so influenced by foreign women (perhaps a reference to ORMUSA's origin in Costa Rica or simply to the fact that ORMUSA members called themselves feminist). Many women who either left the COM or refused to join felt that the coalition was highly controlled by the FMLN, at least in the early nineties. So in 1991 a different coordinating body, known as Concertación, or the Coalition (Concertación de Mujeres por la Paz, la Dignidad, y la Igualdad), was founded with twenty-four member organizations, including ORMUSA. Years later, there were still major disagreements between some members of the coalitions about what it meant to be an advo-

NOTES TO PAGE 88

cate for women's rights. Concertación members tended to see their coalition as more autonomous and more feminist than the COM. Betty, who directed CONAMUS (one of the founders of the COM and the first women's organization in El Salvador to use the word *feminist* to describe its work) compared the two differently. In her opinion, the members of Concertación were "radical feminists" while the COM had a more holistic vision of "feminism, gender, class. . . . At bottom the conception of feminism is what differentiates the two bands" (Betty, interview, July 23, 1994; Scarlet, interview, July 1, 1996; Dignas 1993, 117; Stephen 1997, 68–69, 291).

6. ORDEN (Organización Democrática Nacionalista or Democratic Nationalist Organization) was a right-wing peasant organization founded by the military in the sixties to keep order in the countryside (Montgomery 1995, 106). By the mid-seventies, as Yamilet's story illustrates, the presence of ORDEN was also felt in the cities.

7. In the early eighties students were much more likely to be killed than members of the general population. While college students comprised only three-fifths of one percent of the population of El Salvador in 1980 (27,100 out of 4,525,000), and high school students comprised slightly more than one and a half percent of the population (73,000 out of 4,525,000), students made up a much larger percentage of the victims of state violence: 7.2 percent of those who were killed in the early 1980s and 17.3 percent of those who were disappeared, most of whom were murdered after being tortured. My impression from the secondary literature on El Salvador as well as my own interviews is that college students were more likely targets than high school students although high school students were hardly immune (Booth and Walker 1989, 148, 156; Valdés and Gomáriz 1995, 106).

Jorge Castañeda reported similar findings regarding the vulnerability of intellectuals (especially students) to state violence: 64 percent of the people that the Brazilian dictatorship (1964–78) acknowledged killing "were so-called intellectual workers, of which half were students. . . . In the larger universe of those 'officially' tortured by the regime, intellectual workers represented 55 percent of the total." While Castañeda claimed those who "died as a result of [state] repression . . . [comprised] a sample more or less identifiable with the guerrilla movement" (1994, 78), I think caution is called for regarding the direction of causality. It is doubtless true that many of those who were tortured were guerrillas, but there were also many people who became guerrilla supporters after their detention and torture for a much lesser crime (like supporting a strike or participating in a human rights group or even fitting the state's profile of a guerrilla) led them to lose hope in the efficacy of peaceful resistance.

8. The national and international feminist events that Salvadoran activists attended in the early nineties included the fifth Latin American feminist gathering in Argentina in 1990, the First National Women's Meeting in El Salvador in 1991, the first Central American feminist gathering in Nicaragua in 1992, the second national feminist gathering in El Salvador in 1993, the sixth Latin American feminist gathering in El Salvador in 1993, the regional forum in El Salvador in 1995, and meetings of the Central American Feminist Current, founded in 1995 (interviews; Murguialday 1996a; Stephen 1997).

9. Officially, twenty-eight organizations and numerous individuals belonged to the Women 94 coalition (Mujeres 94 1993). But three women who belonged to either the MAM (Movimiento de Mujeres Mélida Anaya Montes) or Mujer Ciudadana told me, in separate interviews, that forty groups participated. Also, the authors of a study on women's roles during and after the war estimated that "more than forty women's and feminist organizations" participated in the coalition (Vázquez 1996, 56). The disagreement may be due to the difficulty of defining membership.

10. The probably overblown rhetoric of "election of the century" (*elecciones del siglo*) was used to indicate that the 1994 general election was a significant turning point, as in fact it was. First and foremost, it was the first time ever that the left was included, publicly and legally, in electoral politics. Second, it was an election in which voters chose between candidates for executive, legislative, local, and Central America–wide offices (contests that were typically staggered in different years). Finally, it was the first election held in times of peace since the seventies (and even those elections were highly compromised since the winners of the two presidential elections of the seventies were not permitted to take office and instead had to flee into exile).

11. Not surprisingly, the platform is very long. One version of the platform lists seventy-eight demands, another lists sixty-three. An illustrated popular education booklet lists thirty-three. Posters were distributed with a list of fourteen demands. Finally, an even more reduced list of ten demands was presented to the parties (Mujeres 94 1993a, 1993b, 1994; Soro et al. 1994; U.S.–El Salvador Institute for Democratic Development 1994).

12. According to a member of Woman Citizen (Mujer Ciudadana), there were disagreements within the coalition because of the breadth of Women 94, in which "there are organizations that call themselves women's organizations and there are those that call themselves feminist organizations and that is a big difference" (interview, July 28, 1994). As a compromise, the word *feminist* never appeared in any version of the platform.

13. In Latin America, the phrase *free and voluntary motherhood* is generally understood as a euphemism for contraception and abortion rights.

14. After the election, Ms. Salguero Gross became president of the National Assembly, the first woman to hold such a position in the history of El Salvador.

15. *Si Nicaragua venció, El Salvador vencerá.*

16. A dominant current in military thought in El Salvador (and elsewhere in Latin America) blamed politics for a whole host of social problems including instability, poverty, and economic underdevelopment. "Acceptance of this ideology of antipolitics also entailed the denial of the legitimacy of labor protest, strikes, political party claims of representing diverse interests, and more generally, of opposition to government authority, policies and programs" (Loveman and Davies 1997b, 5).

17. On incipient feminism during the war in El Salvador, see Kampwirth 2002, 76–81; Stephen 1997.

18. Though the autonomy struggles in the two countries took place at the same time if measured in years, they took place at very different times if measured in relationship to the end of the guerrilla struggles. While calls for feminist autonomy began at the time of the end of the guerrilla war in El Salvador, they began nearly a decade after the guerrilla war ended in Nicaragua. Of course, the guerrilla wars ended differently in the two countries: with a negotiated settlement in El Salvador and with the successful overthrow of the old regime in Nicaragua. Because the FSLN controlled the state for over a decade, it had considerable control over would be feminist dissidents within the revolutionary coalition. Feminism existed as an undercurrent in social movement politics within Nicaragua throughout the revolutionary decade. But it could not break the surface (i.e., feminists could not seek complete autonomy) because, until it lost the 1990 election, the Sandinista Party had enough political and economic power to keep possibly threatening feminist currents submerged. In contrast, the FMLN never had control of the state and its concomitant economic and political power and so had less control over feminists within the revolutionary coalition.

19. The Half-Moon Lesbian Feminist Collective was founded in San Salvador in 1992 (with the support of the Dignas), though by 1996 it had effectively ceased to exist. In 1996 plans were announced for the first Gay Cultural Center in El Salvador. On gay and lesbian rights organizing in Nicaragua, see chapter 2.

20. The one case in which the influence apparently ran from El Salvador to Nicaragua was in the building of broad feminist coalitions to influence electoral politics: Women 94 of El Salvador preceeded the National Women's Coalition of Nicaragua by two years. But no Nicaraguan ever mentioned the Women 94 coalition when discussing the National Women's Coalition in interviews (even though the women I interviewed knew that I intended to compare Nicaragua with El Salvador), nor did I ever see any references to Women 94 in written accounts of the National Women's Coalition. That silence—in marked contrast to

the frequency with which Salvadorans referred to Nicaraguan feminism—makes me think that Women 94 preceded the National Women's Coalition simply because the first postautonomy national election in El Salvador was in 1994, while the first postautonomy election in Nicaragua was not held until 1996.

21. The Nicaraguan feminist movement is the most significant movement in Central America, with the partial exception of that of Costa Rica. But Costa Rica is dramatically different from all the other Central American countries in that it has a much larger middle class and a longer history of electoral democracy. (For a comparison of women's movements in the five Central American countries in the seventies and early eighties, see Navas 1985; for a comparison of the same cases in the nineties, see Montenegro 1997.)

22. The new feminist vanguardism did differ in important ways from the vanguardism of the guerrillas. While vanguardism for the guerrillas—informed by Marxist-Leninist theory—meant that a party with special knowledge would guide, advise, and sometimes command party followers, the regional vanguardism of Nicaraguan feminism was much more horizontal. Salvadoran feminists were under no obligation to accept the advice of the Nicaraguans but the fact that they often chose to accept it testifies to the fact that Nicaragua remained a regional vanguard years after the formal period of the revolution (1979–90) had ended.

23. Lynn Stephen discusses a wide range of factors that initiated the feminist autonomy battle in El Salvador, including international factors. One of those internationally influenced factors were works on gender and the nature of power that a number of the Dignas read in 1990 and 1991; those readings included the works of the Chilean feminist Julieta Kirkwood, which had been recommended to them by Nicaraguans (Stephen 1997, 71–77, 82–84, 291n13).

24. The Colectivo de Mujeres de Matagalpa, founded in 1987, had performed this and similar plays at least as early as 1990, for in that year I saw one of those plays performed in Managua.

25. The press release did not even directly call for the legalization of abortion, instead observing that "this is a topic that should be addressed seriously, overcoming the common confusion in debates on the subject between concerns of religion and public health services in a secular state like ours, understanding it above all as a problem of public health that, when not resolved, leads to serious problems of maternal sickness and death" (Dignas et al. 1996).

26. *La Boletina,* a free bimonthly feminist magazine that the staff of Puntos de Encuentro began publishing in 1991, had a larger circulation than any other publication in Nicaragua by the late nineties.

27. The participants in the workshop on how to replicate the model of *La Boletina* included women from Las Dignas, Flor de Piedra, Movimiento de Mujeres

Mélida Anaya Montes (MAM), Instituto de Investigación, Capacitación y Desarrollo de la Mujer (IMU), and Asociación de Madres Demandantes. That feminist exchange was made possible with support from Oxfam (*Boletina* 1998, 71).

28. Betsy Hartmann (1995) has argued that international development aid, especially from those agencies that make large grants, has been highly skewed in favor of services aimed at reducing the rate of population growth. For years, many international agencies failed to fund any health services except for contraceptives. Recently, that policy has been adapted in light of the observation that low population growth rates are always associated with low infant mortality rates (since to ensure at least one surviving adult child, it is risky for mothers to limit births if infant and child mortality is high). The change in programs like that of USAID was to add maternal and infant health care to contraceptive programs. But such narrowly defined health programs neglect to address a long list of women and children's other health needs, to say nothing of those of men. This neglect is particularly serious, given that the same U.S. government that promotes maternal and infant health programs also encourages elimination of many public health services through neoliberal policies.

29. But AID's policy of giving grants to women's groups without political restrictions was not to last. As a result of Public Law 106–113 passed by the U.S. Congress, starting in February 2000 an NGO that received a grant from USAID had to certify that they were willing to meet three conditions: "that it would not perform abortions either in the country where it was based or in a foreign country; that it would not violate any of the laws of that country with respect to abortion; that it would not participate in activities or actions to change the laws or policies of the government regarding the theme [of abortion]" (Creatividad Feminista 2000). If members of that organization were unwilling to sign the certificate and give up their rights to express political opinions within their own country, they would not receive the AID funds they had been promised. So while the right in the United States had not yet managed to deny American women the right to express opinions in favor of abortion rights or to have an abortion, it had succeeded in placing those restrictions on women of other countries.

30. Xochitl noted that at least four organizations—CONAMUS, AMS, ADEMUSA, and ORMUSA—received substantial funds from USAID (interview, July 30, 1996)

Chapter 4

1. Translated excerpts from the booklet are available (under the name *Declaration of the Lacandón Jungle*) in Marcos 1995b, 51–54 and Womack 1999,

NOTES TO PAGES 113–114

247–49. The original text, in Spanish, is available on the EZLN and FZLN websites (http://www.ezln.org and http://www.fzln.org.mx).

2. The Revolutionary Women's Law:

"In its just struggle for the liberation of our people, the EZLN incorporates women into the revolutionary struggle without concern for their race, creed, color or political affiliation, the only requirement is to take up the demands of exploited people and to commit to obey and enforce the laws and regulations of the revolution Additionally, in light of the situation of working women in Mexico, the following just demands for equality and justice are incorporated into the Revolutionary Women's Law.

First—All women, without regard to their race, creed, color, or political affiliation have the right to participate in the revolutionary struggle in any place or degree in accordance with their will and ability.

Second—Women have the right to work and to receive a fair salary.

Third—Women have the right to choose the number of children that they can have and care for.

Fourth—Women have the right to participate in the concerns of their communities and to be elected freely and democratically to political offices.

Fifth—Women and children have the right to primary health care and basic nutrition.

Sixth—Women have a right to an education.

Seventh—Women have the right to choose their partners and should not be forced to contract matrimony.

Eighth—No woman should ever be hit or physically abused by her relatives or by outsiders. The crimes of attempted rape and rape will be severely punished.

Ninth—Women can occupy positions of leadership in the organization and can hold military ranks in the revolutionary armed forces.

Tenth—Women will have all the rights and obligations that are spelled out in the revolutionary laws and regulations" (EZLN 1993).

3. While the earliest platform of the FMLN of El Salvador did not address gender issues, the Nicaraguan FSLN's formal platform (first presented in 1969) contained a few feminist elements, explicitly condemning discrimination against women and calling for equality between women and men (FDR/FMLN 1986, 205–9; FSLN 1986, 81–189; Lobao 1990, 222–23). But the Sandinistas' Historic Platform, though unusual in mentioning the problem of gender inequality, did not go nearly as far as the Zapatista's Revolutionary Women's Law in addressing that problem.

4. The Women's Group of San Cristóbal was founded as a coalition of church women, housewives, university students, and indigenous women who came to-

gether to protest a series of rapes in the city of San Cristóbal de las Casas in 1989. Originally an organization that worked against sexual violence, it later expanded its focus to include domestic violence. In the aftermath of the 1994 Zapatista uprising, the Women's Group, an organization that had been comprised largely of urban mestiza women, increased its work with indigenous women, especially in response to the military's use of violence against indigenous women. For more on the Women's Group of San Cristóbal, see Freyermuth and Fernández 1995, Kampwirth 2002.

5. For analysis of the EZLN's negotiations with the government and the paramilitary violence that accompanied those negotiations in the first four years of the public rebellion (1994–98), see Hernández Castillo 1998; Hernández Navarro 1998, 7–10; Kampwirth 1998c, 15–19; Stahler-Sholk 1998, 11–14.

6. On the Zapatistas and civil society, see Harvey 1998, 204–11; Leyva 1998; Marcos 1995c, 51–61, 80–82, 148–49, 215–18, 227, 229–51; Womack 1999, 245–303.

7. On the new man see Leiner 1994, 10, 26–27, 34; for feminist criticism of the new man see I. Rodríguez 1996a, 1996b; Vázquez, Ibáñez, and Murguialday 1996, 61–65.

8. On indigenous people's organizing before the rebellion, also see Benjamin 1996; Burguete 1999; Collier 1994; González and Quintanar 1999; Harvey 1998, 1994; Hernández Cruz 1999; Leyva and Ascencio 1996; Renard 1997.

9. The CEOIC coalition was not to last for long, precisely because it was such a broad coalition, encompassing groups that were openly supportive of the PRI as well as those that supported the demands of the Zapatistas. In June 1994 the CEOIC would split in two, with one part becoming the official CEOIC (that is, allied with the PRI, the official party) and the other maintaining its oppositional stance, eventually renaming itself the State Democratic Assembly of the People of Chiapas (Asamblea Estatal Democrática del Pueblo Chiapaneo) (Gómez Núñez 1999, 193–94; Hernández Arellano 1999, 264).

10. For a list of the autonomous regions and maps identifying their locations, see Lomelí 1999, 257–60; a list is also available in García, López, and Nava 1999, 212.

11. For many years, Amado Avendaño was the editor of a newspaper, *El Tiempo*, that was more critical of the government of Chiapas than any other. He was also a public defender of indigenous rights before he entered politics in 1994 as the gubernatorial candidate of the leftist PRD (Partido de la Revolución Democrática). Openly supported by the Zapatistas, he was seriously injured (and three of his fellow passengers were killed) when his car was hit head-on by an unidentified vehicle, without license plates or local registration, while he was on his way to a campaign event in July 1994. While it is possible that the collision was nothing more than an accident, PRD activists are unusually vulnerable

to accidents involving unmarked cars, leading many to think that it was actually an assassination attempt. Avendaño was not the first such victim of anti-PRD violence in Chiapas: between the beginning of 1994 and March 8, 1996, one hundred activists in the PRD (twenty women and eighty men) were assassinated (CIACH, CONPAZ, and SIPRO 1997, 100).

12. Governing by obeying, a collectivist notion, is the idea that good leaders obey the will of their people.

13. Lidia told me the story of a typical ethnic offense, of a bus trip in which a mestiza woman used her hand to cover the empty seat next to her to keep her, an indigenous woman, from sitting down. She confronted the woman: "'Why?' She said that she was with her son and I said to her, 'But he is already sitting.'" Again, she asked the woman, "'And I can't sit down next to you?'" At that point the mestiza didn't know what to say and Lidia finally sat down. She concluded her story, "That's why we're in the struggle" (interview, February 1995).

Deep-seated and often petty racism of the sort Lidia described was not unusual in Chiapas. Well into the twentieth century indigenous people who walked along the narrow sidewalks of San Cristóbal were expected to jump off those sidewalks if a mestizo crossed their path. As recently as 1995 a dark-skinned taxi driver (who volunteered that he himself was of indigenous descent) ranted at length while I rode in his taxi about the laziness and stupidity of indigenous people, claiming that they would even drink gasoline if told it was good for them.

14. The full text of the accords appears in the book *Chiapas 2* (EZLN/Gobierno Federal 1996).

15. A last-ditch effort to save the talks was attempted by the congressional commission that had participated in the negotiation process: it would write up a document that would address the concerns of both sides and each side would have the option of accepting or rejecting, but not modifying. On November 30 the EZLN accepted the document, despite some serious flaws from the perspective of the rebels. Immediately afterward the same document was presented to the minister of the interior, who also accepted it on behalf of the government but asked for time to show it to President Zedillo, who was out of the country. The president sent it back with a series of "observations" (additions or deletions), which the Zapatistas finally rejected on January 11, 1997, arguing that Zedillo had violated the premise of this round of negotiations, that the two parties could accept or reject, but that neither could claim to accept the agreement while imposing new conditions (Hernández Navarro 1997, 88; the original text that was submitted by the congressional commission and agreed to by both the EZLN and the government, alongside the federal gov-

ernment's subsequent changes, is reprinted in *Chiapas 4* [Cocopa/Ejecutivo 1997, 201–8]). The San Andrés Accords were not voted on until April 2001, after President Zedillo had stepped down and Vicente Fox had taken over as president. But the indigenous rights bill that was passed by the Mexican Congress had been altered in significant ways. Most seriously, from the indigenous rights movement perspective, the promise of autonomy for indigenous communities was greatly watered down from the original agreement. Both the Zapatistas and the National Indigenous Congress rejected that bill as inconsistent with the agreement originally signed in 1995 (López y Rivas 2001; Thompson 2001, A9).

16. On women and autonomy, also see Gutiérrez and Palomo 1999.

17. All quotes in the section on the ANIPA conference were comments made by participants that I recorded in my fieldnotes.

18. I say that militarization was a form of economic violence since the frequency of military checkpoints meant that most indigenous people found it very difficult to leave their villages so as to go to the fields or market. Also, the presence of thousands of soldiers, who were affluent in comparison to the local people, was highly inflationary. Arriving at the market after enduring the humiliation of military checkpoints, people often found that goods were far more expensive than they had been: the soldier's demands drove prices up. Finally, the economic freedom of women was even more restricted than that of men. After three Tzeltal sisters were gang-raped at a military checkpoint in 1994, many women were afraid to leave their villages, even if it meant making do with very little at home.

19. This claim, that many pretend that indigenous Mexicans do not exist, is not exaggerated. If one's only experience of Mexico were that of television, it would be logical to assume that Mexico is a European country. One evening in February 1995, I watched several hours of soap operas (all produced in Mexico) and found that the characters were all wealthy and light skinned, with the sole exception of one indigenous character, a maid, who provided comic relief in an otherwise dramatic program. At the end of that evening of soap operas, Jacobo Zabludovsky, the European featured host of the top-rated news program, *Veinticuatro horas,* came on to report the PRI's perspective on the news (on Zabludovsky, see Preston 1998c, A3).

20. According to an activist in the Independent Front of Indigenous People (Frente Independiente de los Pueblos Indígenas, or FIPI), 70 percent of the independent indigenous organizations were in ANIPA (interview, July 3, 1997).

21. Alison Brysk discusses a similar problem with transnational Indian rights organizing, noting that though "Indian leaders and organizations have acquired similar skills and capacities in a short period, they still lag behind

almost all other movements." For those who would play the role of the "supportive outsiders," she suggests that they "avoid becoming interlocutors between the tribal village and the state," and work toward increasing the capacity of indigenous leaders to act independently through "training to build the capacity for future community control," including training in "communications technology, and media strategies" (2000, 295–96).

22. While the Zedillo administration had threatened to arrest Zapatistas who left the state of Chiapas, it did not have the legal right to place a blockade on the EZLN: within the framework of the 1995 legislation that set out the terms for the peace process—the Law for Dialogue, Conciliation, and Peace with Dignity in Chiapas—the Zapatistas should have been permitted to participate in peaceful politics in Mexico City without being threatened with arrest. The legislation set out the goals of promoting opportunities for members of the EZLN to "participate in poltical actions within the peaceful channels that are offered by the state of law, with absolute respect for their dignity and guarantees as Mexican citizens" (quoted in Hernández Navarro 1997, 86).

23. In Mexico City, Ramona finally had access to the health care that was unavailable in her jungle community. There she got the kidney transplant she so desperately needed, and her health improved (National Commission 1996a, 1).

24. On December 22, 1997, members of a paramilitary organization with links to the ruling party, the PRI, killed forty-five unarmed people in the highland town of Acteal. Anti-Zapatista paramilitary organizations have been active in indigenous Chiapas since at least 1995, killing individuals who either supported the EZLN or who refused to side with either the PRI or the EZLN (as was the case for the people killed in Acteal, most of whom belonged to an organization known as the Bees). What was new was that members of the paramilitary organizations had not previously killed so many people at one time. Because of its brutality, the Acteal massacre attracted the attention of the international press, reminding outsiders that the war between the Zapatista's supporters and the PRI's supporters was hardly over by 1997, despite what were already years of intermittent peace talks. On Acteal and its implications, see Aubry and Inda 1998; Hernández Castillo 1998; Hernández Navarro 1998; Kampwirth 1998c; Stahler-Sholk 1998.

25. The carrot-and-stick metaphor draws on horse training techniques. One may tame a horse through the offer of rewards (carrots), punishments (sticks), or some combination of the two. It is a good metaphor for politics in general, but not for democratic politics: even those who rely on carrots rather than sticks use the carrots to bend the horse to the will of the trainer. The idea is to not let the horse make her own choices.

26. On Mexican clientelism also see Fox 1994b; Hellman 1994a, 1994b.

27. For a vivid and detailed discussion of the PRI's use of clientelism in the 2000 presidential campaign, see Dillon 2000, 1A. But despite those efforts, in 2000, for the first time in more than seven decades, the PRI failed to win the presidential election. The PRI lost the presidency due to a combination of significant electoral reforms passed under the outgoing administration of Ernesto Zedillo (that greatly reduced the possibilities of fraud), combined with the increasing ineffectiveness of clientelism among younger and educated Mexicans. The PRI's Francisco Labastida would have won the 2000 election had the PRI been able to exclude voters younger than forty or those with at least a high school education (*New York Times* 2000, A6). In many predominantly indigenous and poor states, like Chiapas, the PRI did quite well in 2000, despite the new electoral laws, winning eleven of twelve seats in the National Congress (Cuéllar and Urrutia 2000).

28. During a visit to Chiapas in June 1997, President Ernesto Zedillo promised one billion, one hundred and eighty million pesos for "social development" in the state, the greatest amount that had ever been promised to any state for poverty alleviation (Gallegos 1997, 3). These federal funds, along with the efforts of national and international NGOs, had a measureable effect: while in 1989 "Chiapas registered a 33 percent rate of moderate to severe malnutrition, a 1997 study showed that malnutrition had fallen to 20 percent" (Cruz 1997, 41).

29. The groups that ran the workshop were: the Women's Group of San Cristóbal (Grupo de Mujeres de San Cristóbal), the Organization of Indigenous Doctors of the State of Chiapas (Organización de Médicos Indígenas del Estado de Chiapas, or OMIECH), the J'Pas Joloviletik Artesan's Union (Unión de Artesanas J'Pas Joloviletik), and the women's commission of CONPAZ (Comisión de Mujeres de CONPAZ), a coalition of NGOs that were active in promoting indigenous rights.

30. The IMSS (Instituto Mexicano de Seguridad Social) is the Mexican social security institute, while Solidaridad was a social welfare program instituted by the administration of Carlos Salinas de Gortari.

31. From the EZLN perspective, the political demands were of greater importance than the economic and social demands because the long-term viability of economic and social gains depended on political gains. Without democracy, economic promises could be taken away as easily as they were given; with effective democracy, politicians could be held accountable for their economic promises.

32. An alternative acronym Aedepch (which reflects the pronounciation better than the official acronym, AEDPCH) is used in the Zapatista communiqué.

33. While my formal interviews were with women, I often found myself conducting unplanned interviews with men. In part, that was because nearly all the indigenous organizations were led by men, and I often had difficulty getting the names of women to interview without first seeking the permission of the male heads of the organizations. Moreover, men were the ones most likely to be fluent in Spanish. It was striking to me that, while male indigenous activists were happy to tell me about their support for the Zapatistas, women who belonged to the same organizations were far more reticent. In one case, women in an artesan's cooperative (that I had heard was run by the EZLN) told me they knew nothing about the Zapatistas but then asked me to wait for their men. I asked the men the same questions and was told, as I had thought, that the cooperative was a Zapatista cooperative. While I learned a number of things from these informal interviews with men, I did not count them among the interviews that tallied in the introduction.

34. One supporter of the decision to negotiate with the government was clearly scarred by the experience. Four years after the fact he was still angry at the way others had responded: "For the popular sector and those middle-class intellectuals—the so-called NGOs—to be 'autonomous' meant to have no relations of any sort with the government, although many of them were professors or university researchers . . . and they received salaries paid for by a government institution. But they never questioned that . . . [instead] they forcefully questioned the decision . . . to sit down to negotiate with the federal government. Those negotiating groups were to find a way to resolve the hundreds of requests that the 'government in transition' had accumulated . . . the 'rebel government' did not have the capacity to meet those demands since, as was obvious, it was a symbolic government" (Gómez Núñez 1999, 199). But the strongest condemnation of their choice to negotiate came not from the NGO sector or the members of the Rebel Government, but from the EZLN. Gómez Núñez found the EZLN's condemnation of AEDPCH's decision to negotiate hard to understand, "given that the EZLN itself had sat down to negotiate with the government from February to March 1994. . . . Apparently, the top leaders of the EZLN, and their advisers, were bothered that we autonomous organizations, from our birth have always had a will of our own" (200).

35. A list of those groups appears in Gómez Nuñez 1999, 203n105.

36. The Acteal massacre was hardly the first incidence of paramilitary violence. In fact it differed from previous incidences mainly in that so many people were killed at once. Until that point murders in the highlands were more selective: one or two or three every few days. The attorney general of the state of Chiapas estimated that approximately five hundred people died in paramilitary-related violence in 1997 alone (Mariscal 1997b).

37. A study conducted in 2000 found that fifteen groups of armed civilians operated in the state of Chiapas. Ten of those groups were paramilitary groups while the others were groups of armed civilians, without obvious links to the military and the PRI (Elizalde 2000). For an excellent analysis of four years of low-intensity warfare in Chiapas, see Castro Apreza 1999.

38. "Effective suffrage, no reelection" was the slogan that informed the first phase of the Mexican revolution of 1910, when Francisco Madero sought to reform politics after four decades of dictatorial rule by José Porfirio Díaz. The party that was founded through the revolution, the PRI, stuck to the letter of the law—presidents would never serve more than one six-year term—though one could debate whether the party (which ruled over national politics for more than seventy years without interruption) truly stuck to the spirit of the law.

39. It would be problematic to use Marcos as my only source (since he has a vested interest in portraying Zapatista communities as highly democratic), but Marcos's description of women's lives within Zapatista communities is quite consistent with what I heard during my interviews from both sympathizers and critics of the Zapatistas (including one government official).

40. Marcos is probably referring to the Revolutionary Women's Law.

41. In April 2000, I returned to Chiapas, expecting to find that support for the EZLN had fallen, given that the state was more militarized than it had been during my previous visit, in 1997, and that, I presumed, life had become more difficult for Zapatista supporters. To my surprise, none of the people I interviewed agreed with that hypothesis. To the contrary, from what they had seen the EZLN had gained more supporters than it had lost. One reason may have been that the EZLN had made efforts to recruit in new communities. Another was that it was much easier to seize land in areas controlled by the EZLN than in areas controlled by the PRI. While the PRI could offer an array of clientelistic benefits, those projects tended to run out eventually, while land was far more permanent.

One woman who had done development work in indigenous communities for decades told me that in 1994 and 1995 the people she knew seemed to be passing through very hard times; the pressures of war meant that they were not able to feed or clothe themselves or their children as before. But after 1995 many of them looked better, often even better than before 1994. While they were hardly rich, many were surviving fine, suggesting that they could wait out more years of war. A final reason many women supported the rebels was because if their men supported the EZLN, they felt obliged to let them attend Zapatista affiliated gatherings and conventions. The chance to visit new places, in some cases including the ocean, and to be treated with respect and affection when they arrived was identified by many women as an improvement in their lives.

Chapter 5

1. A world systemic opening is a situation in which the superpower or superpowers choose not to intervene militarily or politically in other countries, or at least not to do so as quickly as in the past.

2. By referring to feminism within the Iranian revolution as "softly veiled," I do not wish to understate its significance or the courage of its proponents. Indeed, feminist demands had to be veiled in a religious discourse if they were to made at all. The extent to which some women made them in the nineties was truly impressive, given the hostility to gender equality that had informed the revolution. For instance, the journal *Zanan* (Women), founded in 1991, was an amalgam of what might be called feminine features (on topics like food, health, food, diet, fashion, exercise, and medicine) along with explicitly feminist features, including essays by foreign feminists like Virginia Woolf, Charlotte Perkins Gilman, Mary Wollstonecraft, Evelyn Reed, Alison Jaggar, Nadine Gordimer, and Susan Faludi, reviews of literary work by Iranian women, and sociological studies. A major feature of the journal was a systematic review of scripture from a feminist perspective which, ironically, might not have been possible without the revolution. Over the course of the eighties and nineties many women were trained as theologians and so they were well prepared to make carefully documented arguments that other theologians were forced to take seriously (Afary 1996, 45–46; 1997, 104–8).

3. In Nicaragua, Honduras, and Peru women gained the right to vote in 1955, followed in last place by Paraguay, where women received voting rights in 1961 (Valdés and Gomáriz 1995, 139).

4. I use the term *authoritarian socialism* more often than *communism* (which I take to be synonymous in the Eastern European context) because it more accurately describes life in mid-twentieth-century Poland by distinguishing between the political and the economic aspects of that life. Also, I think the term *authoritarian socialism* highlights the similarities between Poland and other countries that have experienced revolutions. While the overthrow of communist states had never before occurred, many authoritarian governments have been overthrown by mass movements. As in those previous cases, it seems that the Polish regime was overthrown because it was authoritarian, not because it was socialist, a fact that the term *communism* may obscure.

5. The widely held belief that communism in Poland was imposed from the outside was strongly grounded in historical fact. In February 1945 leaders of the three most powerful allied powers—the United States, Britain, and the Soviet Union—met in the Soviet town of Yalta to plan the end to the war and to decide how to divide up Europe once the war was over. The agreement they reached

placed Poland (along with most of the other Central and Eastern European countries) in the Soviet sphere of influence; the Polish map was even redrawn (gaining a hundred miles in the west and losing those miles in the east) to suit the interests of outsiders. Before the forties had come to a close, Polish economics and politics were remade in the image of the Soviet Union (D. S. Mason 1992). Authoritarian socialism in Poland, despite its rhetorical claims to be revolutionary, was hardly the result of a revolution. Instead, it was something akin to a colonial imposition.

6. That the women's section of Solidarity was founded with the encouragement and money of foreigners is another parallel with the Latin American cases, where interest in women's programs within male-dominated revolutionary organizations increased dramatically when foreigners expressed an interest in funding such programs.

7. While that bill did not pass, restrictions were placed on access to abortion in 1990, requiring that a written application for permission to have an abortion be approved by two gynecologists, an internist, and a psychologist. According to a 1993 revision of the abortion law, threats to the pregnant woman's life could be taken into account, but the specialists did not have to save the woman's life by permitting the abortion. In response to the tightening of restrictions on Polish women's previous access to legal abortion, supporters of abortion rights collected one and a half million signatures demanding a referendum on the abortion issue. While politicians refused to permit a popular vote on the issue, a 1996 revision of the abortion law loosened restrictions somewhat, permitting some abortions (with doctor's approval) before the twelfth week of pregnancy if having a child would present a hardship (Novak 1999, 26–29, 46).

8. Zoilamérica Narváez's accusations that her stepfather, top Sandinista Daniel Ortega, raped her is one case when death threats were made (against her and her feminist supporters; see chapter 2). But the threats came too late in the development of the movement; a decade earlier the feminist movement might have subdued by such threats, but by the late nineties the movement was too well institutionalized to be easily eliminated.

9. In a revision of her 1997 article, Moghadam discusses issues that are related to my sixth factor. She notes that the recent growth of transnational feminist networks shapes the context in which revolutionary movements emerge; contemporary revolutionary movements are likely to be more feminist than such movements were in the past. This is not to say that radical antifeminist movements cannot emerge, but transnational feminist networks can make it difficult for them to govern. For example, "The international isolation of the Taliban is a success story of the global feminist movement" (Moghadam 2003, 165).

10. Catholic Church leaders have consistently lobbied against using the word *gender* in international documents, in favor of the word *sex*, demonstrating that they understand basic feminist theory. For a feminist theorist, gender roles are socially constructed, while sex roles are biological. The fact that women are typically responsible for the care of children of all ages is a gender role (which could be changed). In contrast, sex roles are roles that are truly biological, like the fact that women get pregnant, give birth, and nurse infants. If Church leaders accepted the widespread use of the word *gender*, they would be admitting that there is nothing natural about most inequality between men and women and that in turn might require efforts to promote gender equality.

11. In 1999 the average life expectancy in Cuba was almost seventy-six, while the average life expectancy in Russia was slightly over sixty-five. Infant mortality rates also illustrated the differences in access to health care: the 1999 infant mortality rate was 7.81 deaths per thousand live births in Cuba; 23 per thousand in Russia. For comparison, in the United States in 1999 the average life expectancy was 76.23 years while the infant mortality rate was 6.33 deaths per thousand live births.

Cuba's health indicators, approaching those of First World countries, were particularly notable, given that Cuba remained poor at the end of the twentieth century. While per capita income in the United States was $31,500 in 1999, that of Russia was $4,000, and of Cuba only $1,560. Figures such as these suggest that health is a function of government priorities and distribution of basic necessities (like good nutrition), much more than overall societal wealth (*CIA World Factbook*, http://www.odci.gov/cia/ publications/factbook).

12. One of the many paradoxes of the Cuban revolution is that major gains for women, as measured in statistical terms, have been accompanied by minuscule changes at the level of private life. Why private life has not changed more despite forty some years of revolution in the public sphere is a question worth investigating (Teresa Walsh, personal communication, October 17, 1998).

13. One creative way in which the FMC dealt with its ambivalent status— neither a government agency nor an independent NGO—was by claiming to be both. At the United Nations Women's Conference in Beijing, the FMC participated in both the governmental and the nongovernmental meetings (Lutjens 1997, 32).

14. Knowing that a natural tendency is for people to say what they think the questioner wants to hear, I had purposely set up the question to make it as easy as possible for her to say that the FMC disagreed with the party at times, by saying that disagreement was normal. Although I set up the question in that way, she could not bring herself to say anything negative about the party or even about an individual bureaucrat.

15. On the position of gays through the early nineties, see Leiner 1994, 21–59.

16. Popular Power (Poder Popular) was a system of representative government, institutionalized in the seventies, in which people voted for representatives at the neighborhood level (choosing from between two to seven candidates, some of whom represented them in Cuba's National Assembly). For a discussion and critique of Popular Power, see Bengelsdorf 1994, 107–33, 155–65.

17. It is difficult to be sure if, for theoretical purposes, the old regime should be that of Batista or Castro. In all the other cases I considered the old regime to be the one overthrown by the revolutionary coalition. If I applied the same logic here, that would be the government of the Batista era. Yet in all the other cases, the period I was examining was the period fairly immediately following the overthrow of the old dictatorship. In the case of Cuba, that period would the sixties, maybe including the seventies, but certainly not the early twenty-first century. At some point, the memory of the old dictatorship fades so much that it no longer counts as the old regime; given that the majority of Cubans were born during the revolution, I think that point has come. Those people, born with the revolution, will remember the Castro years the same way that young and middle-aged Poles remember the years of the authoritarian-socialist government in their country. As in Poland, the nature of those memories will shape their opinions of women's emancipation.

18. Of course, *patriarchal feminism* is a term laden with contradictions. The term is problematic because the leaders of the Cuban women's movement typically rejected the term *feminism* and also because feminism is a project of opposition to patriarchal domination, a project that seemingly may not be prefaced with the word *patriarchal.* From one perspective patriarchal feminism is the equivalent of antipatriarchal patriarchy, which makes little or no sense. And yet, from another perspective, the term aptly describes a project of women's emancipation that was promoted from the summit of power, apparently by a single man.

19. It is much more likely that Cuba will follow the path of Poland than that of Iran, given the far greater religious and cultural distance between Cuba and Iran than between Cuba and Poland, although with regard to the personalized nature of women's emancipation (promoted by the shahs in Iran and Fidel in Cuba), Cuba had more in common with Iran than Poland.

20. The fact that the Cuban revolution came to power through a nationalistic revolution does not absolutely preclude the possibility that Cubans would choose to reject the revolution or some aspects of the revolution: "As in Cuba, communism resulted in the Soviet Union after a national revolution; yet the overwhelming rejection of the dicatorship was evident in the political transition in the U.S.S.R." (López 1999, 1).

21. Four representatives of the FMC attended the 1987 encuentro in Taxco (Mexico), and Cuban women also attended the following encuentro, in 1990 in San Bernardo (Argentina), though not the following one, held in 1993 in San Salvador. At San Bernardo some considered holding the following encuentro in Cuba but were told by one of the Cubans that it would be "impossible" to meet there (Lutjens 1997, 32; Sternbach et al. 1992, 224, 231, 234).

22. The influence that those international meetings sometimes had was illustrated for me when I asked Odessa, the regional FMC director, about the federation's future plans. The first thing she did was to pull out a brochure entitled "National Action Plan for Follow-up to the Beijing Conference—Republic of Cuba"; she then showed how she had followed the guidelines that emerged from that international feminist conference as a framework for her own local planning (interview, October 21, 1998).

23. The organizations that received *La Boletina* were the women's studies program in the faculty of psychology at the University of Havana (Cátedra de la Mujer—Facultad de Psicología), the American office of the International Federation of Democratic Women (FDIM—Oficina Regional para América), two different Provincial Centers for Health Promotion and Education (Centro Provincial de Promoción y Educación para la Salud), the National Center for Health Promotion and Education (Centro Nacional de Promoción y Educación para la Salud), the Federation of Cuban Women (Federación de Mujeres Cubanas, or FMC), the Ministry of Education (Ministerio de Educación—MINED-ICCP), two different offices of the Cuban Radio and Television Institute (Instituto Cubano de Radio y Televisión), and an organization known by the acronym ETIAH (Ana Leonor Paíz, personal communication, September 28, 1999).

Bibliography

Acevedo, Angela Rosa, et al. 1996. *Los derechos de las mujeres en Nicaragua: Un análisis de género.* Managua: Imprimatur Artes Gráficas.

Acevedo García, Marina. 1995. "Margaritas: Una experiencia de frontera." In *Chiapas: Una modernidad inconclusa,* ed. Diana Guillén, 148–92. Mexico City: Instituto Mora.

Adam, Barry. 1993. "Nicaragua: Homosexuality without a Gay World." *Journal of Homosexuality* 24, nos. 3–4: 171–81.

Afary, Janet. 1996. "Steering between Scylla and Charybdis: Shifting Gender Roles in Twentieth-Century Iran." *NWSA Journal* 8, no. 1 (Spring): 28–49.

———. 1997. "The War against Feminism in the Name of the Almighty: Making Sense of Gender and Muslim Fundamentalism." *New Left Review* 224 (July–August): 89–110.

Afshar, Haleh. 1985. "Women, State, and Ideology in Iran." *Third World Quarterly* 7, no. 2 (April): 256–78.

Alfonso, Pablo. 1985. *Cuba, Castro, y los Católicos: Del humanismo revolucionario al marxismo totalitario.* Miami: Ediciones Hispamerican Books.

Alvarez, Sonia. 1990. *Engendering Democracy in Brazil: Women's Movements in Transition Politics.* Princeton: Princeton University Press.

———. 1998. "Latin American Feminisms 'Go Global': Trends of the 1990s and Challenges for the New Millennium." In *Cultures of Politics, Politics of Cultures: Re-Visioning Latin American Social Movements,* ed. Sonia Alvarez, Evelina Dagnino, and Arturo Escobar, 293–324. Boulder: Westview.

Alvarez, Sonia, Evelina Dagnino, and Arturo Escobar, eds. 1998. *Cultures of Politics, Politics of Cultures: Re-Visioning Latin American Social Movements.* Boulder: Westview.

AMES (Asociación de Mujeres de El Salvador). 1981. "Participación de la mujer latinoamericana en las organizaciones sociales y políticas: Reflexiones de las mujeres salvadoreñas." Paper presented at the Primer Seminario Latinoamericano de Investigación sobre la Mujer, San José, Costa Rica (November 8–14). Available from the Women's International Resource Exchange Service (WIRE), 2700 Broadway, New York, NY, 10025.

AMNLAE (Asociación de Mujeres Nicaragüenses Luisa Amanda Espinoza). 1990. "Propuesta de AMNLAE a la Constitución." Reprinted in Clara Murguialday, *Nicaragua, Revolución, y Feminismo, 1977–89.* Madrid: Editorial Revolución.

Anderson, Thomas P. 1971. *Matanza: El Salvador's Communist Revolt of 1932.* Lincoln: University of Nebraska Press.

ANIPA (Asamblea Nacional Indígena Plural por la Autonomía). n.d. *Proyecto de iniciativa para la creación de las regiones autónomas.* N.p. Booklet.

Arana, Mario. 1997. "General Economic Policy." In *Nicaragua without Illusions: Regime Transition and Structural Adjustment in the 1990s,* ed. Thomas Walker, 81–96. Wilmington, Del.: Scholarly Resources.

Arjomand, Said Amir. 1986. "Iran's Islamic Revolution in Comparative Perspective." *World Politics* 38, no. 3 (April): 383–414.

Asociación de Madres Demandantes por la Cuota Alimenticia, IMU, Dignas, and MAM. 1996. *La Prensa Gráfica* (San Salvador), paid advertisement, June 27.

Aubrey, Andrés, and Angélica Inda. 1997. "¿Quienes son los 'paramilitares'?" *La Jornada,* December 23. http://www.jornada.unam.mx

———. 1998. "Who Are the Paramilitaries in Chiapas?" *NACLA Report on the Americas* (North American Congress on Latin America) 31, no. 5 (March/April): 8–9. Translation of Aubrey and Ina 1997.

Babb, Florence. 2001. *After the Revolution: Mapping Gender and Cultural Politics in Neoliberal Nicaragua.* Austin: University of Texas Press.

Barnes, William. 1998. "Incomplete Democracy in Central America: Polarization and Voter Turnout in Nicaragua and El Salvador." *Journal of Interamerican Studies and World Affairs* 40, no. 3 (Fall): 63–101.

Barricada. 1992. "Más Cambio para Managua: agua potable, alcantarillado, pupitres." Paid advertisement, October 21, 2B.

———. 1995. "La señora Chamorro debe una disculpa. April 26.

Barricada internacional. 1996a. "Finding Common Ground to Build On: National Women's Coalition." Vol. 16, no. 394 (March): 19–20.

———. 1996b. "Sharing Out the Spoils: Alemán Names His Cabinet." Vol. 16, no. 403 (December): 6–7

———. 1990. "Results of the February 25, 1990 elections." March 10.

Barrig, Maruja. 1998. "Female Leadership, Violence, and Citizenship in Peru." In *Women and Democracy: Latin America and Central and Eastern Europe,* ed. Jane Jaquette and Sharon Wolchik, 104–24. Baltimore: Johns Hopkins University Press.

Barrios Ruiz, Walda, and Leticia Pons Bonals. 1995. *Sexualidad y religión en los altos de Chiapas.* Tuxtla Gutiérrez: Universidad Autónoma de Chiapas.

Barton, Christopher P. 1988. "The Paradox of a Revolutionary Constitution: A Reading of the Nicaraguan Constitution." *Hastings International and Comparative Review* 12, no. 1 (Fall).

Bayard de Volo, Lorraine. 2001. *Mothers of Heroes and Martyrs: Gender Identity Politics in Nicaragua, 1979–1999.* Baltimore: Johns Hopkins University Press.

Becarril, Andrea. 2000. "Fallido intento para desconocer el triunfo de Salazar." *La Jornada,* August 21.

Becerra, Ricardo, Pedro Salazar, and José Woldenburg. 1997. *La reforma electoral de 1996: Una descripción general.* Mexico City: Colección Popular, Fondo de Cultura Económica.

Belli, Gioconda. 1998. "En el escándulo NO está el pecado: Continuación de entrevista a Zoilamérica Narváez." *El Nuevo Diario,* September 22: C1–2.

Bellinghausen, Hermann. 1997. "Buscarán ONG nuevas vías para la paz en chiapas: Hace Hugo Trujillo, de Conpaz, un balance autocrítico de esa organización." *La Jornada,* November 26.

Bendaña, Alejandro. 1991. *Una tragedia campesina: Testimonios de la resistencia.* Managua: COMPANIC.

Bengelsdorf, Carollee. 1994. *The Problem of Democracy in Cuba: Between Vision and Reality.* New York: Oxford University Press.

Benjamin, Thomas. 1996. *A Rich Land, a Poor People: Politics and Society in Modern Chiapas.* Albuquerque: University of New Mexico Press.

Berkin, Carol R., and Clara M. Lovett, eds. 1980. *Women, War, and Revolution.* New York: Holmes and Meier.

Blachman, Morris, and Kenneth Sharpe. 1992. "The Transition to 'Electoral' and Democratic Politics in Central America: Assessing the Role of Political Parties." In *Political Parties and Democracy in Central America,* ed. Louis Goodman, William LeoGrande, and Johanna Forman. Boulder: Westview.

Blandón, María Teresa, ed. 1994. *Memorias del Sexto encuentro feminista latinoamericano y del Caribe.* Managua: Imprenta UCA.

———. 2001. "The Coalición Nacional de Mujeres: An Alliance of Left-Wing Women, Right-Wing Women, and Radical Feminists in Nicaragua." In

Radical Women in Latin America: Left and Right, ed. Victoria González and Karen Kampwirth. University Park: Penn State University Press.

Boff, Leonardo. 1985. *Church, Charism, and Power: Liberation Theology and the Institutional Church.* New York: Crossroad.

Boletina, La. 1991. "Desempleo de las obreras industriales en Managua." No. 2 (September–October): 17–18.

———. 1992. "Un aporte de Puntos de Encuentro a la comunicación entre mujeres." No. 5 (March–April).

———. 1993. No. 10 (January).

———. 1996a. No. 25 (March).

———. 1996b. No 28 (October–December).

———. 1997a. "Ministerio de la Familia: No todo lo que brilla es oro!" No. 31 (July–August): 20–30.

———. 1997b. "Los puntos en agenda del 'Ministro de la Familia.'" No. 30 (April–June): 12–19.

———. 1998. "Con mujeres salvadoreñas: Para que inventar la pólvora si ya existe *La Boletina!*" No. 35 (May–July): 71–72.

———. 1999. Letter to the editor from Bárbara Rojas Echeverría, Holguín, Cuba. No. 39 (April–June): 89.

———. 2000. "Comisarías de la Mujer en peligro de extinción." No. 41 (January): 36–39. "Puntos de Encuentro," Managua.

Bolt González, Mary. 1996. *Sencillamente diferentes: La autoestima de las mujeres lesbianas en los sectores urbanos de Nicaragua.* Managua: Centro Editorial de la Mujer (CEM).

Booth, John. 1985. *The End and the Beginning: The Nicaraguan Revolution.* Boulder: Westview.

Booth, John, and Thomas W. Walker. 1989. *Understanding Central America.* Boulder: Westview

Borge, Tomás. 1984. *Carlos, the Dawn Is No Longer beyond Our Reach: The Prison Journals of Tomas Borge Remembering Carlos Fonseca, Founder of the FSLN.* Vancouver: New Star Books.

Bossert, Thomas John. 1985. "Health Policy: The Dilemma of Success." In *Nicaragua: The First Five Years,* ed. Thomas Walker. New York: Praeger.

Brandt, Deborah. 1985. "Popular Education." In *Nicaragua: The First Five Years,* ed. Thomas Walker. New York: Praeger.

Braslavsky, Cecilia. 1992. "Educational Legitimation of Women's Economic Subordination in Brazil." In *Women and Education in Latin America:*

Knowledge, Power, and Change, ed. Nelly Stomquist. Boulder: Lynne Rienner.

Brenes, Ada Julia, Ivania Lovo, Olga Luz Restrepo, Sylvia Saakes, and Flor de María Zúniga, eds. 1991. *La mujer nicaragüense en los años ochenta.* Managua: Ediciones Nicarao.

Brown, Timothy. 2001. *The Real Contra War: Highlander Peasant Resistence in Nicaragua.* Norman: University of Oklahoma Press.

Brysk, Alison. 2000. *From Tribal Village to Global Village: Indian Rights and International Relations in Latin America.* Stanford: Stanford University Press.

Buckley, Mary. 1989. "The 'Woman Question' in the Contemporary Soviet Union." In *Promissory Notes: Women in the Transition to Socialism,* ed. Sonia Kruks, Rayna Rapp, and Marilyn B. Young, 251–81. New York: Monthly Review Press.

Bunster-Burotto, Ximena. 1986. "Surviving beyond Fear: Women and Torture in Latin America." In *Women and Change in Latin America,* ed. June Nash and Helen Safa, 297–325. South Hadley, Mass.: Bergin and Garvey Press.

Burbach, Roger. 1986. "The Conflict at Home and Abroad: U.S. Imperialism vs. the New Revolutionary Societies." In *Transition and Development: Problems of Third World Socialism,* ed. Richard Fagen, Carmen Diana Deere, and José Luis Coraggio. New York: Monthly Review Press.

Burdick, John. 1992. "Rethinking the Study of Social Movements: The Case of Christian Base Communities in Urban Brazil." In *The Making of Social Movements in Latin America: Identity, Strategy, and Democracy,* ed. Arturo Escobar and Sonia Alvarez, 171–84. Boulder: Westview.

Burguete Cal y Mayor, Aracely. 1999. "Empoderamiento indígena tendencias autonómicas en la región altos de Chiapas." In *México: Experiencias de autonomía indígena,* ed. Aracely Burguete Cal y Mayor. Copenhagen: Grupo Internacional de Trabajo sobre Asuntos Indígenas (IWGIA).

Byrne, Hugh. 1996. *El Salvador's Civil War: A Study of Revolution.* Boulder: Lynne Rienner.

Cabezas, Omar. 1985. *Fire from the Mountain: The Making of a Sandinista.* New York: Plume.

Castañeda, Jorge G. 1994. *Utopia Unarmed: The Latin American Left after the Cold War.* New York: Vintage.

———. 1995. *The Mexican Shock.* New York: New Press.

Castro, Daniel. 1999a. "The Iron Legions." In *Revolution and Revolutionaries: Guerrilla Movements in Latin America,* ed. Daniel Castro, 191–99. Wilmington, Del.: Scholarly Resources.

————, ed. 1999b. *Revolution and Revolutionaries: Guerrilla Movements in Latin America.* Wilmington, Del.: Scholarly Resources.

Castro, Yolanda, and Nellys Palomo. 1995. "Roban la tienda de artesanías de la organización J'Pas Joloviletik." Letter to *La Jornada,* December 1: 71.

Castro Apreza, Inés. 1999. "Quitarle el agua al pez: La guerra de baja intensidad en Chiapas (1994–1998)." In *Chiapas 8,* ed. Neus Espreste, 123–41. Mexico City: Ediciones Era.

CCRI (Comité Clandestino Revolucionario Indígena). 1995a. "Da a conocer propuestas del EZLN: Explica el EZLN por qué se requiere otra constitución y un gobierno de transición." In *Los hombres sin rostro II,* ed. Mario Monroy and Carlos Zarco, 107–10. Mexico City: Impretei. Original communique dated July 27, 1994.

————. 1995b. "EZLN: 'No' a la propuesta de firmar los acuerdos." In *Los hombres sin rostro II,* ed. Mario Monroy and Carlos Zarco, 78–82. Mexico City: Impretei. Original communique dated June 10, 1994.

————. 1996. "Llama el EZLN a crear un frente político nacional." *La Jornada,* January 2.

Ceceña, Ana Esther, José Zaragoza, and Equipo Chiapas. 1995. "Cronología del Conflicto: 1 enero—1 diciembre 1994." In *Chiapas 1,* ed. Neus Espresate, 149–79. Mexico City: Ediciones Era.

CEMUJER (Centro de Estudios de la Mujer "Norma Virginia Guirola de Herrera"). 1992. *Norma: Vida insurgente y feminista.* San Salvador: Talleres Gráficos UCA.

Chamorro, Edgar. 1987. *Packaging the Contras: A Case of CIA Disinformation.* Monograph Series, no. 2. New York: Institute for Media Analysis.

Chinchilla, Norma. 1990. "Revolutionary Popular Feminism in Nicaragua: Articulating Class, Gender, and National Sovereignty." *Gender and Society* 4, no. 3 (September).

————. 1993. "Women's Movements in the Americas: Feminism's Second Wave." *NACLA Report on the Americas* 27, no. 1 (July–August).

————. 1994. "Feminism, Revolution, and Democratic Transitions in Nicaragua." In *The Women's Movement in Latin America,* ed. Jane Jaquette. Boulder: Westview.

————. 1997. "Nationalism, Feminism, and Revolution in Central America." In *Feminist Nationalism,* ed. Lois West, 201–19. New York: Routledge.

Christian, Shirley. 1986. *Nicaragua: Revolution in the Family.* New York: Vintage Books.

CIACH (Centro de Información y Análisis de Chiapas). 1997a. "The Attempt on the Life of Bishop Samuel Ruiz and the Effects of Polarization in Chiapas." *La Opinión,* bulletin no. 80: 1–5.

———. 1997b. "The Covert War Waged by Gunmen, White Guards, and Paramilitary Forces." *La Opinión,* bulletin no. 79 (November 11): 1–6.

CIACH, CONPAZ (Coordinación de Organismos No Gubernamentales por la Paz), and SIPRO (Servicios Informativos Procesados). 1997. *Para entender Chiapas: Chiapas en cifras.* Mexico City: Impretei.

CIEM (Centro de Investigación y Estudios Municipales). 1989. "Encuestas al sector comerciantes y al sector juvenil en la tercera región: Resultados, referidos a la población femenina)." Unpublished document, Managua(?), in author's possession.

Cochran, Augustus B., and Catherine V. Scott. 1992. "Class, State, and Popular Organizations in Mozambique and Nicaragua." *Latin American Perspectives* 19, no. 2, issue 73 (Spring).

Cock, Jacklyn. 1994. "Women and the Military: Implications for Demilitarization in the 1990s in South Africa." *Gender and Society* 8, no. 2 (June): 152–69.

Cocopa/Ejecutivo. 1997. "Balance comparativo entre la propuesta de reformas constitucionales presentada por la Cocopa y las observaciones del Ejecutivo." In *Chiapas 4,* ed. Neus Espresate, 201–8. Mexico City: Ediciones Era.

Codina, Teresa. 1992. "Lesbos en el nuevo mundo." *Pensamiento propio* 10: 2–4.

Colburn, Forrest. 1994. *The Vogue of Revolution in Poor Countries.* Princeton: Princeton University Press.

Collier, George. 1994. *Basta! Land and the Zapatista Rebellion in Chiapas.* San Francisco: Food First Books.

———. 2000. "Zapatismo Resurgent: Land and Autonomy in Chiapas." *NACLA Report on the Americas* 33, no. 5 (March–April): 20–25, 47.

Collinson, Helen, ed. 1990. *Women and Revolution in Nicaragua.* Atlantic Highlands, N.J.: Zed Books.

Comisaría de la Mujer y la Niñez. n.d. "Mujer: Niña: Niño: Vos tenés derecho al respeto." Unpublished document, Managua, in author's possession.

Comité Nacional Feminista. 1994. "Aquelarre." Unpublished manuscript, Managua, in author's possession.

Concha, Miguel. 1996. "El derecho a defender." *La Jornada,* December 14.

CONPAZ (Coordinación de Organismos No Gubermentales por la Paz). 1994. *La guacamaya,* no. 1 (February).

Conroy, Michael. 1986. "U.S. Economic Policy as Economic Aggression." In *Nicaragua, Unfinished Revolution: The New Nicaragua Reader,* ed. Peter Rosset and John Vandermeer. New York: Grove Press.

COOPIBO-Nicaragua. 1995. *Seminario, "Fortalecimiento de la organizacion de mujeres rurales" memorias.* Managua: Imprenta Universitaria (UCA).

Crahan, Margaret. 1987. "Religion and Revolution: Cuba and Nicaragua." Working paper no. 174, Latin American Program, Wilson Center, Smithsonian Institution, Washington D.C.

Creatividad Feminista. 2000. "Prohibe AID a las ONG hablar o promover el tema del aborto a cambio de financiamiento." http://www.creatividadfeminista.org/noticias/usaid.htm, May 19.

Criquillón, Ana. 1995. "The Nicaraguan Women's Movement: Feminist Reflections from Within." In *The New Politics of Survival: Grassroots Movements in Central America,* ed. Minor Sinclair, 209–37. New York: Monthly Review Press.

———. n.d. (1988?) "Acabamos con el Mito del Sexo Debil: La Historia del Programa de Mujeres en la ATC." In Programa de Mujeres del Consejo Internacional de Educación de Adultos y la Asociación de Trabajadores del Campo. *La luna también tiene su propia luz: La lucha por el desarrollo de la conciencia de las mujeres entre las trabajadores rurales nicaragüenses.* Unpublished manuscript, Managua(?), in author's possession.

Cruz, Angelse. 1997. "Desnutrido en algún grado, cuarentatres por ciento de niños indígenas: Encuesta del INN." *La Jornada,* June 28, 41.

Cuadra, Scarlet. 1990. "Electorado feminino por la revolución." *Barricada,* January 13.

———. 1996. "Accusations from All Sides." *Barricada internacional* 16, no. 402 (November): 16–17.

Cuadra, Scarlet, Guillermo Fernández, and Francis Lurys Ubeda. 1992. "Seeking Unity in Diversity: The Nicaraguan Women's Conference." *Barricada internacional* 12, no. 347 (March): 22–31.

Cuéllar, Mireya, and Alonso Urrutia. 2000. "Fox, presidente electo con 43.43 por ciento de los votos: IFE, Labastida obtuvo 36.88 por ciento y Cárdenas 17." *La Jornada,* July 7.

Danner, Mark. 1993. "The Truth of El Mozote." *New Yorker,* December 6.

Delgado, Violeta. 2003. "The Experiences and Achievements of the Women's Network against Violence." *Envío* 22, no. 261 (April): 11–20

DePalma, Anthony. 1994. "Mexican State Gets Two Chiefs, One Official, One Itinerant." *New York Times,* December 9.

Dickey, Christopher. 1985. *With the Contras: A Reporter in the Wilds of Nicaragua.* New York: Simon and Schuster.

Diebold de Cruz, Paula, and Mayra Pasos de Rappacioli. 1975. "Report on the Role of Women in the Economic Development of Nicaragua." Report prepared for USAID, Office of Planning and Development, Managua.

Dignas, Las (Mujeres por la Dignidad y la Vida). 1993. *Hacer política desde las mujeres: Una propuesta feminista para la participación política de las mujeres salvadoreñas.* San Salvador: Las Dignas.

———. 1995. *Las mujeres ante, con, contra, desde, sin, tras . . . el poder político.* San Salvador: Las Dignas.

Dignas, MAM, IMU, MSM, and Asociación de Mujeres Demandantes de la Cuota Alimenticia. 1996. "Comunicado de Prensa." Unpublished document.

Dillon, Sam. 2000. "In Mexican Campaign, Money Still Buys Votes." *New York Times,* June 19: A1.

Doble jornada. 1994a. "Ley Revolucionaria de Mujeres."

———. 1994b. "Las mujeres de Chiapas, protagonistas invisibles." February 7.

Dodson, Michael, and Laura Nuzzi O'Shaugnessy. 1985. "Religion and Politics." In *Nicaragua: The First Five Years,* ed. Thomas Walker. New York: Praeger.

Dunkerley, James. 1982. *The Long War: Dictatorship and Revolution in El Salvador.* London: Junction Books.

Eber, Christine. 1995. *Women and Alcohol in a Highland Maya Town: Water of Hope, Water of Sorrow.* Austin: University of Texas Press.

———. 2002. "Seeking Our Own Food: Indigenous Women's Power and Autonomy in San Pedro, Chenalhó, Chiapas (1980–1998)." In *Rereading Women in Latin America and the Caribbean: The Political Economy of Gender,* ed. Jennifer Abbassi and Sheryl Lutjens, 231–45. Lanham, Md.: Rowman and Littlefield.

Eber, Christine, and Brenda Rosenbaum. 1993. "'That We May Serve beneath Your Hands and Feet': Women Weavers in Highland Chiapas, Mexico." In *Crafts in the World Market: The Impact of Global Exchange on Middle-American Artesans,* ed. June Nash. Albany: SUNY Press.

Elizalde, Triunfo. 2000. "Suman 15 los grupos armados que operan en Chiapas: Identificados como paramilitares, diez de las organizaciones." *La Jornada,* June 1.

Engels, Friedrich. 1975. *The Origin of the Family, Private Property, and the State.* New York: International Publishers.

Enloe, Cynthia. 1990. *Bananas, Beaches, and Bases: Making Feminist Sense of International Politics.* Berkeley: University of California Press.

Enríquez, Laura J. 1991. *Harvesting Change: Labor and Agrarian Reform in Nicaragua, 1979–1990.* Chapel Hill: University of North Carolina Press.

———. 1997. *Agrarian Reform and Class Consciousness in Nicaragua.* Gainesville: University Press of Florida.

Envío. 1996–97a. "A New Period For the Nation: The Thirty-Three Days that Shook Nicaragua." Vol. 15, nos. 185–86 (December–January).

———. 1996–97b. "The Roots of the Electoral Crisis: The Thirty-Three Days that Shook Nicaragua." Vol. 15, nos. 185–86 (December–January).

———. 1998a. "Cuban Women's History—Jottings and Voices." Vol. 17, no. 208 (November): 27–43.

———. 1998b. "A Test in Ethics For a Society in Crisis." Vol. 17, no. 200 (March): 3–9.

Escalante Gonzalbo, María de la Paloma. 1995. "Cambio y políticas modernizadoras en Chiapas." In *Chiapas: Una modernidad inconclusa,* ed. Diana Guillén, 11–41. Mexico City: Instituto Mora.

Escobar Morales, César. n.d. *Aprendemos a convivir: Civica, moral, y urbanidad, sexto grado.* Lima: Editorial Labrusa.

Everingham, Mark. 1996. *Revolution and the Multiclass Coalition in Nicaragua.* Pittsburgh: University of Pittsburgh Press.

Ewen, Alexander. 1994. "Mexico: The Crisis of Identity." *Akwe:kon: A Journal of Indigenous Issues* 11, no. 2. (Summer): 28–40.

EZLN (Ejército Zapatista de Liberación Nacional). 1993. "Ley revolucionaria de mujeres." *El despertador Mexicano: Organo informativo del EZLN México* no. 1 (December): 17–18.

———. 1995. "Llamado del EZLN al diálogo nacional." In *¿Chiapas, y las mujeres, qué?* ed. Rosa Rojas, 2:67–70. Mexico City: Ediciones la Correa Feminista.

———. 1996. *Crónicas intergalácticas EZLN: Primer Encuentro Intercontinental por la Humanidad y Contra el Neoliberalismo.* Mexico City: Prensa Salinillas.

EZLN/Gobierno Federal. 1996. "Acuerdos sobre derechos y cultura indígena" [San Andrés Accords]. In *Chiapas 2,* ed. Neus Espresate, 133–71. Mexico City: Ediciones Era.

Fagen, Richard R. 1969. *The Transformation of Political Culture in Cuba.* Stanford: Stanford University Press.

————. 1986. "The Politics of Transition." In *Transition and Development: Problems of Third World Socialism,* ed. Richard R. Fagen, Carmen Diana Deere, and José Luis Coraggio. New York: Monthly Review Press.

Fagen, Richard, Carmen Diana Deere, and José Luis Coraggio, eds. 1986. *Transition and Development: Problems of Third World Socialism.* New York: Monthly Review Press.

Falquet, France. 1995. *La violencia cultural del sistema educativo: Las mujeres indígenas víctimas de la escuela.* Doc. 044-V-95. San Cristóbal de las Casas: Instituto de Asesoría Antropológica para la Región Maya.

Farhi, Farideh. 1990. *States and Urban-Based Revolutions: Iran and Nicaragua.* Urbana: University of Illinois Press.

Fauné, María Angélica. 1995. *Mujeres y familias centroamericanas: Principales problemas y tendencias.* Vol. 3. San José: PNUD.

FDR/FMLN (Frente Revolucionario Democrático/Frente Farabundo Martí para la Liberación Nacional). 1986. "Proposal for a Provisional Government." In *El Salvador: Central America in the New Cold War,* ed. Marvin Gettleman et al. New York: Grove Press.

Ferguson, Ann. 1993. "Women's Studies Conference, University of Havana, March 15–17, 1993." *NWSA Journal* 5, no. 3 (Fall): 343–48.

Fernández, Manuel. 1984. *Religión y revolución en Cuba (Veinticinco años de lucha ateísta).* Miami: Saeta Ediciones.

Fernández Ampié, Guillermo. 1996. "Muddy Waters: 'Final Provisional Results' Announced." *Barricada internacional,* no. 402 (November): 7–8.

Fernández Poncela, Anna. 1996. "The Disruptions of Adjustment: Women in Nicaragua." *Latin American Perspectives* 23, no. 1, issue 88 (Winter): 49–66.

Figueroa, Martha. 1996. "Las mujeres en Chiapas y el conflicto armado." Unpublished manuscript in author's possession.

Fink, Marcy. 1992. "Women and Popular Education in Latin America." In *Women and Education in Latin America: Knowledge, Power, and Change,* ed. Nelly Stromquist. Boulder: Lynne Rienner.

FIPI and CADDIAC (Frente Independiente de Pueblos Indios, Comité de Apoyo y Defensa de los Derechos Indios, A.C.). 1994. *Garantías individuales: Los derechos humanos en la constitución, Campaña Nacional de Alfabetización en Derechos Humanos.* Mexico City: Talleres de Editorial Praxis.

Fitzsimmons, Tracy. 2000. "A Monstrous Regiment of Women? State, Regime, and Women's Political Organizing in Latin America." *Latin American Research Review* 35, no. 2: 216–29.

Flood, Merielle. 1994. "Changing Gender Relations in Zinacantán, Mexico." *Research in Economic Anthropology* 15: 145–73.

Flynn, Patricia. 1983. "Women Challenge the Myth." In *Revolution in Central America,* ed. John Althoff et al., Stanford Central American Network. Boulder: Westview.

Foran, John. 1992. "A Theory of Third World Social Revolutions: Iran, Nicaragua, and El Salvador Compared." *Critical Sociology* 19, no. 2: 3–27.

———. 1993. "Theories of Revolution Revisited: Toward a Fourth Generation?" *Sociological Theory* 11 (March): 1–17.

———. 1994. "The Iranian Revolution of 1977–79: A Challenge for Social Theory." In *A Century of Revolution: Social Movements in Iran,* ed. John Foran, 160–88. Minneapolis: University of Minnesota Press.

———. 1997a. "The Comparative-Historical Sociology of Third World Social Revolutions: Why a Few Succeed, Why Most Fail." In *Theorizing Revolutions,* ed. John Foran, 227–67. New York: Routledge.

———. 1997b. "Discourses and Social Forces: The Role of Culture and Cultural Studies in Understanding Revolutions." In *Theorizing Revolutions,* ed. John Foran, 203–26. New York: Routledge.

———, ed. 1997c. *Theorizing Revolutions.* New York: Routledge.

Foran, John, Linda Klouzal, and Jean Pierre Rivera. 1997. "Who Makes Revolutions? Class, Gender, and Race in the Mexican, Cuban, and Nicaraguan Revolutions." *Research in Social Movements, Conflict, and Change* 20: 1–60.

Forbis, Melissa. 2000. "Hacia la autonomía: Zapatista Women and the Development of a New World." Unpublished manuscript in author's possession.

Foweraker, Joe. 1993. *Popular Mobilization in Mexico: The Teachers' Movement, 1977–87.* Cambridge: Cambridge University Press.

Fox, Jonathan. 1994a. "The Challenge of Democracy: Rebellion as Catalyst." *Akwe:kon: A Journal of Indigenous Issues* 11, no. 2 (Summer): 13–19.

———. 1994b. "The Difficult Transition from Clientelism to Citizenship: Lessons from Mexico." *World Politics* 46 (January): 151–84.

Freeman, Jo. 1975. *The Politics of Women's Liberation.* New York: David McKay.

Freyermuth Enciso, Graciela, and Mariana Fernández Guerrero. 1995. "Migration, Organization and Identity: The Case of a Women's Group from San Cristóbal de las Casas." *Signs: Journal of Women in Culture and Society* 20, no. 4 (Summer): 970–95.

FSLN (Frente Sandinista de Liberación Nacional). 1986. "The Historic Program of the FSLN." In *Nicaragua, Unfinished Revolution: The New*

Nicaragua Reader, ed. Peter Rosset and John Vandermeer. New York: Grove Press.

Fundación 16 de Enero. 1993. "Diagnostico de la situación actual de la mujer ex combatiente." Unpublished manuscript, San Salvador, in author's possession.

Funk, Nanette, and Magda Mueller, eds. 1993. *Gender Politics and Post-Communism: Reflections from Eastern Europe and the Former Soviet Union.* New York: Routledge.

Gaceta, La (Managua). 1987. "Constitución Política." January 9.

Gallegos, Elena. 1997. "El gobierno está en favor del diálogo, dice Zedillo en Chiapas: La justica social es posible cuando trabajamos juntos, indica." *La Jornada,* June 30, 3.

Garaizábal, Cristina. 1996. Introduction to *Mujeres-montaña: Vivencias de guer-rilleras y colaboradoras del FMLN,* by Norma Vázquez, Cristina Ibáñez, and Clara Murguialday, 13–19. Madrid: Editorial Horas y Horas.

García, Ana Isabel, and Enrique Gomáriz. 1989. *Mujeres centroamericanas.* San José: FLACSO.

García Oliveras, Julio A. 1979. *José Antonio Echeverría: La lucha estudiantil contra Batista.* Havana: Editorial Política.

García Torres, Ana Esther, Esmeralda López Armenta, and Alma Nava Martínez. 1999. "Municipio autónomo de Polhó." In *Chiapas 8,* ed. Neus Espreste, 211–15. Mexico City: Ediciones Era.

Garfield, Richard M., and Eugenio Taboada. 1986. "Health Service Reforms in Revolutionary Nicaragua" In *Nicaragua, Unfinished Revolution: The New Nicaragua Reader,* ed. Peter Rosset and John Vandermeer. New York: Grove Press.

Gargallo, Francesca. 1987. "La relación entre participación política y conciencia feminista en las militantes salvadoreñas." *Cuadernos americanos nueva epoca,* year 1, vol. 2 (March–April): 58–76.

Garza Caligaris, Anna María. 1991. "Sobre mujeres indígenas y su historia." *Anuario CEI* (Centro de Estudios Indígenas) 3: 31–42. San Cristóbal de las Casas: Universidad Autónoma de Chiapas.

Garza Caligaris, Anna María, and Bárbara Cadenas Gordillo. 1994. "Derechos reproductivos en los altos de Chiapas." *Anuario IEI* (Instituto de Estudios Indígenas) 4. San Cristóbal de las Casas: Universidad Autónoma de Chiapas.

Gente. 1991. "El feminismo a la Nica." *Barricada* (Managua), March 8: 10.

Gil, José. 1997. "Formal integración del FZLN; campaña nacional por la paz, primera tarea." *La Jornada,* September 17.

————. 1998. "El gobierno, sin voluntad para solucionar el caso chiapaneco." *La Jornada,* August 19.

Gil, José, and Rosa Rojas. 1996. "Irá Marcos a la clausura del foro en San Cristóbal." *La Jornada,* January 7.

Golden, Tim. 1994a. "Mexican Rebel Leader Sees No Quick Settlement." *New York Times,* February 20.

————. 1994b. "Mexico's Two Faces: Is Political Change Top Priority?" *New York Times,* February 24.

————. 1994c. "Rebels Battle for Hearts of Mexicans" *New York Times,* February 26.

Goldman, Wendy Z. 1993. *Women, the State, and Revolution: Soviet Family Policy and Social Life, 1917–1936.* New York: Cambridge University Press.

Goldstone, Jack A., Ted Robert Gurr, and Farrokh Moshiri, eds. 1991. *Revolutions of the Late Twentieth Century.* Boulder: Westview.

Gómez Nuñez, Marcelino. 1999. "Regiones autónomas pluriétnicas (RAP): Los muchos senderos de las autonomías de facto." In *México: Experiencias de autonomía indígena,* ed. Aracely Burguete Cal y Mayor, 192–209. Copenhagen: Grupo Internacional de Trabajo sobre Asuntos Indígenas.

Gómez Treto, Raúl. 1988. *The Church and Socialism in Cuba.* Maryknoll, N.Y.: Orbis Books.

González, Victoria. 1995. "La historia del feminismo en Nicaragua, 1837– 1956." *La Boletina* (Puntos de Encuentro, Managua), no. 22, 7–15.

————. 1996. "Mujeres somocistas: 'La Pechuga' y el corazón de la dictadura nicaragüense (1936–1979)." Paper presented at the Tercer Congreso Centroamericano de Historia, Universidad de Costa Rica, San José, July 15–18.

————. 2001. "Somocista Women, Right-Wing Politics, and Feminism in Nicaragua, 1936–1979." In *Radical Women in Latin America: Left and Right,* ed. Victoria González and Karen Kampwirth. University Park: Penn State University Press.

González, Victoria, and Karen Kampwirth. 2001. Introduction to *Radical Women in Latin America: Left and Right,* ed. Victoria González and Karen Kampwirth. University Park: Penn State University Press.

González Hernández, Miguel, and Elvia Quintanar Quintanar. 1999. "La construcción de la región autónoma norte y el ejercicio del gobierno municipal." In *México: Experiencias de autonomía indígena,* ed. Aracely Burguete Cal y Mayor, 210–33. Copenhagen: IWGIA.

González Suarez, Enrique, and Fabio González Suarez. 1986. *La Mobilización Popular Frente a la Crisis Alimentaria.* Managua: INIES.

Goodwin, Jeff. 1997. "State-Centered Approaches to Revolution." In *Theorizing Revolution,* ed. John Foran. London: Routledge.

Gorman, Stephen M., and Thomas W. Walker. 1985. "The Armed Forces." In *Nicaragua: The First Five Years,* ed. Thomas W. Walker, 91–117. New York: Praeger.

Goven, Joanna. 1993. "The Gendered Foundations of Hungarian Socialism: State, Society, and the Anti-Politics of Anti-Feminism, 1948–1990." Ph.D. dissertation, University of California, Berkeley.

Greenberg-Lake. 1989. "Nicaragua National Election Survey." Press release, December 13, in author's possession.

———. 1990. "Results of a Poll Conducted for Hemisphere Initiatives." Report, January, in author's possession.

Grenier, Yvon. 1999. *The Emergence of Insurgency in El Salvador: Ideology and Political Will.* Pittsburgh: University of Pittsburgh Press.

Grupo de Mujeres de San Cristóbal, Organización de Médicos Indígenas del Estado de Chiapas, and Comisión de Mujeres de CONPAZ. 1994. "Memorias del encuentro-taller: 'Los Derechos de las Mujeres en Nuestras Costumbres y Tradiciones.'" May 19–20.

Guerra, Luz Grant. 1993. "The Salvadoran Women's Movement: An Autonomous Movement for Social and Structural Change." Master's thesis, University of Texas, Austin.

Guillén, Diana. 1995. "Del paraíso al infierno terrenal: La iglesia como canal de participación política." In *Chiapas: Una modernidad inconclusa,* ed. Diana Guillén, 42–71. Mexico City: Instituto Mora.

———. 1997. "Mediaciones y rupturas: El orden político en Chiapas." Paper presented at Latin American Studies Association conference, Guadalajara, April 17–19.

Gutiérrez, Margarita, and Nellys Palomo. 1999. "Autonomía con Mirada de Mujer." In *México: Experiencias de autonomía indígena,* ed. Aracely Burguete Cal y Mayor, 54–86. Copenhagen: IWGIA.

Hartmann, Betsy. 1987. *Reproductive Rights and Wrongs: The Global Politics of Population Control and Contraceptive Choice.* New York: Harper and Row.

———. 1995. *Reproduction Rights and Wrongs: The Global Politics of Population Control.* Revised edition. Boston: South End Press.

Harvey, Neil. 1994. *Rebellion in Chiapas: Rural Reforms, Campesino Radicalism, and the Limits to Salinismo.* Transformation of Rural Mexico, no. 5. San Diego: Center for U.S.-Mexican Studies.

———. 1998. *The Chiapas Rebellion: The Struggle for Land and Liberty.* Durham: Duke University Press.

Hauser, Ewa, Barbara Heyns, and Jane Mansbridge. 1993. "Feminism in the Interstices of Politics and Culture: Poland in Transition." In *Gender Politics and Post-Communism: Reflections from Eastern Europe and the Former Soviet Union,* ed. Nanette Funk and Magda Mueller, 257–73. New York: Routledge.

Hayes, Kathleen. 1996. *Women on the Threshold: Voices of Salvadoran Baptist Women.* Macon: Smyth and Helwys.

Hellman, Judith Adler. 1994a. *Mexican Lives.* New York: New Press.

———. 1994b. "Mexican Popular Movements: Clientelism and the Process of Democratization." *Latin American Perspectives* 21 (Spring).

Henríquez, Elio. 1996. "Amenazas de muerte contra veintiocho integrantes de la Conpaz." *La Jornada,* November 7.

Henríquez, Elio, and Rosa Rojas. 1995. "Asegura Aedpch que cuarenta de sus militantes han sido asesinados en este año y 860 luchadores sociales han sido encarcelados." *La Jornada,* November 14.

Hernández Arellano, Ricardo. 1999. "Ocosingo: Poder local y buen gobierno: La experiencia del consejo municipal plural ampliado." In *México: Experiencias de autonomía indígena,* ed. Aracely Burguete Cal y Mayor, 261–80. Copenhagen: Grupo Internacional de Trabajo sobre Asuntos Indígenas.

Hernández Castillo, Rosalva Aída. 1994. "La 'fuerza extraña' es mujer." *Ojarasca* (Mexico City), no. 30 (March): 36–37.

———. 1995. "De la Comunidad a la Convención Estatal de Mujeres: Las Campesinas Chiapanecas y sus Demandas de Género." In *La explosión de comunidades en Chiapas,* ed. Grupo Internacional de Trabajo sobre Asuntos Indígenas. Copenhagen: IWGIA.

———, ed. 1998. *La otra palabra: Mujeres y violencia en Chiapas, antes y después de acteal.* Mexico City: CIESAS, COLEM, CIAM.

Hernández Cruz, Antonio. 1999. "Autonomía Tojolab'al: Genesis de un proceso." In *México: Experiencias de autonomía indígena,* ed. Aracely Burguete Cal y Mayor, 171–91. Copenhagen: IWGIA.

Hérnandez López, Julio. 1998. "Astillero." *La Jornada,* January 8.

Hernández Navarro, Luis. 1997. "Entre la memoria y el olvido: Guerrillas, movimiento indígena, y reformas legales en la hora del EZLN." In *Chiapas 4,* ed. Neus Espresate, 69–92. Mexico City: Ediciones Era.

———. 1998. "The Escalation of the War in Chiapas." *NACLA Report on the Americas* 31, no. 5 (March–April): 7–10.

Herrera, Morena. 1997. Pensándose a sí mismas: El Salvador." In *Movimiento de mujeres en Centroamérica,* ed. Sofía Montenegro, 223–335. Managua: Programa Regional La Corriente.

Heyck, Denis Lynn Daly. 1990. *Life Stories of the Nicaraguan Revolution.* New York: Routledge.

Hidalgo, Onécimo, and Mario B. Monroy. 1994. "El estado de Chiapas en cifras." In *Pensar Chiapas, repensar Mexico: Reflexiones de las ONGs mexicanas sobre el conflicto,* ed. Mario B. Monroy. Mexico City: Convergencia de Organismos Civiles por la Democracia.

Hipsher, Patricia. 2001. "Right- and Left-Wing Women in Post-Revolutionary El Salvador: Feminist Autonomy and Cross-Political Alliance Building for Gender Equality." In *Radical Women in Latin America: Left and Right,* ed. Victoria González and Karen Kampwirth. University Park: Penn State University Press.

Hiriart, Berta. 1995. "Las Cubanas y sus milagros: Bajo el lema 'Comunicar es unir' Cubanas organizan encuentro mujer y comunicación." *Fempress* 164: 9.

Hirshon, Sheryl. 1983. *And Also Teach Them to Read.* Westport, Conn.: Lawrence Hill.

Horton, Lynn. 1998. *Peasants in Arms: War and Peace in the Mountains of Nicaragua, 1979–1994.* Athens: Ohio University Press.

Huerta, Juan Ramón. 1998. *El silencio del patriarca: La linea es no hablar de esto.* Managua: El Renacimiento.

Hughes, Donna. 1998. "Khatami and the Status of Women in Iran." *Z Magazine,* October: 22–24.

Hunt, Lynn. 1992. *The Family Romance of the French Revolution.* Berkeley: University of California Press.

Huntington, Samuel. 1968. *Political Order in Changing Societies.* New Haven: Yale University Press.

INEC (Instituto Nacional de Estadísticas y Censos). 1989. *Encuesta sociodemográfica nicaragüense, tabulaciones básicas.* 4 vols. Managua: Talleres Gráficos de INEC.

———. 1990. *Nicaragua: Diez años en cifras.* Managua: Talleres Gráficos de INEC.

INEGRI (Instituto Nacional de Estadística Geografía e Informática). 1992. *Estados Unidos Mexicanos: Perfil sociodemografico, undécimo censo general de población y vivienda, 1990.* Aguascalientes: INEGRI.

INSS (Instituto Nicaragüense de Seguridad Social). 1981. "Analysis comparativo entre la ley anterior y la nueva ley organica de seguridad social." Unpublished document, Managua, May, in author's possession.

INSSBI (Instituto Nicaragüense de Seguridad Social y Bienestar). 1986. "Dirección de orientación y protección familiar: Acciones en el area jurídico social familiar en Nicaragua." Unpublished document, Managua, in author's possession.

————. 1990. "Bienestar social en diez años de revolución." *El Nuevo Diario,* February 16.

Instituto de Historia del Movimiento Comunista y de la Revolución Socialista de Cuba. 1985. *Historia del Movimiento Obrero Cubano, 1865–1958.* Havana: Editora Política.

Isbester, Katherine. 2001. *Still Fighting: The Nicaraguan Women's Movement, 1977–2000.* Pittsburgh: University of Pittsburgh Press.

Jaimes Guerrero, M. A. 1995. "An Indigenous American Intifada." In *First World, Ha Ha Ha: The Zapatista Challenge,* ed. Elaine Katzenberger. San Francisco: City Lights Books.

Jaquette, Jane S. 1973. "Women in Revolutionary Movements in Latin America." *Journal of Marriage and the Family* 35 (May): 344–54.

————, ed. 1989. *The Women's Movement in Latin America: Feminism and the Transition to Democracy.* Boston: Unwin Hyman.

Jaquette, Jane, and Sharon Wolchik, eds. 1998. *Women and Democracy: Latin America and Central and Eastern Europe.* Baltimore: Johns Hopkins University Press.

Jonas, Susanne, and Nancy Stein. 1989. "Elections and Transitions: The Guatemalan and Nicaraguan Cases." In *Elections and Democracy in Central America,* ed. John A. Booth and Mitchell A. Seligson. Chapel Hill: University of North Carolina Press.

————. 1990. "The Construction of Democracy in Nicaragua." In *Democracy in Latin America: Visions and Realities,* ed. Susanne Jonas and Nancy Stein. New York: Bergin and Garvey Publishers.

Jornada, La. 1996a. "Alianza Cívica: el gobierno, obligado a un viraje en el diálogo en Chiapas." September 11.

————. 1996b. "¿Quien se esfuerza por la paz? El gobierno, 21.9 por ciento; el EZLN, 75.6 por ciento." September 10.

————. 1997. "Mas de 200 muertes desde 1995, saldo de acciones paramilitares: Datos de grupos defensores de derechos humanos: Datos de grupos defensores de derechos humanos." December 28.

———. 1998. "Chiapas: Recambios en el Vacio." January 8.

Jubb, Nadine. 2001. "Enforcing Gendered Meanings and Social Order: The Participation of the National Police in the Nicaraguan Women's and Children's Police Stations." Paper presented at the Latin American Studies Association, Washington D.C., September 6–8.

Junta de Gobierno. 1984. *Evaluación del decenio de las naciones unidas para la mujer: Igualdad, desarrollo, y paz, 1976–1985.* Managua: Oficina de la Mujer.

Kaltefleiter, Caroline. 1995. "Revolution Girl Style Now: Trebled Reflexivity and the Riot Grrrl Network." Ph.D. dissertation, Ohio University.

Kampwirth, Karen. 1993. "Democratizing the Nicaraguan Family: Struggles over the State, Households, and Civil Society." Ph.D. dissertation. University of California, Berkeley.

———. 1994. "'The Movement Came to Fill an Emptiness': Lesbian Feminists Talk about Life in Post-Sandinista Nicaragua." *Sojourner: The Women's Forum,* December, 16–17.

———. 1996a. "Confronting Adversity with Experience: The Emergence of Feminism in Nicaragua." *Social Politics* 3, nos. 2–3 (Summer–Fall).

———. 1996b. "Creating Space in Chiapas: An Analysis of the Strategies of the Zapatista Army and the Rebel Government in Transition." *Bulletin of Latin American Research* 15, no. 2 (May): 261–67.

———. 1996c. "Gender Inequality and the Zapatista Rebellion: Women's Organizing in Chiapas, Mexico." Paper presented at American Political Science Association annual conference, San Francisco, August 29–September 1.

———. 1996d. "The Mother of the Nicaraguans: Doña Violeta and the UNO's Gender Agenda." *Latin American Perspectives* 23, no. 1, issue 88 (Winter): 67–86.

———. 1997. "Social Policy." In *Nicaragua without Illusions: Regime Transition and Structural Adjustment in the 1990s,* ed. Thomas Walker, 115–29. Wilmington, Del.: Scholarly Resources.

———. 1998a. "Feminism, Antifeminism and Electoral Politics in Postwar Nicaragua and El Salvador." *Political Science Quarterly* 113, no. 2 (Summer): 259–79.

———. 1998b. "Legislating Personal Politics in Sandinista Nicaragua, 1979–1992." *Women's Studies International Forum* 21, no. 1: 53–64.

———. 1998c. "Peace Talks, But No Peace." *NACLA Report on the Americas* 31, no. 5 (March–April): 15–19.

———. 2001. "Women in the Armed Struggles in Nicaragua: Sandinistas and Contras Compared." In *Radical Women in Latin America: Left and Right,* ed. Victoria González and Karen Kampwirth. University Park: Penn State University Press.

———. 2002. *Women and Guerrilla Movements: Nicaragua, El Salvador, Chiapas, Cuba.* University Park: Penn State University Press.

———. 2003. "Arnoldo Alemán Takes on the NGOs: Antifeminism and the New Populism in Nicaragua." *Latin American Politics and Society* 45 no. 2: 133–58.

Kanoussi, Dora, ed. 1998. *El zapatismo y la política.* Mexico City: Plaza y Valdés Editores.

Keane, John. 1988. *Democracy and Civil Society.* London: Verso.

Keddie, Nikki, ed. 1995. *Debating Revolutions.* New York: NYU Press.

Kenez, Peter. 1986. *The Birth of the Propaganda State: Soviet Methods of Mass Mobilization, 1917–1929.* Cambridge: Cambridge University Press.

Kirk, Robin. 1997. *The Monkey's Paw: New Chronicles from Peru.* Amherst: University of Massachusetts Press.

Kruks, Sonia, Rayna Rapp, and Marilyn B. Young, eds. 1989. *Promissory Notes: Women in the Transition to Socialism.* New York: Monthly Review Press.

Kruks, Sonia, and Ben Wisner. 1989. "Ambiguous Transformations: Women, Politics, and Production in Mozambique." In *Promissory Notes: Women in the Transition to Socialism,* ed. Sonia Kruks, Rayna Rapp, and Marilyn B. Young, 148–71. New York: Monthly Review Press.

Lacayo, Rolando D., and Martha Lacayo de Arauz. 1981. *Decretos-leyes para gobierno de un país.* Vol. 5. Managua: Editorial Unión.

Laclau, Ernesto, and Chantal Mouffe. 1985. *Hegemony and Socialist Strategy: Towards a Radical Democratic Politics.* New York: Verso.

Lancaster, Roger N. 1988. *Thanks to God and the Revolution: Popular Religion and Class Consciousness in the New Nicaragua.* New York: Columbia University Press.

———. 1992. *Life Is Hard: Machismo, Danger, and the Intimacy of Power in Nicaragua.* Berkeley: University of California Press.

Lapidus, Gail Warshofsky. 1978. *Women in Soviet Society: Equality, Development, and Social Change.* Berkeley: University of California Press.

Larios, Roberto. 1991. "Gobierno cede a chantaje EU: Confirman proyecto para renunciar a indemnización de diecisiete mil millones: Pretenden derogar ley que obliga a continuar juicio de La Haya." *Barricada,* April 5.

Larner, Marvin. 1990. "Struggle to Rule Nicaragua Begins: Hints of Dynasty." *Christian Science Monitor,* March 1.

LASA (Latin American Studies Association). 1985. Epilogue ("The 1984 Elections"). In *Nicaragua: The First Five Years,* ed. Thomas W. Walker. New York: Praeger.

Lázaro, Juan. 1990. "Women and Political Violence in Contemporary Peru." *Dialectical Anthropology* 15: 233–47.

Legorreta Díaz, María del Carmen. 1998. *Religión, política, y guerrilla en Las Cañadas de la Selva Lacandona.* Mexico City: Cal y Arena.

Leiner, Marvin. 1994. *Sexual Politics in Cuba: Machismo, Homosexuality, and AIDS.* Boulder: Westview.

León, Irene. 1994. "Sexto encuentro feminista de América Latina y el Caribe: Una utopia para todos." In *Memorias del sexto encuentro feminista latinoamericano y del Caribe,* ed. María Teresa Blandón. Managua: Imprenta UCA.

Leyva Solano, Xochitl. 1998. "The New Zapatista Movement: Political Levels, Actors, and Political Discourse in Contemporary Mexico." In *Encuentros Antropológicos: Power, Identity, and Mobility in Mexican Society,* ed. Valentina Napolitano and Xochitl Leyva Solano, 35–55. London: Institute of Latin American Studies.

Leyva Solano, Xochitl, and Gabriel Ascencio Franco. 1996. *Lacandonia al filo del agua.* Mexico City: Centro de Investigaciones y Estudios Superiores en Antropología Social.

Lind, Amy. 1992. "Power, Gender, and Development." In *The Making of Social Movements in Latin America,* ed. Arturo Escobar and Sonia Alvarez. Boulder: Westview.

Lloyd, Jane-Dale, and Laura Pérez Rosales, eds. 1995. *Paisajes rebeldes: Una larga noche de rebelión indígena.* Mexico City: Universidad Iberoamericano.

Lobao, Linda M. 1990. "Women in Revolutionary Movements: Changing Patterns of Latin American Revolutionary Struggle." *Dialectical Anthropology* 15: 211–32.

Lomelí González, Arturo. 1999. "Pueblos indios y autonomías zapatistas." In *México: Experiencias de autonomía indígena,* ed. Aracely Burguete Cal y Mayor, 234–60. Copenhagen: IWGIA.

Long, Kristi. 1996. *We All Fought for Freedom: Women in Poland's Solidarity Movement.* Boulder: Westview.

López, Juan J. 1999. "The Nontransition in Cuba: Problems and Prospects for Change." Paper presented at American Political Science Association annual conference, September 2–5.

López, Yolanda, Juan Balboa, and Elio Henríquez. 1995. "Bloque Aedpch las carreteras de accesso a Oaxaca, Tabasco, y Veracruz: Veinte municipios afectados." *La Jornada,* November 21.

López y Rivas, Gilberto. 2001. "Traición en el Congreso." *La Jornada,* April 30.

Loveman, Brian, and Thomas M. Davies, Jr. 1997a. "Guerrilla Warfare, Revolutionary Theory, and Revolutionary Movements in Latin America." Introduction to *Guerrilla Warfare* by Che Guevara. Wilmington, Del.: Scholarly Resources.

———. 1997b. *The Politics of Antipolitics: The Military in Latin America.* Wilmington, Del.: Scholarly Resources.

Luciak, Ilja. 1995. "Women in the Transition: The Case of the Female FMLN Combatants in El Salvador." Paper presented at Latin American Studies Association conference, Washington, D.C., September 28–30.

———. 1998. "Gender Equality and Electoral Politics on the Left: A Comparison of El Salvador and Nicaragua." *Journal of Interamerican Studies and World Affairs* 40 (Spring): 39–66.

———. 2000. "Gender Equality and Democratization in Central America: The Case of the Revolutionary Left." Paper presented at Latin American Studies Association conference, Miami, March 16–18.

———. 2001a. *After the Revolution: Gender and Democracy in El Salvador, Nicaragua, and Guatemala.* Baltimore: Johns Hopkins University Press.

———. 2001b. "Gender Equality, Democratization, and the Revolutionary Left in Central America: Guatemala in Comparative Perspective." In *Radical Women in Latin America: Left and Right,* ed. Victoria González and Karen Kampwirth. University Park: Penn State University Press.

Lumsden, Ian. 1996. *Machos, Maricones, and Gays: Cuba and Homosexuality.* Philadelphia: Temple University Press.

Lungo, Mario. 1989. *La lucha de las masas en el Salvador.* San Salvador: UCA Editores.

Lupiáñez Reinlein, José. 1985. *El movimiento estudiantil en Santiago de Cuba, 1952–53.* Havana: Editorial de Ciencias Sociales.

Lutjens, Sheryl. 1995. "Reading between the Lines: Women, the State, and Rectification in Cuba." *Latin American Perspectives* 22, no. 2, issue 85 (Spring): 100–24.

————. 1997. "The Politics of Revolution in Latin America: Feminist Perspectives on Theory and Practice." Paper presented at Latin American Studies Association conference, Guadalajara, April 17–19.

Luzón, José Luis. 1987. *Economía, población, y territorio en Cuba (1899–1983)* Madrid: Ediciones Cultura Hispánica.

MacDowell Santos, M. Cecilia. 2000. "Gender, the State, and Citizenship: Women's Police Stations in São Paulo, Brazil." In *Irrumpiendo en lo público: Seis facetas de las mujeres en América Latina,* ed. Sara Poggio and Monteserrat Sagot, 63–92. San José: Maestría Regional en Estudios de la Mujer, Universidad de Costa Rica.

Macías, Anna. 1982. *Against All Odds: The Feminist Movement in Mexico to 1940.* Westport, Conn.: Greenwood Press.

Maloof, Judy. 1999. *Voices of Resistance: Testimonies of Cuban and Chilean Women.* Lexington: University Press of Kentucky.

Marcos. 1994. "The First Zapatista Uprising: An Extract of a Letter from Subcommander Marcos." *Akwe:kon: A Journal of Indigenous Issues* 11, no. 2 (Summer).

————. 1995a. "Nota a la Asamblea Estatal Democrática del Pueblo Chiapaneco." *La Jornada,* May 20.

————. 1995b. *Shadows of Tender Fury: The Letters and Communiqués of Subcomandante Marcos and the Zapatista Army of National Liberation.* New York: Monthly Review Press.

————. 1995c. "To the Men and Women Who, in Different Languages and by Different Paths, Believe in a More Human Future and Struggle to Achieve It Today." Unpublished translation, in author's possession.

————. 1996a. "The Future Must Be Made by and for Women: Marcos." *Libertad* (National Commission for Democracy in Mexico), no. 2 (March).

————. 1996b. "Llama el EZLN a un encuentro intercontinental antiliberalismo." *La Jornada,* January 30.

————. 1997. "No desaparecerá por decreto la rebeldía indígena: Marcos al CNI." *La Jornada,* October 13.

Marel García, Gladys. 1996. *Memoria e identidad: Un estudio específico (1952–1958).* Havana: Editorial de Ciencias Sociales.

Mariscal, Angeles. 1997a. "Detenidos por la matanza declaran su filiación prísta; Otros se dijeron miembros del Partido Cardenista, indica la PGR; Delinquen las personas, no las instituciones, señala Palacios Alcocer;

Rindió declaración el secretario de Gobierno, acusado de negligencia; Rifles AK-47, entre las armas utilizadas, indica Jorge Madrazo." *La Jornada,* December 26.

———. 1997b. "En tres años 11 mil 443 desplazados; en 1997, 500 muertes violentas." *La Jornada,* December 31.

Marquis, Christopher. 1990. "Preocupa a EU 'nepotismo' en Nicaragua: Afirma el nuevo *Herald.*" *Barricada,* December 20.

Mason, David S. 1992. *Revolution in East-Central Europe.* Boulder: Westview.

Mason, T. David. 1992. "Women's Participation in Central American Revolutions." *Comparative Political Studies* 25, no. 1 (April): 63–89.

Massell, Gregory. 1974. *The Surrogate Proletariat: Moslem Women and Revolutionary Strategies in Soviet Central Asia, 1919–1929.* Princeton: Princeton University Press.

Mattelart, Michele. 1980. "Chile: The Feminine Version of the Coup d'Etat." In *Sex and Class in Latin America,* ed. June Nash and Helen Safa, 279–301. South Hadley, Mass.: J. F. Bergin Publishers.

Maxfield, Sylvia, and Richard Stahler-Sholk. 1985. "External Constraints." In *Nicaragua: The First Five Years,* ed. Thomas Walker. New York: Praeger.

McAdam, Doug. 1982. *Political Process and the Development of Black Insurgency, 1930–1970.* Chicago: University of Chicago Press.

McClintock, Cynthia. 1992. "Theories of Revolution and the Case of Peru." In *The Shining Path of Peru,* ed. David Scott Palmer. New York: St. Martin's Press.

———. 1998. *Revolutionary Movements in Latin America: El Salvador's FMLN and Peru's Shining Path.* Washington, D.C.: United States Institute of Peace Press.

MED (Ministerio de Educación). 1984. *Cinco años de educación en la revolución, 1979–1984.* Managua: MED.

———. 1988. "Evolución del financimiento educativo, 1978–1988." Unpublished document, Managua.

———. 1990a. *Lineamientos del Ministerio de Educación en el nuevo gobierno de salvación nacional.* Managua: MED.

———. 1990b. "Principales indicadores del sistema educativo, años 1979–1990." Unpublished document, Managua. Includes data for 1978.

Mendoza Ramírez, Martha Patricia. 1995. "La intervención política en la Selva Lacandona." In *Chiapas: Una modernidad inconclusa,* ed. Diana Guillén, 114–47. Mexico City: Instituto Mora.

Midlarsky, Manus, and Kenneth Roberts. 1985. "Class, State, and Revolution in Central America: Nicaragua and El Salvador Compared." *Journal of Conflict Resolution* 29, no. 2 (June): 163–93.

MINSA (Ministerio de Salud). 1989. *Programa y norma de planificación familiar.* Managua: Impresiones EINM.

———. 1991. *Plan maestro de salud, 1991–1996.* Managua: MINSA.

———. 1993a. *Política nacional de salud.* Managua: Ediciones Internacionales.

———. 1993b. *Política nacional de salud: Sesión extraordinaria.* Managua: n.p.

Mintz, Sidney. 1964. Foreword to *Sugar and Society in the Caribbean: An Economic History of Cuban Agriculture* by Ramiro Guerra y Sánchez. New Haven: Yale University Press.

Mintz, Steven, and Susan Kellogg. 1988. *Domestic Revolutions: A Social History of American Family Life.* New York: Free Press.

Moghadam, Valentine. 1994. "Islamic Populism, Class, and Gender in Postrevolutionary Iran." In *A Century of Revolution: Social Movements in Iran,* ed. John Foran, 189–222. Minneapolis: University of Minnesota Press.

———. 1997. "Gender and Revolutions." In *Theorizing Revolutions,* ed. John Foran, 137–67. London: Routledge.

———. 1999. "Revolution, Religion, and Gender Politics: Iran and Afghanistan Compared." *Journal of Women's History* 10, no. 4 (Winter): 172–95.

———. 2003. "Is the Future of Revolutions Feminist? Rewriting 'Gender and Revolutions' for a Globalizing World." In *The Future of Revolutions: Rethinking Radical Change in the Age of Globalization,* ed. John Foran, 159–68. London: Zed Books.

Moghissi, Haideh. 1996. *Populism and Feminism in Iran: Women's Struggle in a Male-Defined Revolutionary Movement.* New York: St. Martin's Press.

Molyneux, Maxine. 1984. "Women in Socialist Societies: Problems of Theory and Practice." In *Of Marriage and the Market: Women's Subordination Internationally and Its Lessons,* ed., Kate Young, Carol Wolkowitz, and Roslyn McCullagh, 55–90. London: Routledge and Kegan Paul.

———. 1986. "Mobilization without Emancipation?" In *Transition and Development: Problems of Third World Socialism,* ed. Richard Fagen, Carmen Diana Deere, and José Luis Coraggio. New York: Monthly Review Press.

———. 1988. "The Politics of Abortion in Nicaragua: Revolutionary Pragmatism—or Feminism in the Realm of Necessity?" *Feminist Review,* no. 29 (May): 114–32.

———. 2000. "Gender, State, and Institutional Change: The Federación de Mujeres Cubanas." In *Hidden Histories of Gender and the State in Latin America*, ed. Elizabeth Dore and Maxine Molyneux, 291–321. Durham: Duke University Press.

———. 2001. *Women's Movements in International Perspective: Latin America and Beyond*. New York: Palgrave.

Montenegro, Sofía, ed. 1997. *Movimiento de mujeres en Centroamérica*. Managua: Programa Regional La Corriente.

Montgomery, Tommie Sue. 1983. "Liberation and Revolution: Christianity as a Subversive Activity in Central America." In *Trouble in Our Backyard: Central America and the United States in the Eighties*, ed. Martin Diskin. New York: Pantheon Books.

———. 1995. *Revolution in El Salvador: From Civil Strife to Civil Peace*. Boulder: Westview.

Morales Carazo, Jaime. 1989. *La contra*. Mexico City: Imprimatur Artes Gráficas.

Morales Henríquez, Viktor. 1980. *De Mrs. Hanna a La Dinorah: Principio y fin de la dictadura somocista, historia de medio siglo de corrupción*. Managua(?): n.p.

Moreno, Elsa. 1997. *Mujeres y política en el Salvador*. San José: FLACSO.

Morquecho, Gaspar. 1994. "Sin paz ni democracia." In *A Propósito de la insurgencia en Chiapas*, ed. Silvia Soriano Hernández, 145–55. Mexico City: Asociación para el Desarrollo de la Investigación Científica y Humanística de Chiapas.

———. 1995a. "Comenzó la Cuarta Asamblea Nacional Indígena Plural: Se reúnen en San Cristóbal delegaciones de doce estados y del extranjero." *La Jornada*, December 9: 16.

———. 1995b. "Encuentro en San Cristóbal de las Casas: Piden mujeres que su sentir se refleje en un proyecto de ley, 'Estamos aquí porque queremos ser escuchadas,' dijeron." *La Jornada*, December 8: 25.

———. 1995c. "Las Mujeres en la Asamblea Democrática Estatal del Pueblo Chiapaneco." In *¿Chiapas, y las mujeres, qué?* Mexico City: Ediciones la Correa Feminista.

Mujeres 94. 1993a. "Plataforma de las mujeres salvadoreñas." Unpublished document, August 31, in author's possession.

———. 1993b. "Plataforma de las mujeres salvadoreñas: Edición popular." Unpublished document, August, in author's possession.

———. 1994. "Compromisos de los candidatos(as) con el movimiento de mujeres de el Salvador." Unpublished document, March 8, in author's possession.

Murguialday, Clara. 1990. *Nicaragua, revolución, y feminismo (1977–1989)*. Madrid: Editorial Revolución.

———. 1996a. *Montañas con recuerdos de mujer: Una mirada feminista a la participación de las mujeres en los conflictos armados en Centroamérica y Chiapas*. Memorias del Foro Regional, San Salvador, December 1995. San Salvador:Las Dignas.

———. 1996b. "Mujeres, transición democrática, y elecciones: El Salvador en tiempos de posguerra." *Nueva sociedad* (Caracas), no. 141 (January–February): 34–42.

Murillo, Rosario. 1991. "Mónica Boltodano: Las Mujeres Sandinistas." *Ventana* (suppl. to *Barricada*), no. 472 (June 3).

Nash, June. 1993. "Maya Household Production in the World Market: The Potters of Amatenango del Valle, Chiapas, Mexico." In *Crafts in the World Market: The Impact of Global Exchange on Middle-American Artesans*, ed. June Nash. Albany: SUNY Press.

———. 2001. *Mayan Visions: The Quest for Autonomy in an Age of Globalization*. New York: Routledge.

Nashat, Guity. ed. 1983. *Women and Revolution in Iran*. Boulder: Westview.

NCDM (National Commission for Democracy in Mexico). 1996a. "Ramona Recovering!" *Libertad*, no. 7 (November–December): 1.

———. 1996b. " . . . Y la Comandante Ramona rompió el cerco militar." *Libertad*, no. 7 (November–December): 5.

———. 1997a. "Commandante Ramona inaugura Convención Nacional de Mujeres." *Libertad*, no. 10 (September–October): 3.

———. 1997b. "Ik'otik: We Are the Wind." *Libertad*, no. 11 (October–November): 1.

Navas, María Candelaria. 1985. "Los movimientos femeninos en Centroamerica, 1970–1983." In *Movimientos populares en Centroamérica*, ed. Daniel Camacho and Rafael Menjívar. San José: EDUCA, FLACSO, UNU, IISUNAM.

———. 1987. "Las organizaciones de mujeres en el Salvador, 1975–1985." Master's thesis (Latin American Studies) Universidad Nacional Autonoma de Mexico.

Navas, María Candelaria, Nancy Orellana, and Liza Domínguez. 2000. *La experiencia organizativa de las mujeres rurales en la transición post-guerra (1992–1999)*. San Salvador: Oxfam America, FUNDE, IMU.

Nazzari, Muriel. 1983. "The 'Woman Question' in Cuba: An Analysis of Material Constraints on Its Solution." *Signs: Journal of Women in Culture and Society* 9, no. 2 (Winter): 246–63.

Nelson, Sara. 2002. "Constructing and Negotiating Gender in Women's Police Stations in Brazil." In *Rereading Women in Latin America and the Caribbean: The Political Economy of Gender,* ed. Jennifer Abbassi and Sheryl Lutjens, 197–212. Lanham, Mass.: Rowman and Littlefield.

New York Times. 2000. "A Portrait of Mexican Voters." July 4: A6.

Nicaragua. Asamblea Nacional. 1992. *Ley de reformas al código penal.* Law 150. July 8.

———. Presidencia de la Republica. 1997. "Ley de Organización, competencias, y procedimientos del poder ejecutivo." Unpublished document, Managua.

Novak, Monica. 1999. "A Period of Transition and Redefinition: Post-Communist Polish Female Identity through the Lens of the Private/Public Distinction." Honor's thesis, Knox College.

Núñez, Orlando, Gloria Cardenal, Amanda Lorío, Sonia Agurto, Juan Morales, Javier Pasquier, Javier Matus, and Rubén Pasos. 1998. *La guerra y el campesinado en Nicaragua.* Managua: Editorial Ciencias Sociales.

Núñez Téllez, Carlos. 1981. "El problema fundamental de la mujer: Participar en las transformaciones revolucionarias." Transcript of speech given at fourth anniversary of AMNLAE, Managua, September 29.

———. 1986. "La revolución es también transformadora de las relaciones personales y organización de las nuevas formas de vida." Unpublished document.

Oficina de la Mujer/AMNLAE. 1988. *Aportes al análisis del maltrato en la relación de pareja.* Managua: Libros Especiales, S.A. (DILESA).

Olivera, Mercedes. 1994. "Aguascalientes y el movimiento social de las mujeres chiapanecas." In *A propósito de la insurgencia en Chiapas,* ed. Silvia Soriano Hernández, 57–80. Mexico City: Asociación para el Desarrollo de la Investigación Científica y Humanística de Chiapas.

———. 1995. "Practica feminista en el Movimiento Zapatista de Liberación Nacional." In *¿Chiapas, y las mujeres, qué?* Vol. 2, ed. Rosa Rojas, 168–84. Mexico City: Ediciones la Correa Feminista.

———. 1996. "El ejército zapatista y la emancipación de las mujeres chiapanecas." In *Montañas con recuerdos de mujer: Una mirada feminista a la participación de las mujeres en los conflictos armados en Centroamérica y Chiapas,* ed. Clara Murguialday, 47–57. San Salvador: Algier's Impresores.

Oquist, Paul. 1992. "The Sociopolitical Dynamics of the 1990 Nicaraguan Elections." In *The 1990 Elections in Nicaragua and Their Aftermath,* ed.

Vanessa Castro and Gary Prevost, 1–40. Lanham, Mass.: Rowman and Littlefield.

Organización de Mujeres Guatemaltecas Refugiadas en México. 1999. "Mamá Maquín." In *Nuestra experiencia ante los retos del futuro*. San Cristóbal de las Casas: Editorial Fray Bartolomé de las Casas.

Padilla, Martha Luz, Clara Murguialday, and Ana Criquillón. 1987. "Impact of the Sandinista Agrarian Reform on Rural Women's Subordination." In *Rural Women and State Policy*, ed. Carmen Diana Deere and Magdalena León, 124–41. Boulder: Westview.

Paige, Jeffery M. 1975. *Agrarian Revolution*. New York: Free Press.

———. 1997. *Coffee and Power: Revolution and the Rise of Democracy in Central America*. Cambridge, Mass.: Harvard University Press.

Pardo-Maurer, R. 1990. *The Contras, 1980–1989: A Special Kind of Politics*. New York: Praeger.

Payne, Leigh. 2000. *Uncivil Movements: The Armed Right and Democracy in Latin America*. Baltimore: Johns Hopkins University Press.

Pearce, Jenny. 1986. *Promised Land: Peasant Rebellion in Chalatenango, El Salvador*. London: Latin American Bureau.

Pérez-Alemán, Paola. 1990. *Organización, identidad, y cambio: Las campesinas en Nicaragua*. Managua: Centro de Investigación y Acción para la Promoción de los Derechos de la Mujer (CIAM).

———. 1992. "Economic Crisis and Women in Nicaragua." In *Unequal Burden: Economic Crises, Persistent Poverty, and Women's Work*, ed. Lourdes Benería and Shelley Feldman. Boulder: Westview.

Pérez Rojas, Niurka. 1979. *Características sociodemográficas de la familia cubana, 1953–1970*. Havana: Editorial de Ciencias Sociales.

Pérez-Stable, Marifeli. 1987. "Cuban Women and the Struggle for 'Conciencia.'" *Cuban Studies* 17: 57–72.

———. 1993. *The Cuban Revolution: Origins, Course, and Legacy*. New York: Oxford Press.

Pérez U., Matilde, and Elio Henríquez. 1995. "Denuncia Aedpch la violencia contra indígenas ante la Procuraduría Estatal." *La Jornada*, October 6.

Peterson, Anna L. 1997. *Martyrdom and the Politics of Religion: Progressive Catholicism in El Salvador's Civil War*. Albany: SUNY Press.

Petrich, Blanche. 1996. "Crece en México la violencia hacia mujeres indígenas y activistas: AI." *La Jornada*, March 10.

Pizarro Leongómez, Eduardo. 1996. *Insurgencia sin revolución: La guerrilla en Colombia en una perspectiva comparada*. Bogotá: Tercer Mundo Editores.

Prensa, La. 1990. "Violeta: Mis muletas son símbolo de Nicaragua." January 22.

————. 1991. "Honores en Washington a Chamorro." April 15.

Prensa Gráfica 1996. "Piden despenalizar el aborto." June 21: 3.

Preston, Julia. 1996. "Zapatista Tour Offers Mud, Sweat, and Radical Chic: La Realidad Journal." *New York Times,* August 13: A5.

————. 1997. "Indian Rebels Draw Throng to a Rally in Mexico City." *New York Times,* September 14.

————. 1998a. "Feuding Indian Villages Bringing Mexican Region to Brink of War." *New York Times,* February 2: A1, A6.

————. 1998b. "Mexico Accuses Policeman of Helping Arm Mass Killers." *New York Times,* January 13: A6.

————. 1998c. "News (and State) Anchor Weighs His: Mexico City Journal." *New York Times,* January 20: A3.

Raleigh, Morrella S. 1994. "Riot Grrls and Revolution." Master's thesis, Bowling Green State University.

Ramírez Cuevas, Jesús. 1997. "Jamás atendió la policía estatal los llamados de auxilio: Testigos." *La Jornada,* December 30.

Randall, Margaret. 1981. *Sandino's Daughters: Testimonies of Nicaraguan Women in Struggle.* Vancouver: New Star Books.

————. 1992. *Gathering Rage: The Failure of Twentieth-Century Revolutions to Develop a Feminist Agenda.* New York: Monthly Review Press.

————. 1993. "To Change Our Own Reality and the World: A Conversation with Lesbians in Nicaragua." *Signs: Journal of Women in Culture and Society* 18: 907–24.

————. 1994. *Sandino's Daughters Revisited.* New Brunswick, N.J.: Rutgers University Press.

Ready, Kelley. 2001. "A Feminist Reconstruction of Fatherhood within Neoliberal Constraints: La Asociación de Madres Demandantes in El Salvador." In *Radical Women in Latin America: Left and Right,* ed. Victoria González and Karen Kampwirth. University Park: Penn State University Press.

Ready, Kelley, Lynn Stephen, and Serena Cosgrove. 2001. "Women's Organizations in El Salvador: History, Accomplishments, and International Support." In *Women and Civil War: Impact, Organizations, and Action,* ed. Krishna Kumar, 183–203. Boulder: Lynne Rienner.

Reca Moreira, Inés, et al. 1990. *Análisis de las investigaciones sobre la familia cubana, 1970–1987.* Havana: Editorial de las Ciencias Sociales.

Reif, Linda L. 1986. "Women in Latin American Guerrilla Movements: A Comparative Perspective." *Comparative Politics* 18, no. 2 (January): 147–69.

Renard, María Cristina. 1997. "Movimiento campesino y organizaciones políticas: Simojovel-Huitiupán (1974–1990)." In *Chiapas 4*, ed. Neus Espresate, 93–110. Mexico City: Ediciones Era.

Reséndez Fuentes, Andrés. 1995. "Background Women: *Soldaderas* and Female Soldiers in the Mexican Revolution." *Americas* 51, no. 4 (April): 525–53.

Richards, Gareth. 1996. "A Plan of Action: The Women's Coalition." *Barricada internacional*, no. 402 (November): 29.

Robinson, William I. 1992. *A Faustian Bargain: U.S. Intervention in the Nicaraguan Elections and American Foreign Policy in the Post–Cold War Era*. Boulder: Westview.

Rodríguez, Candelaria. 1994. "Se repenaliza en Chiapas el aborto." In *Chiapas, ¿y las mujeres, qué?* ed. Rosa Rojas, 135–38. Mexico City: Ediciones la Correa Feminista.

Rodríguez, Ileana. 1990. *Registradas en la Historia: Diez años de quehacer feminista en Nicaragua*. Managua: Centro de Investigación y Acción para los Derechos de la Mujer (CIAM).

———. 1996a. "Amor y patria: Desarmando el estado nacional." In DIGNAS. eds. *Montañas con recuerdos de mujer: Una mirada feminista a la participación de las mujeres en los conflictos armados en Centroamérica y Chiapas*, ed. Clara Murguialday, 3–19. San Salvador: Algier's Impresores.

———. 1996b. *Women, Guerrillas, and Love: Understanding War in Central America*. Minneapolis: University of Minnesota Press.

Rodríguez Araujo, Octavio. 1995. "Tiempo y olvido." *La Jornada,* June 8.

Roiz Murillo, William. 1995. "Alfabetizadores rechazan afirmaciones de Chamorro, Tünnerman: Doña Violeta sabe que no fue asi." *Barricada,* April 27.

Rojas, Rosa, ed. 1994. *Chiapas, ¿y las mujeres, qué?* Mexico City: Ediciones La Correa Feminista.

———. 1995a. "De la primera Convención Nacional de Mujeres a la Consulta Nacional del EZLN (cronología de los principales sucesos relacionados con las mujeres en torno al conflicto chiapaneco)." In *Chiapas, ¿y las mujeres, qué?* ed. Rosa Rojas, 3–70. Mexico City: Ediciones La Correa Feminista.

———. 1995b. Introduction to *Chiapas, ¿y las mujeres, qué?* Vol. 2, ed. Rosa Rojas, v–xii. Mexico City: Ediciones La Correa Feminista.

———. 1995c. "Negociaciones Gobierno Federal–EZLN: Primera fase de la mesa 1, grupo 4, sintesis indicativa, situación, derechos y cultura de la mujer indígena." In *Chiapas, ¿y las mujeres, qué?* ed. Rosa Rojas, 232–37. Mexico City: Ediciones La Correa Feminista.

———. 1995d. "Segunda Fase de la Mesa de Larrainzar: Retroseso en los consensos del Grupo de Mujeres." In *Chiapas, ¿y las mujeres, qué?* ed. Rosa Rojas, 238–87. Mexico City: Ediciones La Correa Feminista.

Rojas, Rosa, and José Gil. 1996a. "Pide una profunda reforma del estado." *La Jornada,* January 8.

———. 1996b. "Se prorroga el Foro Nacional." *La Jornada,* January 9.

Rojas, Rosa, and Elio Henríquez. 1995. "Acuerdos de Larráinzar sobre reconocimiento constitucional del sistema juridico indígena y sobre varios rubros de derechos de la mujer indígena." *La Jornada,* November 17.

Rojas Requena, Iliana, Mariana Ravenet Ramírez, and Jorge Hernández Martínez. 1985. *Sociología y desarrollo rural en Cuba.* Havana: Editorial de Ciencias Sociales.

Rosemberg, Fúlvia. 1992. "Education, Democratization, and Inequality in Brazil." In *Women and Education in Latin America: Knowledge, Power, and Change,* ed. Nelly Stromquist. Boulder: Lynne Rienner.

Rosenbaum, Brenda. 1993. *With our Heads Bowed: The Dynamics of Gender in a Mayan Community.* Albany, N.Y.: Institute for Mesoamerican Studies.

Ross, John. 1995. *Rebellion from the Roots: Indian Uprising in Chiapas.* Monroe, Maine: Common Courage Press.

Rosset, Peter, and John Vandermeer, eds. 1986. *Nicaragua, Unfinished Revolution: The New Nicaragua Reader.* New York: Grove Press.

Rovira, Guiomar. 1995. "Mujeres indígenas: Protagonistas de la historia." *La guillotina* 31 (August–September): 14–20.

———. 1997. *Mujeres de maíz.* Mexico City: Ediciones Era.

Ruchwarger, Gary. 1985. "Las organizaciones de masas sandinistas y el proceso revolucionario." In *La revolución en Nicaragua: Liberación nacional, democracia popular, y transformación económica,* ed. Richard Harris and Carlos Vilas. Mexico City: Ediciones Era.

Ruiz Hernández, Margarito. 1999. "La Asamblea Nacional Indígena Plural por la Autonomía (ANIPA)." In *México: Experiencias de autonomía indígena,* ed. Aracely Burguete Cal y Mayor, 21–53. Copenhagen: IWGIA.

Ruiz Hernández, Margarito, and Aracely Burguete Cal y Mayor. 1998. "Chiapas: Organización y lucha indígena al final del milenio (1974–1998)." *Asuntos Indígenas,* no. 3: 27–33.

Ruiz Ortiz, Juana María. 1991. "El mandato de la mujer." *Anuario CEI II, 1989–1990,* 65–71. Tuxtla Gutiérrez: Universidad Autonoma de Chiapas.

Rus, Jan. 1995. "Local Adaptation to Global Change: The Reordering of Native Society in Highland Chiapas, Mexico, 1974–1994." *European Review of Latin American and Caribbean Studies* 58 (June): 71–89.

Russo, Tim. 2000. "A Day in a Zapatista Autonomous Community." *NACLA Report on the Americas* 33, no. 5 (March–April): 23.

Rust, Paula. 1995. *Bisexuality and the Challenge to Lesbian Politics: Sex, Loyalty, and Revolution.* New York: New York University Press.

Saadatmand, Yassaman. 1995. "Separate and Unequal Women in Islamic Republic of Iran." *Journal of South Asian and Middle Eastern Studies* 18, no. 4 (Summer): 1–24.

Salas, Elizabeth. 1990. *Soldaderas in the Mexican Military: Myth and History.* Austin: University of Texas Press.

Sanasarian, Eliz. 1983. "An Analysis of Fida'i and Mujahadin Positions on Women's Rights." In *Women and Revolution in Iran,* ed. Guity Nashat, 97–108. Boulder: Westview.

Sargent, Lydia, ed. 1981. *Women and Revolution: A Discussion of the Unhappy Marriage of Marxism and Feminism.* Boston: South End Press.

Schirmer, Jennifer. 1993. "The Seeking of Truth and the Gendering of Consciousness." In *Viva: Women and Popular Protest in Latin America,* ed. Sarah Radcliffe and Sallie Westwood. New York: Routledge.

Schroeder, Susan. 1982. *Cuba: A Handbook of Historical Statistics.* Boston: G. K. Hall.

Schultz, Barry, and Robert Slater, eds. 1990. *Revolution and Political Change in the Third World.* Boulder: Lynne Rienner.

Schwab, Theodore, and Harold Sims. 1985. "Relations with the Communist States." In *Nicaragua: The First Five Years,* ed. Thomas Walker. New York: Praeger.

Scott, Catherine V. 1994. "'Men in Our Country Behave Like Chiefs': Women and the Angolan Revolution." In *Women and Revolution in Africa, Asia, and the New World,* ed. Mary Ann Tétreault, 89–108. Columbia: University of South Carolina Press.

SEDEPAC (Servicio, Desarrollo, y Paz, A.C.). 1996. *Propuestas de las mujeres indígenas al Congreso Nacional Indígena.* Mexico City: Benjamín Alvarez.

Selbin, Eric. 1997. "Revolution in the Real World: Bringing Agency Back In." In *Theorizing Revolutions,* ed. John Foran. London: Routledge.

———. 1999. *Modern Latin American Revolutions*. 2d ed. Boulder: Westview.

Shayne, Julia. 1999. "Gendered Revolutionary Bridges: Women in the Salvadoran Resistance Movement (1979–1992)." *Latin American Perspectives* 26, no. 3, issue 106 (May): 85–102.

Sheldon, Kathleen. 1994. "Women and Revolution in Mozambique: A luta continua." In *Women and Revolution in Africa, Asia, and the New World,* ed. Mary Ann Tétreault, 33–61. Columbia: University of South Carolina Press.

Shnookal, Deborah. 1991. *Cuban Women Confront the Future: Vilma Espín.* Melbourne: Ocean Press.

Siemienska, Renata. 1998. "Consequences of Economic and Political Changes for Women in Poland." In *Women and Democracy: Latin America and Central and Eastern Europe,* ed. Jane Jaquette and Sharon Wolchik, 125–52. Baltimore: Johns Hopkins University Press.

Skocpol, Theda. 1979. *States and Social Revolutions.* Cambridge: Cambridge University Press.

———. 1994. *Social Revolutions in the Modern World.* Cambridge: Cambridge University Press.

Slater, David. 1994. "Power and Social Movements in the Other Occident: Latin America in an International Context." *Latin American Perspectives* 21 (Spring): 11–37.

Smith, Christian. 1991. *The Emergence of Liberation Theology: Religion and Social Movement Theory.* Chicago: University of Chicago Press.

———. 1997. *Resisting Reagan: The U.S. Central America Peace Movement.* Chicago: University of Chicago Press.

Smith, Lois, and Alfred Padula. 1996. *Sex and Revolution: Women in Socialist Cuba.* New York: Oxford Press.

Smith, Steven Kent. 1997. "Renovation and Orthodoxy: Debate and Transition within the Sandinista National Liberation Front." *Latin American Perspectives* 24, no. 2, issue 93 (March): 102–16.

Soriano Hernández, Silvia. 1994. "Del ejército de la virgen al ejército zapatista." In *A propósito de la insurgencia en Chiapas,* ed. Silvia Soriano Hernández, 17–41. Mexico City: Asociación para el Desarrollo de la Investigación Científica y Humanística de Chiapas.

Soro, Julio. 1992. "Revolución en la revolución: Las mujeres salvadoreñas y la construcción de la democracia." Unpublished manuscript.

Soro, Julio, Lissette Gonzáles, Clara Luz de Osorio, Elvira Portillo, and Ana Dora de Vega. 1994. *Como los partidos políticos incluyen a las mujeres en sus plataformas políticas.* San Salvador: Red por la Unidad y el Desarollo de las Mujeres Salvadoreñas.

Spence, Jack. 1994. *El Salvador, Elections of the Century: Results, Recommendations, Analysis.* Cambridge, Mass.: Hemisphere Initiatives.

Spence, Jack, Hemisphere Initiatives, and Washington Office on Latin America. 1997. *Democracy Weakened? A Report on the October 20, 1996, Nicaraguan Elections.* Cambridge, Mass.: Hemisphere Initiatives.

Stacey, Judith. 1983. *Patriarchy and Socialist Revolution in China.* Berkeley: University of California Press.

Stahler-Sholk, Richard. 1998. "The Lessons of Acteal." *NACLA Report on the Americas* 31, no. 5 (March–April): 11–14.

Stanley, William. 1996. *The Protection Racket State: Elite Politics, Military Extortion, and Civil War in El Salvador.* Philadelphia: Temple University Press.

Stavenhagen, Rodolfo. 1999. Prologue ("Hacia el derecho de autonomía en México") to *México: Experiencias de autonomía indígena,* ed. Aracely Burguete Cal y Mayor, 7–20. Copenhagen: IWGIA.

Stephen, Lynn. 1994a. "Convención Estatal de Mujeres Chiapanecas." Unpublished document, November 11.

———. 1994b. "Democratic Convention in Chiapas" *Peacework,* October: 6.

———. 1994c. "Eyewitness Report on the National Democratic Convention, Chiapas, Mexico." *Reporter on Latin America and the Caribbean,* November– December: 5.

———. 1994d. *Hear My Testimony: María Teresa Tula, Human Rights Activist of El Salvador.* Boston: South End Press.

———. 1995. "The Zapatista Army of National Liberation and the National Democratic Convention." *Latin American Perspectives* 22, no. 4, issue 87 (Fall): 88–99.

———. 1997. *Women and Social Movements in Latin America: Power from Below.* Austin: University of Texas Press.

Stephens, Beth. 1988. "Changes in the Laws Governing the Parent-Child Relationship in Post-Revolutionary Nicaragua." *Hastings International and Comparative Law Review* 12, no. 1 (Fall): 137–71.

Sternbach, Nancy Sporta, Marysa Navarro-Aranguren, Patricia Chuchryk, and Sonia Alvarez. 1992. "Feminisms in Latin America: From Bogotá to San Bernardo." In *The Making of Social Movements in Latin America: Identity, Strategy, and Democracy* ed. Arturo Escobar and Sonia Alvarez, 207–39. Boulder: Westview.

Stolcke, Verena Martinez-Alier. 1989. *Marriage, Class, and Colour in Nineteenth-Century Cuba: A Study of Racial Attitudes and Sexual Values in a Slave Society.* Ann Arbor: University of Michigan Press.

Stoll, David. 1990. *Is Latin America Turning Protestant? The Politics of Evangelical Growth.* Berkeley: University of California Press.

Stoner, K. Lynn. 1991. *From the House to the Streets: The Cuban Women's Movement for Legal Reform, 1898–1940.* Durham: Duke University Press.

Stromquist, Nelly P., ed. 1992. *Women and Education in Latin America: Knowledge, Power, and Change.* Boulder: Lynne Rienner

Suchlicki, Jaime. 1969. *University Students and Revolution in Cuba, 1920–1968.* Coral Gables: University of Miami Press.

Sulloway, Frank J. 1996. *Born to Rebel: Birth Order, Family Dynamics, and Creative Lives.* New York: Pantheon Books.

Tejera Gaona, Héctor. 1996. "Las causas del conflicto en Chiapas." In *La sociedad rural frente al nuevo milenio.* Vol. 4, *Los nuevos actores sociales y procesos políticos en el campo,* ed. Hubert C. De Grammont and Héctor Tejera Gaona. Mexico City: Plaza y Valdés.

Tétreault, Mary Ann, ed. 1994. *Women and Revolution in Africa, Asia, and the New World.* Columbia: University of South Carolina Press.

Thompson, Ginger. 2001. "Mexico Congress Approves Altered Rights Bill." *The New York Times,* April 30: A9.

Toledo Tello, Sonia. 1986. "El papel de la cultura en el proceso de subordinación de las mujeres indígenas de Chiapas." *Anuario* 1: 73–87. San Cristóbal de las Casas: Universidad Autonoma de Chiapas.

Townsend, Janet, Ursula Arrevillaga Matías, Socorro Cancino Córdova, Silvana Pachecho Bonfíl, and Elia Pérez Nasser. 1994. *Voces femeninas de las selvas.* Mexico City: Colegio de Postgraduados, Centro de Estudios del Desarollo Rural.

UNICEF (United Nations Children's Fund). 1988. *Analysis de la situación de la mujer en el Salvador.* San Salvador: n.p.

Univisión. 1989. News release, November 14.

Urrutia, Alonso, and Candelaria Rodríguez. 1995a. "Eduardo Robledo Solicitó licensia, pidió a Samuel Ruiz y Avendaño que renuncien" *La Jornada,* February 15.

———. 1995b. "Robledo se fue cuando estaba más fortalecido que nunca: Ganaderos." *La Jornada,* February 16.

U.S.–El Salvador Institute for Democratic Development. 1994. "Platform of the Women of El Salvador." Unpublished document.

Valdés, Teresa, and Enrique Gomáriz. 1995. *Mujeres latinoamericanas en cifras.* Santiago: Ministerio de Asuntos Sociales de España/FLACSO Chile.

Valle, Sonia del. 1998. "Las muertas vivas de Chiapas: Testimonio de una justicia pendiente." *Doble Jornada* (supplement to *La Jornada*), January 5.

Vázquez, Norma, Cristina Ibáñez, and Clara Murguialday. 1996. *Mujeres-montaña: Vivencias de guerrilleras y colaboradoras del FMLN.* Madrid: Editorial Horas y Horas.

Venegas, Juan Manuel. 1997. "Madrazo: En Acteal, conflicto intercomunitario." *La Jornada,* December 27.

Venegas, Juan Manuel, and Angeles Mariscal. 1998. "Albores Guillén sustituye a Ruiz Ferro; riesgo de choques: EZLN." *La Jornada,* January 8.

Verdery, Katherine. 1994. "From Parent-State to Family Patriarchs: Gender and Nation in Contemporary Eastern Europe." *Eastern European Politics and Societies* 8, no. 2 (Spring): 225–55.

Vilas, Carlos. 1986. *The Sandinista Revolution: National Liberation and Social Transformation in Central America.* New York: Monthly Review Press.

———. 1995. *Between Earthquakes and Volcanoes: Market, State, and the Revolutions in Central America.* New York: Monthly Review Press.

Villafuerte Solís, Daniel, and María del Carmen García Aguilar. 1994. "Los altos de Chiapas en el contexto del neoliberalismo: Causas y razones del conflicto indígena." In *A propósito de la insurgencia en Chiapas,* ed. Silvia Soriano Hernández, 83–119. Mexico City: Asociación para el Desarrollo de la Investigación Científica y Humanística en Chiapas.

Walker, Thomas. 1981. *Nicaragua, the Land of Sandino.* Boulder: Westview.

———, ed. 1985. *Nicaragua: The First Five Years.* New York: Praeger.

———, ed. 1987. *Reagan versus the Sandinistas: The Undeclared War on Nicaragua.* Boulder: Westview.

Waylen, Georgina. 1994. "Women and Democratization: Conceptualizing Gender Relations in Transition Politics." *World Politics,* March: 327–54.

———. 1998. "Gender, Feminism, and the State: An Overview." In *Gender, Politics, and the State,* ed. Vicky Randall and Georgina Waylen. London: Routledge.

Wickham-Crowley, Timothy P. 1992. *Guerrillas and Revolution in Latin America: A Comparative Study of Insurgents and Regimes since 1956.* Princeton: Princeton University Press.

————. 1997. "Structural Theories of Revolution." In *Theorizing Revolutions,* ed. John Foran. London: Routledge.

Williams, Philip. 1989. *The Catholic Church and Politics in Nicaragua and Costa Rica.* Pittsburgh: University of Pittsburgh Press.

Williams, Philip, and Knut Walter. 1997. *Militarization and Demilitarization in El Salvador's Transition to Democracy* Pittsburgh: University of Pittsburgh Press.

Wolf, Eric R. 1969. *Peasant Wars of the Twentieth Century.* New York: Harper and Row.

Womack, John. 1999. *Rebellion in Chiapas: An Historical Reader.* New York: New Press.

Wright, Robin. 2000. *The Last Great Revolution: Turmoil and Transformation in Iran.* New York: Knopf.

Zeitlin, Maurice. 1967. *Revolutionary Politics and the Cuban Working Class.* Princeton: Princeton University Press.

Zwerling, Philip, and Connie Martin. 1985. *Nicaragua: A New Kind of Revolution.* Chicago: Lawrence Hill Books.

Index

abortion politics, 65, 102–3, 175–76, 182, 209n7, 216n13, 218nn24–25, 229n7

Abejas, Las (Chiapas), 154, 224n24

Acteal massacre, 142, 154–56, 160, 224n24, 226n36

ADEMUSA (Asociación de Mujeres Salvadoreñas) (El Salvador), 77, 89–90, 107–8

ADIM (Asociación para el Desarrollo Integral de la Mujer) (El Salvador), 77

AEDPCH (Asamblea Estatal Democrática del Pueblo Chiapaneco) (Chiapas), 149–52, 221n9, 226n34

agrarian reform, women and, 204n14

Alemán, Arnoldo, 69–72, 212n25

Alvarez, Sonia, 8, 100, 205–6n22

AMNLAE (Asociación de Mujeres Nicaragüenses Luisa Amanda Espinoza) (Nicaragua), 28–30, 33–36, 54, 56–57, 64, 203n10, 207n25; compared to FMC (Federación de Mujeres Cubanas), 186–87, 193

AMS (Asociación de Mujeres Salvadoreñas) (El Salvador), 77

Ana María (major). See EZLN

ANIPA (Asamblea Nacional Indígena

Plural por la Autonomía) (Chiapas), 136–38, 154, 223n20

antifeminism: defined, 48; in Iran, 45, 166–67; as legacy of revolution, 3, 165–83, 195; in Nicaragua 26–27, 41–43, 47–48, 207n1; in Poland, 173, 176–77. See also feminism

ARENA (Alianza Nacionalista Republicana) (El Salvador), 92–97

Asociación de Madres Demandantes por la Cuota Alimenticia (El Salvador), 79

Asociación de Mujeres Rurales "Olga Estela Moreno" (El Salvador), 77

Association of Mothers Demanding Child Support (El Salvador), 79

ATC (Asociación de Trabajadores del Campo) (Nicaragua), 31–33, 204n15, 207n25

authoritarian socialism, 172–75, 228nn4–5

autonomous feminism. See feminism

autonomous regions: in Chiapas, 123–24, 130, 221n10. See also indigenous movement

autonomy: and civil society, 116; disputed meanings of, 63–65, 86, 116, 148–49, 153–54, 226n34; and

autonomy: and civil society (*cont.*)
indigenous women, 134–35,
223n16; and resources, 86, 177
Avendaño, Amado, 130–31, 152, 221n11

Bees, The (Chiapas), 154, 224n24
Belli, Humberto, 70–71, 212nn26–27

Catholic Church: in Chiapas, 163, 180;
in El Salvador, 179; in Nicaragua,
44–45, 70, 179; opposition to the
word *gender,* 183, 230n10; in
Poland, 173–75, 177, 181–83. *See
also* liberation theology
CCM (Consejo de Comunidades Mar-
ginales) (El Salvador), 78
CEF (Centro de Estudios Feministas)
(El Salvador), 79
CEMUJER (Centro de Estudios de la
Mujer "Norma Virginia Guirola de
Herrera") (El Salvador), 79, 84
Central America, feminism in, 7,
109–11. *See also* El Salvador,
Nicaragua
Central American Feminist Current, 66
Centro de Mujeres de Masaya
(Nicaragua), 35–36
CEOIC (Coordinadora Estatal de Orga-
nizaciones Indígenas y
Campesinas) (Chiapas), 128, 221n9
CEPSIDA (Colectivo de Educadores
Populares Contra el SIDA), 61
Chamorro, Violeta (doña Violeta),
38–43, 47–48, 52–53, 205nn20–21,
206n23, 207n1. *See also* UNO
Chiapas: autonomous regions in, 123–24,
130; feminism in, 1, 8–9, 16–17;
gender relations in, 1, 15–16, 112–14,
134–35, 161–64; women's organizing

in, 118–22, 134–42, 146–48, 158–60,
199n11. *See also* EZLN
Chiapas State Women's Convention,
119–20
CIAM (Centro de Investigaciones y Acción para la Mujer Latinameri-
cana) (Chiapas), 118
CISPES (Committee in Solidarity with
the People of El Salvador), 91
civil society: and clientelism, 144; con-
trasted to popular organizations,
116–18; and EZLN, 116–18, 123,
221n6
clientelism, 143–54, 224n26, 225n27;
defined, 144; threats to, 163–64
Coalición Nacional de Mujeres
(Nicaragua), 67, 69–70,
211nn23–24
CODEFAM (Comité de Familiares de
Victimas de Violacciones Hu-
manas Marianella García Villas)
(El Salvador), 79
Colectivo de Mujeres de Matagalpa
(Nicaragua), 36, 102, 104, 218n24
Colectivo Lésbico Feminista de la Media
Luna (El Salvador), 79
Collier, George, 123
COM (Coordinación de Organismos de
Mujeres) (El Salvador), 79, 86,
214n5
COMADRES (Comité de Madres y Fa-
miliares de El Salvador), 79
Comisaría de la Mujer y la Niñez
(Nicaragua), 67–69, 210n19
Comité de Mujeres por una Cultura de
Paz (El Salvador), 77
Comité Femenino de la Asociación de
Trabajadores del CEL (El Sal-
vador), 79–80

INDEX

Frente Farabundo Martí para la Liberación Nacional. *See* FMLN
Frente Sandinista de Liberación Nacional. *See* FSLN
FSLN (Frente Sandinista de Liberación Nacional) (Nicaragua): and democracy, 20–21, 201n2; and electoral politics, 37–40, 212n25; and feminism, 46, 206n24; gender relations in, 1, 17–18, 180–81, 202nn3–4, 203n7; health policies, 25–26; legal changes, 21–24, 202nn5–6, 203n7; and lesbians, 57–63, 209nn11–12, 210nn13–14; literacy crusade, 24–25; opposition to, 26–27; social policies, 21–27; as vanguard party, 28, 64; women's proclamation (*proclama*), 37, 205n18. *See also* Nicaragua
FUNIC-MUJER (Nicaragua), 68
FZLN (Frente Zapatista de Liberación Nacional) (Chiapas): and feminism, 143; founding principles, 142–43; and women, 112, 143. *See also* EZLN

GALEES (Grupo de Acción por la Libertad de Expresión de la Elección Sexual) (Cuba), 190–91, 193
gender relations: in Chiapas, 1, 15–16, 112–14, 134–35, 161–64; in Cuba, 230n12; in El Salvador, 1, 16–17; in Iran, 166–69; in Nicaragua, 1, 17–18, 20, 27, 43; in Poland, 172–75, 176–77; transformation of, 20, 178–83
González, Victoria, 207n27, 210n15
Grupo de Mujeres de San Cristóbal (Chiapas), 114, 220n4
Guatemala, 115

guerrillas: EZLN platform compared to FMLN and FSLN platforms, 113, 220nn2–3; feminist legacy, 2, 7–12, 76–77, 87–90, 97, 113–14, 180; gender relations, 14–18; images of, 19–20; percentage of women in, x; prestige within, 9–12, 199n12, 200nn13–14; strategies, xi. *See also* EZLN; FMLN; FSLN
Guirola, Norma, 84

identity politics, 98
IMU (Instituto de Investigación, Capacitación, y Desarrollo de la Mujer) (El Salvador), 77, 84
Indians. *See indigenismo;* indigenous movement; indigenous people
indigenismo, 125–26
indigenous movement, 119, 122–24, 132–40, 221n8; and autonomous regions, 123–24; "govern by obeying," 131, 222n12; and mestizos, 119, 121, 138–40, 157, 222n13, 223n21; and Mexican politics, 132–40, 149–54, 223nn18–19, 226n35; and women, 126–27, 134–42, 146–48, 151, 158–60; and Zapatistas, 119, 122–24, 127–30
indigenous people: and gender relations, 126–27; in Mexican history, 124–27
INI (Instituto Nacional Indigenista) (Chiapas), 132, 145–48, 152–54
INIM (Instituto Nicaragüense de la Mujer), 71
Instituto Mujer Ciudadana (El Salvador), 78
Iran, 166–72; gender inequality and revolution, 166–67; feminism in, 181–83, 228n2; March 8th (International Women's Day) in, 170–72;

275

National Indigenous Forum (Chiapas),
137–38
nationalism, 172–73
National Women's Coalition
(Nicaragua), 67, 69–70, 211nn23–24
neoliberalism: defined, 208n4
Network for Women's Health
(Nicaragua), 64
new man, 117, 221n7
Nicaragua: birth rates in, 209n6;
compared to El Salvador,
96–106, 109–11, 217n18, 217n20;
constitution, debates surrounding,
35–36; contras in, 29–30, 45–46,
203n11, 204nn12–13; electoral politics in, 37–43, 205n19, 206n23;
feminism in, 1, 19–20, 23, 35–38,
56–57, 63–66, 208n3; gender com-
position of workforce, 31, 55–56;
gender relations in, 179–80; legacy
of guerrillas, 19–21; lesbians in, 46,
57–63, 209nn11–12, 210nn13–14;
Sandinismo, 1, 17, 20; unemployment in, 47, 208n2; women's
movement, 28–38, 54–70, 199n11,
209n5; women's secretariats in,
30–35, 55–56. See also AMNLAE;
FSLN; Somoza regime; UNO

"Olga Estela Moreno" Association of
Rural Women (El Salvador), 77
ORDEN (Organización Democrática
Nacionalista) (El Salvador), 88,
215n6
ORMUSA (Organización de Mujeres
Salvadoreñas) (El Salvador), 78,
85–86, 106–7, 214n4
Ortega, Daniel, 23–24, 38–40, 73–74,
206n23, 212n29

Ortega, Zoilamérica, 73–74, 212n29,
213nn30–31, 229n8

paramilitary groups (Chiapas), 154–56,
221n5, 224n24, 226n36, 227n37
Partido de la Revolución Institucional
(Mexico). See PRI
Partido Demócrata (El Salvador): Di-
rección de la Mujer y la Familia,
78
patriarchal feminism. See feminism
Paz y Justicia (Chiapas), 154
PDC (Christian Democrats) (El Sal-
vador), 92–94
Peace and Justice (Chiapas), 154
Peña, Lorena, 95–96, 105
PIE (Partido de la Izquierda Erótica)
(Nicaragua), 37
Poland, 172–77; antifeminism in,
172–73, 176–77; and Catholic
Church, 173–75, 177; feminism
in, 181–83; Solidarity movement,
174–77, 183; women's section
of Solidarity, 176–77, 183,
229n6
PRD (Partido de la Revolución
Democrática), 123
popular organizations, contrasted to
civil society. See civil society
PRI (Partido de la Revolución Institu-
cional), x, 115, 133, 143–55, 157,
225n27, 227n38
Primer Encuentro del Maiz Maya-
Zoque (Chiapas), 153
Pro-Familia (Nicaragua), 68
Programa de la Mujer de ANTA (El Salvador), 80
Puntos de Encuentro (Nicaragua), 101,
103–4, 218nn26–27

134–42, 146–48, 158–60, 199n11; in El Salvador, 75–80, 82–87, 89–95, 99–108, 199n11, 213n1, 214n5, 216nn8–9, 216nn11–12, 217nn17–18
Women's Network against Violence (Nicaragua), 64; in Nicaragua, 28–38, 54–70, 199n11, 203n17, 208n3, 209n5, 211nn23–24, 217n18

Women's program of ANTA (El Salvador), 80
women's organizing, 8
world systemic opening, 166, 173; defined, 228n1

Zamora, Rubén, 92–93
Zapatistas (Chiapas). *See* EZLN; FZLN
Zedillo, Ernesto, 130, 132–34, 157, 222n15